CHOCOLATE IS
FOREVER

Don't miss these other great books
by Maida Heatter:

HAPPINESS IS BAKING

COOKIES ARE MAGIC

MAIDA HEATTER

CHOCOLATE IS FOREVER

CLASSIC CAKES, COOKIES, PASTRIES, PIES, PUDDINGS, CANDIES, CONFECTIONS, and MORE

Illustrations by
ALICE OEHR

Foreword by
DAVID LEBOVITZ

VORACIOUS

LITTLE, BROWN AND COMPANY
New York | Boston | London

Voracious
Little, Brown and Company
Hachette Book Group
1290 Avenue of the Americas, New York, NY 10104
littlebrown.com

First Edition: April 2020

Voracious is an imprint of Little, Brown and Company, a division of Hachette Book Group, Inc. The Voracious name and logo are trademarks of Hachette Book Group, Inc.

The recipes in *Chocolate Is Forever* have been assembled from Maida Heatter's previously published books, including *Happiness Is Baking, Maida Heatter's Cakes, Maida Heatter's Cookies, Maida Heatter's Book of Great Chocolate Desserts, Maida Heatter's Book of Great Desserts, Maida Heatter's New Book of Great Desserts,* and *Maida Heatter's Book of Great Cookies.* They have been minimally updated from their original forms only in the rare instances where the author's personal notes on her books have improved a recipe after its original publication.

The publisher is not responsible for websites (or their content) that are not owned by the publisher.

Design by Toni Tajima

ISBN 978-0-316-46014-9
LCCN 2019950356

10 9 8 7 6 5 4 3 2 1

WOR

Printed in the United States of America

For me, life's problems seem less important and easier to cope with while trussing a chicken, chopping onions, kneading a yeast dough, or icing a cake. And all seems well to me when popovers and soufflés rise to magnificent heights. My mother taught me that cooking is an act of love—and a beautiful, mountainous escape.

contents

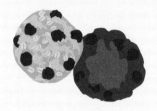

foreword

I worked for over a decade in the kitchen at Chez Panisse. The restaurant was, and still is, one of the best-known eateries in the world. Everyone — from Hollywood stars, to famous chefs, and even American presidents — stopped in for dinner. One particularly memorable evening was when French food and wine expert Richard Olney showed up with cases of Château d'Yquem, the most exquisite — and expensive — wine in the world. Another was the arrival of Julia Child, who towered over everyone when she stepped into the kitchen and yodeled "Hellooo, everybody!" in her unmistakable voice. It sailed across the room, all the way back to the pastry department, where I was rolling out tart dough for that evening's dessert.

It was nice to meet famous actors and to feed celebrities, but the person that I was most excited to see coming into the kitchen was Maida Heatter. When Maida showed up with her gray-white, well-coiffed swoop of hair, she wore her signature smile, wide enough to make everyone put down their knives (or in my case, a rolling pin) to greet her.

That night she didn't hand out the usual brownies that she carried around in her purse, a practice she called "cookie diplomacy." But making and giving away cookies just made her happy. One person, a pilot from Texas, was so delighted with them that he proposed, and she eventually married him.

On the covers of her books, Maida was right at home presiding over a table loaded with dozens of platters of cookies and brownies, either lined up in impeccable rows or arranged by type, shape, and flavor. Cakes and tortes were presented on stands, her smiling face beaming above everything. On the cover of one cookbook, she's leaning on a cookie jar, looking none the worse for wear after probably baking everything for the photographs.

Maida's books invariably had the word "Great" in the title. Anyone else would be accused of boasting, but similar proclamations like "gorgeous," "sensational," "superb," and "perfect" were liberally sprinkled throughout her books. "Delicious" appears about fifty times in the one you're holding. But Maida truly believed that everything that came out of her oven was gorgeous and great, and delicious. And she was right.

Baking never seemed to be a chore for Maida, and even though there were some setbacks in her otherwise sweet life, she always radiated warmth in her headnotes, which never failed to persuade me, and undoubtedly others, to make the recipes that followed. She was especially known for her desserts made with chocolate, an ingredient that figured prominently in all of her books, including *Maida Heatter's Book of Great Chocolate Desserts*. When I wrote a guidebook to chocolate, I knew Maida had to be in it. I adapted her Chocolate Sauerkraut Cake, whose name may raise eyebrows but — you guessed it — is a great chocolate cake. Out of the blue, after my book came out Maida sent a note, in her famously cursive, gloriously expressive handwriting, thanking me for including her, dotting each "i" with a cheerful circle. As a young baker just starting a career as a cookbook author, I was floored to receive that letter, and I've kept it in my desk and even took it with me when I moved abroad. In fact, it's in there right now as I write this. Often when I'm riffling through that desk drawer, looking for a stamp or a pair of scissors, I'll take it out and read it again.

Maida passed away at the age of 102. Her reign as the Queen of Cake was presumably over, but her books continue to remind us of how revered she was by bakers everywhere. With this compilation of her best-loved chocolate desserts, you can create your own memories of Maida, in your own kitchen. You won't get a lovely note from Maida, but if you carry a few packets of brownies (I suggest the Palm Beach Brownies, page 191), who knows? — maybe you'll meet the man, or woman, of your dreams, too.

— David Lebovitz

introduction

After reading any of my books, people who love chocolate realize that I am a member of the club. Actually, I'm the Chairperson of the Board of the Chocolate Lovers Association of the World. (I started as a Brownie and worked my way up.) Chocolate lovers could not wait to corner me or my husband (also a member in good standing) and confess to their chocolate addictions, chocolate splurges, chocolate dreams, fantasies, and uncontrollable cravings and hunger for the stuff.

People always ask what my favorite dessert is. My answer is "anything chocolate." But it is like the line of a song from *Finian's Rainbow,* a Broadway play from many years ago, "When I'm not near the girl I love, I love the girl I'm near." So my favorite dessert is whatever is chocolate and is near: mousse, brownies, pots de crème, Bavarian.

The one question I am asked most often is "What do you do with all the desserts you make while writing a cookbook?" Frankly, we eat an awful lot of them. And we have friends and neighbors, and delivery men, garbage men, gardeners, mailmen, and the butcher, the baker, and the candlestick maker who hope I will never finish testing recipes.

But once, when a new recipe for brownies resulted in a dry, tasteless thing, I did not want to pass it on to anyone. We lived on Biscayne Bay, where the sky is usually alive with seagulls. I didn't know what else to do with the brownie mistake, so I tried it on the gulls. I have never seen them so excited — they were frantic; they have never come so close, nor grabbed the food so hungrily; they fought with each other over every crumb. Then they sat out in the bay for hours waiting for more.

Now I not only have a new and appreciative audience, but a hitherto unknown fact about chocolate: Seagulls *love* it!

In a way, chocolate is like wine — or coffee. It is difficult to say which is the best. A connoisseur will be familiar with them all and will know the subtle differences. Everyone does not agree; it is a matter of taste. So taste as many as you can. Cook with as many as you can. See which you like best.

One final note before you go: I am always dumbfounded when someone tells me about a recipe that did not turn out right, and then they casually add, "But that might be because I used fewer eggs and baked it in a larger pan at a lower temperature and I used oil instead of butter." Read the recipes carefully, follow them exactly, and you will have great success.

Over the course of some of my other books, I have left out chocolate recipes that I loved because I was not certain everyone felt the way I did about chocolate — that is, the more the better. But now, no holds barred, this is it: a true chocolate binge.

Maida Heatter

before you bake

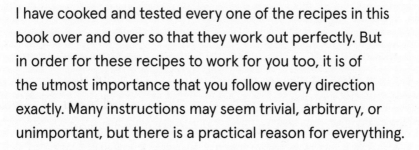

I have cooked and tested every one of the recipes in this book over and over so that they work out perfectly. But in order for these recipes to work for you too, it is of the utmost importance that you follow every direction exactly. Many instructions may seem trivial, arbitrary, or unimportant, but there is a practical reason for everything.

If a recipe says to line a cookie sheet with aluminum foil, it is not because I am a fuddy-duddy and care about keeping cookie sheets clean. In some recipes, you would encounter disaster without the foil. With it, you will squeal with joy at the ease and satisfying excitement of peeling the foil from the smooth, shiny backs of the cookies.

If a cheesecake recipe, for instance, includes directions to refrigerate it for at least 10 hours or longer, it is because the custard would collapse if it were served sooner. With

adequate baking and chilling time it will hold its shape, and serving it (to say nothing of eating it) will be a sensuous thrill.

If brownies are not allowed to stand for the specified time after they come out of the oven, they will squash when you cut them into portions.

I could go on and on, but please, take my word for it. Read the recipes carefully and follow them exactly.

before you bake

1 Read the recipe completely. Make sure you have everything you will need, including the correct-size baking pan.

2 Remove butter, cream cheese, and eggs from the refrigerator.

3 Adjust oven racks and preheat the oven.

4 Prepare the pan according to the directions.

5 Grind or chop nuts.

6 Sift flour (and other dry ingredients) onto a large piece of wax paper or baking parchment.

7 Crack open the eggs (and separate them if necessary).

8 Measure all the other ingredients and organize them into the order called for in the recipe.

ingredients

A Chocolate Primer

I often dreamed about picking chocolate from a chocolate tree and eating my fill. I have never seen a chocolate tree but I have learned that if I did, I could not pick and eat the fruit. It's a long story from the picking to the eating.

· WHAT IS CHOCOLATE? ·

A "chocolate tree" is really a cocoa (cacao) tree — a wide-branching tropical evergreen that grows in many parts of the world, but always within 20 degrees of the equator. Its fruit, a long pod, is split and the seeds (or beans) removed and dried to make the chocolate we know. The cocoa beans are cleaned and roasted to each manufacturer's unique specifications, then shelled, leaving behind cocoa "nibs." The nibs are crushed and heated to separate the cocoa butter from the thick, dark chocolate "liquor." When this liquor is poured into molds and solidified, it becomes unsweetened chocolate. If still more of the cocoa butter is removed and the liquor ground to a powder, it is cocoa.

Sweetened chocolate is created by adding more cocoa butter and sugar to unsweetened chocolate — and the amount of sugar in it determines whether it is **sweet, semisweet, bittersweet,** or **extra-bittersweet.** These are generally interchangeable in cooking and baking, depending on your taste and their availability. Some chocolate bars note the percentage of pure cacao they contain— generally up to 60 percent for semisweet, 70 percent for bittersweet, 80 percent for extra-bittersweet, and 100 percent for unsweetened. I have my favorites and my least favorites as you will see throughout this book. I hope you will search out many varieties and try them all; then you will arrive at your own.

Milk chocolate is quite different and should not be substituted when a recipe calls for bittersweet or semisweet chocolate.

Compound chocolate or **melting chocolate,** unlike "real chocolate," is made with cocoa in place of chocolate liquor — and some vegetable fat other than cocoa butter (either palm kernel oil or coconut oil — or cottonseed or soya oil). Even though these are "natural" ingredients, this mixture is called "imitation chocolate." For the retail trade, the F.D.A. says these chocolates have to be labeled as "chocolate flavored." There are also some completely artificial or synthetic chocolates that contain no ingredients derived from cocoa beans — read the label to find out and avoid these. Whereas real chocolate should be tempered to prevent discoloring or streaking after melting and cooling, compound chocolate does not need to be tempered and will set up (harden) faster than real chocolate. I use compound chocolate especially for making Chocolate Curls (page 240) and Chocolate Cigarettes (page 97), which are long, thin shavings for decoration, and for dipping all kinds of things — try pretzels, saltines, matzohs, etc. You can make these things with real chocolate, but tempering is a precise and complicated process, I think better suited to a laboratory than a home kitchen.

Commercial coating chocolate (also called "dipping chocolate" or "couverture") may be "real" chocolate or compound, just as with other chocolates. It is used for making candy and in bakeries for cooking. The compound chocolate is often simply melted and used as an icing for cookies — frequently just the

ends of finger-shaped cookies or half the diameters of round cookies are dipped into the chocolate.

Pre-melted (or no-melt) chocolate, according to the F.D.A., is not real chocolate; it is a combination of powdered cocoa and hydrogenated vegetable oil. It has a less pronounced chocolate flavor.

White chocolate, according to the F.D.A., is also not really chocolate because it does not contain chocolate liquor. It is pure cocoa butter with sugar, milk, and flavoring — although some brands have additional ingredients. It tastes like very sweet, very mild milk chocolate.

Dutch-process cocoa is not a brand name; it is so called because it was created in Holland by a Dutchman named Coenraad van Houten, who discovered the process of adding alkali very sparingly to cocoa to neutralize the acidity, make it less bitter, and deepen the color. The label will say either "Dutch-process" or "processed with alkali." It may be domestic or imported. I usually use Droste. You may use any unsweetened cocoa in cooking or baking, but I much prefer the richer and darker flavor of Dutch-process. In some recipes, it's best to strain the cocoa before use. To do so, push it through a fine sieve or strainer.

· TO STORE CHOCOLATE ·
Chocolate should be stored where it is cool and dry and the temperature is about 68 to 78 degrees. When the temperature is cold, as in the refrigerator, chocolate will "sweat"

when it is brought to room temperature. When the temperature is too warm, chocolate can develop a "bloom" (a pale exterior). This is simply caused by a slight percentage of the cocoa butter that has separated and risen to the surface. It is OK; the chocolate is not spoiled; use it.

· TO MELT CHOCOLATE ·
When melting chocolate with no other ingredient, the container *must* be absolutely dry. Even the merest drop of moisture will cause the chocolate to "tighten" or "seize," becoming a pasty, gritty mess. (If it should tighten, stir in 1 tablespoon vegetable shortening for each 3 ounces of chocolate.) Melt chocolate by stirring it slowly in the top of a double boiler over hot, but not boiling, water. The reason for this is that boiling water might bubble up and get into the chocolate. Some people swear by melting chocolate in a microwave oven.

Chocolate should melt slowly — it burns easily. To be sure chocolate doesn't get overheated and burn, it is always advisable to remove it from over the hot water before it is completely melted and then stir it until it is entirely melted and smooth. Milk chocolate should be melted even more slowly than other chocolates.

Unsweetened chocolate will run (liquefy) as it melts; sweet, semisweet, and milk chocolates hold their shape when melted and must be stirred. Some semisweet chocolates might not melt as smoothly as unsweetened. If the chocolate is not smooth, stir it briskly with a rubber spatula, pressing against any lumps until it becomes smooth. Various chocolates have different

consistencies when they are melted. Unsweetened chocolate is the thinnest, and milk chocolate the thickest. When you melt chocolate in or with milk (or when you mix melted chocolate and milk), if the mixture is not smooth and the chocolate remains in little flecks, beat it with an electric mixer, wire whisk, or an egg beater until smooth.

Butter

Whenever butter is called for it means unsalted (sweet) butter.

Coffee

Instant espresso or coffee in a recipe means dry — powdered or granules.

Instant coffee powder will dissolve more easily than granules. If you happen to have granules on hand, it is easy to powder it yourself. Whirl some in the blender, then strain it and return the coarse part to the blender to grind until it is all powdered. Medaglia d'Oro instant espresso is finely powdered and works very well. It is generally available at specialty food stores and Italian markets.

Cream

· TO WHIP CREAM ·

Heavy cream may be whipped with an electric mixer, a rotary beater, or a large, balloon-type wire whisk. It will whip more easily and give better results if the cream, bowl, and beaters are cold. The bowl should be metal (but not copper), as that gets and stays colder. Place the bowl and beaters in the refrigerator or freezer just before using them; they should be thoroughly chilled. If the room is very warm, the bowl in which you are whipping the cream should be placed in a larger bowl of ice and water.

Do not overbeat or the cream will lose its smooth texture; if you beat even more it will turn into butter. If you use an electric beater, a handy safeguard is to stop beating before the cream is completely whipped and then finish the job with a wire whisk. This allows less chance for overbeating.

Eggs

These recipes are all based on the use of large eggs, or occasionally extra-large or jumbo eggs.

If directions call for adding whole eggs one at a time, they may all be cracked open ahead of time into one container and poured into the other ingredients, approximately one at a time. Do not crack eggs directly into the batter — you wouldn't know if a piece of shell had been included.

· TO SEPARATE EGGS ·

A new bride, when faced with the direction "separate eggs," placed them carefully on the table about 4 inches apart, and wondered how far they should be from one another…

Eggs separate best (that is, the yolks separate most readily from the whites) when they are cold. Place three small bowls in front of you, one for the whites and the second for the yolks. The third may not be needed, but if you should break the yolk when opening an egg, just drop the whole thing into the third bowl and save it for some other use. When cracking the shell it is important not to use too much pressure or you will break the yolk at the same time.

Some cooks open the egg directly onto the palm of a hand and let the white run through their fingers into a bowl while the yolk remains in their hand. But the most popular

method is to tap the side of the egg firmly on the edge of a bowl to crack the shell. Then, holding the egg in both hands, separate the two halves of the shell, letting some of the white run out into a bowl. Now pour the yolk back and forth from one half of the shell to the other, letting all of the white run out. Drop the yolk into the second bowl.

· TO BEAT EGG WHITES ·

Egg whites may be beaten with an electric mixer, a rotary eggbeater, or a large balloon-type wire whisk. Both the bowl and the beater must be perfectly clean and dry. Just a bit of oil, egg yolk, or grease will prevent the whites from inflating properly.

If you use an electric mixer or a rotary beater, be sure not to use a bowl that is too large, or the whites will be too shallow to get the full benefit of the beater's action. Also, if you use an electric hand mixer or a rotary beater, keep moving it around in the bowl. If you use a mixer on a stand, use a rubber spatula frequently to push the whites from the sides of the bowl into the center. If you use a wire whisk and a bowl, an unlined copper bowl is best, though you may use glass, china, or stainless steel. Do not beat egg whites in an aluminum or plastic bowl.

The beaten whites will have a better — creamier — consistency if you beat some of the sugar into the whites as they begin to hold a shape.

Do not beat egg whites ahead of time. They must be folded in immediately after they are beaten. If it is a cake that you are making, it must then be placed in the oven right away.

Do not overbeat the whites or they will become dry and you won't be able to fold them in without losing the air you have beaten in. Beat only until they hold a shape or a point — "stiff but not dry."

Flour

With only a few exceptions, these recipes call for *sifted* flour. This means that it should be sifted immediately before it is measured. If the flour is not sifted, or if it is sifted long before it is used, it packs down and 1 cup is liable to contain a few spoonfuls more than 1 cup of flour that has been sifted immediately before measuring.

· TO SIFT FLOUR ·

If you have one, use a double or triple sifter (which forces flour through multiple layers of fine mesh); otherwise sift the flour twice using a fine-mesh sieve. Sift onto a piece of wax paper or baking parchment, sifting a bit more than you will need. Use a metal measuring cup. Spoon the sifted flour lightly into the cup. Do not shake the cup or pack the flour down; just scrape any excess off the top with a metal spatula or any flat-sided implement. It is not necessary to wash a flour sifter; just shake it out firmly and store in a plastic bag.

Sugars

When sugar is called for in these recipes, unless otherwise stated, it means granulated white sugar.

Sugar should be measured in the same metal cups as those recommended for flour. If granulated sugar is lumpy it should be strained before use. Brown sugar and confectioners' sugar are best strained also. (Hard lumps in brown sugar will not disappear in mixing or baking.) Unlike flour, sugars may all be strained ahead of time and you may do several pounds at once. Use a very large strainer set over a large bowl and press the sugar through with your fingertips.

· BROWN SUGAR ·
Most brown sugars are made of white granulated sugar to which molasses has been added. Dark brown has a slightly stronger flavor than light brown sugar, but they may be used interchangeably.

You can make your own brown sugar by blending together ½ cup granulated sugar with 2 tablespoons unsulphured molasses. The yield is equivalent to ½ cup brown sugar.

Brown sugar is moist; if it dries out it will harden. It should be stored airtight at room temperature. If your brown sugar has hardened, place a damp paper towel or a slice of apple inside the bag and close the package tightly for 12 hours or more.

· CONFECTIONERS' SUGAR ·
Confectioners' sugar and powdered sugar are exactly the same. They are both granulated sugar that has been pulverized very fine and has had about 3 percent cornstarch added to keep it in a powdery condition. Of these, 4X is the least fine and 10X is the finest; 10X is now the most common. They may be used interchangeably. Store it airtight.

Nuts

I've given weights as well as volume measure for nuts weighing over 2 ounces. If only volume is given, the weight is under 2 ounces.

· TO STORE NUTS ·
All nuts should be stored in the freezer or refrigerator. Always bring them to room temperature before using, and smell them and taste them — rancid nuts would ruin a whole cake or an entire batch of cookies.

· TO BLANCH NUTS ·
To blanch almonds: Cover almonds with boiling water. Let them stand until the water is cool enough to touch. Pick out the almonds one at a time and squeeze each one between thumb and forefinger to squirt off the skin. As each one is skinned, place it on a towel to dry. Then spread the almonds in a single layer in a shallow baking pan and bake in a 200-degree oven for half an hour or so, until they are dry. Do not let them brown. If the almonds are to be split or sliced or slivered, cut them immediately after removing the skin and bake to dry as above.

To blanch hazelnuts: Spread the hazelnuts on a rimmed baking sheet and bake at 350 degrees for 15 minutes, or until the skins parch and begin to flake off. Then, working with a few at a time, place them on a large coarse towel (I use a terrycloth towel). Fold part of the towel over to enclose the nuts and rub firmly against the towel. Or hold that part of the towel between both hands and roll back and forth. The handling and the texture of the towel will cause most of the skins to flake off. Pick out the nuts and discard the skins. Don't worry about the few pieces of skin that remain. This is not as quick and easy as it sounds.

To blanch pistachios: In a small saucepan, bring a few inches of water to a boil. Drop the nuts (no more than ¼ to ½ cup at a time, as the skin is difficult to remove after the nuts have cooled) into the boiling water and let them boil for only a few seconds. They will lose their color if boiled for too long. Remove one nut and pinch the skin off with your fingers. If it slides off easily, immediately drain them all and turn them out onto a paper towel. While they are still warm, pinch off the skins. Now they may be either slivered with a small paring knife or chopped into pieces that are coarse or almost as fine as a powder, when they make a fine decoration.

· TO GRIND NUTS ·

When the instructions say to grind nuts, it means that the nuts should be reduced to a powder, the consistency of coarse flour. *Chopped* nuts are much less fine and are left in visible pieces. To grind nuts in a food processor, use the metal chipping blade; you can also use a nut grinder or blender. If possible, always add some of the flour called for in the recipe. It will help to prevent the nuts from becoming oily. If the recipe does not have any flour, add some of the sugar called for. And do not overprocess.

Dates and Raisins

Raisins and dates must always be fresh and soft — baking will not soften them. They may be softened by steaming them in a vegetable steamer or strainer over boiling water, covered, for about 5 minutes. Dates and raisins should be stored in the refrigerator or freezer.

Orange and Lemon Zest

When grating orange or lemon zests, if your grater has a variety of shaped openings, it is best to grate the zest on the side with the small, round openings, rather than the diamond-shaped ones.

equipment

Double Boiler

Since it is essential to melt chocolate slowly, it is generally best to do it in a double boiler, and many of these recipes specifically call for one. If necessary, you can create a double boiler by placing the ingredients in a heatproof bowl over a saucepan of shallow hot water. The bowl should be wide enough so that its rim rests on the rim of the saucepan and the bowl is supported above the water.

Electric Mixer

Mixing and beating in these recipes may be done with different equipment — an electric hand mixer, any type of stand mixer, or by hand. I use a stand mixer. Susan, my mother's cook for thirty-five years, beat egg whites with a tree branch, in spite of a fantastically well-equipped kitchen. In the country she picked a fresh one as she needed it; in the city, she always washed it carefully and put it away.

Because I use a stand mixer, I have given directions for beating times based on this type of mixer; a handheld mixer might take longer. If you are not using a stand mixer, when directions call for "small bowl of electric mixer," use a bowl with a 7-cup capacity. When directions call for "large bowl of electric mixer," use one with a 4-quart capacity.

Some of these recipes would be too much work without a mixer. Others, especially many of the cookies, may be made using your bare hands for creaming and mixing. Don't be afraid to use your hands.

Measuring Equipment

Success in baking depends on many things. One of the most important is correct oven temperature. I suggest that you buy an oven thermometer, preferably a good one. Hardware stores and quality cookware stores sell them. All oven temperatures in this book are in Fahrenheit.

MEASURING CUPS ·

Glass measuring cups with the measurements marked on the sides are only for measuring liquids. With the cup at eye level, fill carefully to exactly the line indicated. To measure dry ingredients, use the cups that come in sets that include at least four sizes: ¼ cup, ⅓ cup, ½ cup, and 1 cup. Fill to overflowing and then scrape off the extra with a flat spatula or large knife. If you are measuring flour, do not pack it down — but do pack down brown sugar.

MEASURING SPOONS ·

Standard measuring spoons must be used for correct measurements. For dry ingredients, fill to overflowing and then scrape off the excess.

Pastry Bags

Though most bakers prefer the convenience of disposable pastry bags, canvas bags are still available online and at high-end kitchen shops. If you use canvas bags, they should be washed in hot soapy water after use, then just hung up to dry.

It is easier to work with a bag that is too large rather than one that is too small. When filling a pastry bag, unless there is someone else to hold it for you, it is generally easiest if you support the bag by placing it in a tall and wide glass or jar.

Pastry Brushes

There are different types of pastry brushes. Use a good one, or the bristles will come out while you are using it. Sometimes I use an artist's watercolor brush in a large size; it is softer and there are times when I prefer it.

Rolling Pins

If you have many occasions to use a rolling pin (and I hope you will), you really should have different sizes and shapes. Sometimes a very long, thick, and heavy one will be best; for other doughs you will want a smaller, lighter one. The French style, which is extra-long, narrow, and tapered at both ends, is especially good for rolling dough into a round shape, as for a pie crust, while the straight-sided pin is better for an oblong shape.

However, in the absence of any rolling pin at all, other things will do a fair job. Try a straight-sided bottle, tall jar, or drinking glass.

Rubber Spatulas

Rubber spatulas are almost indispensable — do not use plastic; they are not flexible enough. Use rubber spatulas for folding, for some stirring, for scraping bowls, pots, etc. I suggest that you have several. Most spatulas manufactured now are synthetic and heatproof.

Turntable or Lazy Susan

If you ice a cake — either occasionally or often — you will be able to do a much better job (it will be smooth and professional-looking in no time) if you have a cake-decorating turntable. You will be glad if you do. If you don't have one now, you will thank me if I influence you to get one. You will say, "Wow — this is a joy — how did I get along without it — why didn't you tell me sooner?"

A cake-decorating turntable allows a cake to rotate freely as you decorate it. Not that you can't ice a cake without it, but it will not look the same. It works on the same principle as a lazy Susan, and, although a lazy Susan can be used in place of a turntable, it usually does not turn quite so easily.

Turntables are available at specialty kitchen shops and at restaurant and bakery suppliers. They do not have to be expensive. The thing to look for is one that turns very easily. There is no reason why a turntable, if it is not abused, should not last a lifetime or two.

· TO ICE A CAKE ON A TURNTABLE ·

I put the cake on a cake plate and then put the plate on the turntable.

First put the icing on freely just to cover the cake. Then hold a long, narrow metal spatula in one hand, with the blade at about a 30-degree angle against the side or the top of the cake. With your other hand, slowly rotate the turntable. Hold the spatula still as the cake turns and in a few seconds you will have a smooth, sleek, neat-looking cake. It is fun. And exciting.

I also use the turntable when trimming and then fluting the edge of pie crust (you will love using it for this).

techniques

Folding

Many recipes call for folding beaten egg whites and/or whipped cream into another mixture. The egg whites and/or cream have air beaten into them, and folding rather than mixing is done in order to retain the air.

This is an important step and it should be done with care. The knack of doing it well comes with practice and concentration. Remember that you want to incorporate the mixtures without losing any air. That means handling them as little as possible.

If one of the mixtures is heavy, first stir in a bit of the lighter mixture. Then, with a rubber spatula (or occasionally on the lowest speed of an electric mixer), gradually fold the remaining light mixture into the heavier mixture as follows:

Place some of the light mixture on top. With a rubber spatula, rounded side down, cut through the center to the bottom, then toward you against the bottom of the bowl, then up against the side, and finally out over

the top, bringing the heavier ingredients from the bottom over the top. Rotate the bowl slightly with your other hand. Repeat, cutting with the rounded side of the spatula down, rotating the bowl a bit after making each cut. Continue only until both mixtures are combined. Try to make every motion count; do not handle any more than necessary.

Preparing a Cake Pan

To grease a pan: I use butter, which I spread onto the pan with a piece of crumpled wax paper or plastic wrap. Occasionally I also spray the buttered pan with nonstick cooking oil spray.

To dust a pan: For most recipes (but not all), I prefer to coat the buttered pan with bread crumbs rather than flour, because in those recipes there is less chance of sticking if you use crumbs rather than flour. Put a few spoonfuls of crumbs (or flour, when specified) into the buttered pan. Holding the pan over a piece of paper, tilt it in all directions. Tap the pan and shake it back and forth until it is completely coated. Invert the pan over the paper and shake out the excess crumbs or flour. You should have a thin, even coating. Use unseasoned bread crumbs or make your own.

To dust a pan for a dark cake: It is best to use dark crumbs or flour. Simply mix enough unsweetened cocoa powder into fine dry bread crumbs or flour to give the mixture a medium-brown color. It is handy to keep a jar of these already mixed. They last well.

To make homemade bread crumbs: Use sliced white bread with or without the crusts. Place the slices in a single layer on cookie sheets and bake in a 225-degree oven until the bread is completely dry and crisp. (If the bread is so stale that it is completely dry, it is not necessary to bake it.) Break the slices into coarse pieces and grind them in a food processor or blender until the crumbs are rather fine, but not as fine as powder. Strain the crumbs through a coarse strainer and return any chunks to the processor and repeat. Store bread crumbs in an airtight container.

To line a cake pan with parchment: Some recipes call for using baking parchment to line pans. Baking parchment has been coated on both sides with silicone to prevent sticking. It comes in sheets or in a roll and is available in hardware stores and most kitchen shops and supermarkets. To line a pan, place the pan right side up on the paper and trace around it. If it is a tube pan, stick the pencil into the tube and trace the

opening. Cut the paper with scissors. After you have cut the opening for the tube, cut short lines radiating from the tube hole about ½ inch deep and ¼ inch apart to ensure a smooth fit.

Baking a Cake

The minute you put a cake into the oven, set a timer and write down the time that it should be finished. Good insurance.

It is important not to overbake cakes, or they become dry. There are several ways to test for doneness, but the tests vary with different cakes. (All of the recipes here indicate which test or tests to use.) Some cakes will come slightly away from the sides of the pan when done, the top of others will spring back when touched lightly with your fingertip, while others must be tested with a cake tester or a toothpick. Insert it gently straight down into the middle of the cake, going all the way to the pan bottom. If it comes out clean, the cake is done. In most cases, if some moist batter clings to the tester, the cake needs to be baked longer. Test in two or three places to be sure.

Preparing a Cake Plate

When you are ready to ice a cake, begin by tearing off a 10-inch length of wax paper or baking parchment. Fold it crossways into four parts, then cut through the folds with a knife, making four 10 x 3-inch strips. Place them in a square on the cake plate, and put the cake on top, making sure the entire edge is touching paper. As soon as the cake is iced, remove the paper, pulling each strip out by a narrow end and leaving the cake plate clean.

Freezing a Cake

All of the cakes in this book may be frozen before icing (individual layers should be wrapped separately or they will stick together) and most of them can also be frozen after, except where indicated in individual recipes (for instance, 7-Minute Icing doesn't freeze). Iced cakes should be frozen unwrapped and then, when firm, wrapped airtight — plastic wrap is best for this. If you freeze a cake on a plate and then want to remove it from the plate to wrap it, be sure to put wax paper or baking parchment between the cake and the plate or else the cake will stick.

Having frozen every refreezable recipe in this collection, I find that contrary to general opinion it is better to thaw iced cakes before removing the wrapping. They sweat while thawing. If they have been unwrapped the moisture collects on the cake. If they have not been unwrapped, the moisture collects on the outside of the wrapping.

Freezing Cookies

Most cookies freeze quite well. It is always extremely handy (I think it is a luxury) to have cookies in the freezer for unexpected company; they usually thaw quickly, and many can be served frozen direct from the freezer.

(Almost always, when I need a gift for someone, my first thought is cookies. And if they are in the freezer, individually wrapped, all I have to do is plan some attractive packaging for them.)

The same rule about thawing cakes applies to cookies — thaw before unwrapping.

Any cake or cookies that may be frozen can be thawed and refrozen — even several times. I do it often. I would rather refreeze it immediately than let it stand around and get stale.

Label the packages in your freezer — if not, you might wind up with a freezer full of UFOs (Unidentified Frozen Objects).

using ingredients

To Bring Ingredients to Room Temperature

In individual recipes I have indicated the very few times I actually bring ingredients to room temperature before using. Otherwise they may be used right out of the refrigerator. If butter is too hard, cut it into small pieces, and let it stand only until it can be worked with.

To Add Dry Ingredients Alternately with Liquid

Always begin and end with dry ingredients. The procedure is generally to add about one-third of the dry ingredients, half the liquid, the second third of the dry, the rest of the liquid, and finally the last third of the dry.

Use the lowest speed on an electric mixer for this. After each addition mix only until smooth. If your mixer is the type that allows for a rubber spatula to be used while it is in motion, help the blending along by using the rubber spatula to scrape around the sides of the bowl. If the mixer does not have the room, or if it is the handheld kind, stop it frequently and scrape the bowl with the spatula.

a final word

I once put a cake in the oven and then realized that I had forgotten to use the baking powder that the recipe called for. I learned the hard way that it is necessary to organize all the ingredients listed in a recipe — line them up in the order they are called for — before you actually start mixing. As you use an ingredient, set it aside. That way, nothing should be left on the work surface when you are through. A quick look during and after mixing will let you know if something was left out.

SIMPLE CAKES

CHOCOLATE INTRIGUE

NOTE

⌄

To serve this after freezing, thaw it covered in the refrigerator for at least 5 or 6 hours.

Makes 2 small loaves, about 8 portions each Gloria and Jacques Pépin and some of their friends came to our home for a visit one afternoon while I was working on this recipe. They all said yes, they would like some. When it was served, they all raved about it, more than I expected since it is a plain little loaf. They all asked what the exotic flavor was. I asked them to guess. Jacques guessed many spices — a mixture of spices — some of which I had never heard of. And they never did guess what it was. When I told them that it was just a little bit of black pepper, they thought I was kidding; they thought that there must be more to it. They all had seconds.

It is a moist cake with a fine texture and an extremely generous amount of chocolate. It keeps well (preferably in the refrigerator), slices beautifully, and is quick and easy to make.

You need two small loaf pans, preferably 8 x 4 x 2½-inch pans with a 5-cup capacity, but I have also used 8½ x 4½ x 2¾-inch pans with a 6-cup capacity; the cakes were equally delicious in the larger pans, although not quite as high.

3 ounces semisweet chocolate

2 ounces unsweetened chocolate

1 tablespoon instant espresso or coffee powder

1⅓ cups boiling water

1¼ cups *sifted* unbleached all-purpose flour

¼ cup unsweetened cocoa powder (preferably Dutch-process), plus more for serving

1½ teaspoons baking powder

1 teaspoon salt

½ teaspoon finely ground black pepper (preferably freshly ground)

4 ounces (1 stick) unsalted butter

1½ teaspoons vanilla extract

2 cups sugar

3 large eggs

OPTIONAL: Bittersweet Chocolate Sauce with Cocoa (page 41) and/or ice cream

Adjust an oven rack one-third up from the bottom and preheat the oven to 325 degrees. Butter two 5-cup loaf pans (see headnote) and dust all over with bread crumbs. Tap over paper to remove excess crumbs and set aside.

In a small saucepan over moderate heat, place both chocolates with the espresso or coffee and boiling water. Whisk frequently until the chocolates are melted and the mixture is smooth. Transfer to a small pitcher that will be easy to pour from

continues ⌄

(i.e. a 2-cup measuring cup) and set aside to cool to lukewarm.

Sift together the flour, cocoa, baking powder, salt, and pepper and set aside.

In the large bowl of an electric mixer, beat the butter until soft. Beat in the vanilla and then gradually add the sugar and beat well until incorporated. Add the eggs and beat until smooth. Then, on low speed, alternately add the sifted dry ingredients in three additions and the chocolate mixture in two additions. Scrape the bowl as necessary and beat until smooth. Pour the mixture (which will be very liquid) into the prepared pans.

Bake both pans on the same rack for 1 hour and 10 to 15 minutes; cover the pans loosely with foil after about 40 minutes of baking. Bake until a cake tester gently inserted comes out clean; since the cake forms a hard crust on top, it is best to insert the cake tester on the side of the top edge, where there is no crust.

Let the cakes cool in the pans for about 15 minutes. Then cover each pan with a rack,

invert the pan and rack, remove pan, and let the cake cool upside down (the bottom of the cake is moist and tender at this stage).

It is best to wrap the cakes in plastic wrap and refrigerate them for several hours or overnight.

To serve: Cover the top of each cake with a generous layer of unsweetened cocoa powder, sprinkling it on through a wide but fine strainer. Refrigerate.

Work next to the sink so that you can hold the knife under hot running water before making each cut. With a long and sharp knife, cut the cake into small portions. Since it is so light and delicate, work carefully. With a wide metal spatula, transfer the pieces to cake plates.

Serve plain. Or, as an important dessert, serve with Bittersweet Chocolate Sauce with Cocoa and, if you wish, ice cream as well. Pour the sauce on one side of a portion of cake and place the ice cream on the other side.

Bittersweet Chocolate Sauce with Cocoa

1 cup strained unsweetened cocoa powder (preferably Dutch-process)

¾ cup sugar

1¼ teaspoons instant espresso or coffee powder

Pinch of salt

1 cup boiling water

1 tablespoon plus 1½ teaspoons dark rum

In a heavy 5- to 6-cup saucepan, stir together the cocoa, sugar, espresso or coffee, and salt to mix. Add the water and stir with a wire whisk.

Place over moderate heat and stir and scrape the pan constantly with a rubber spatula until the mixture comes to a boil. Immediately reduce the heat to low and let barely simmer, stirring and scraping the pan constantly with a rubber spatula, for 3 minutes.

Remove from the heat. Strain. Stir in the rum. Place in a covered jar and refrigerate.

Check the sauce ahead of time. If it has become too thick to serve, let it stand at room temperature and stir it a bit.

Pour the sauce into a pitcher and serve quickly while it is cold.

86-PROOF CHOCOLATE CAKE

12 portions This is an especially moist and luscious dark chocolate cake, generously flavored with bourbon and coffee. Sensational! It is made in a fancy pan and is served without icing. I have made this at demonstrations all around the country. It is one of my favorite cakes to teach because people can't wait to make it.

NOTE

Of course you can substitute rum, Cognac, or Scotch whisky for the bourbon; or Amaretto, the suggestion of a friend of mine in Ohio.

- 5 ounces unsweetened chocolate
- 2 cups *sifted* all-purpose flour
- 1 teaspoon baking soda
- ¼ teaspoon salt

- ¼ cup instant coffee or espresso powder
- Boiling water
- Cold water
- ½ cup bourbon (see Note)
- 8 ounces (2 sticks) unsalted butter

- 1 teaspoon vanilla extract
- 2 cups sugar
- 3 large eggs
- OPTIONAL: additional bourbon
- OPTIONAL: confectioners' sugar

Adjust rack one-third up from bottom of the oven and preheat oven to 325 degrees. You will need a 9-inch Bundt pan (this is the smaller size; it is called a mini Bundt pan) or any other fancy tube pan with a 10-cup capacity. Butter the pan (even if it is a nonstick pan). Then dust the whole inside of the pan with fine, dry bread crumbs. Invert over a piece of paper and tap lightly to shake out excess crumbs. Set the pan aside.

Place the chocolate in the top of a small double boiler over hot water on low heat. Cover and cook only until melted; then remove the top of the double boiler and set it aside, uncovered, to cool slightly.

Sift together the flour, baking soda, and salt and set aside.

In a 2-cup glass measuring cup, dissolve the coffee in a bit of boiling water. Add cold water to the 1½-cup line. Add the bourbon. Set aside.

Cream the butter in the large bowl of an electric mixer. Add the vanilla and sugar and beat to mix well. Add the eggs one at a time, beating until smooth after each addition. Add the chocolate and beat until smooth.

Then, on low speed, alternately add the sifted dry ingredients in three additions with the coffee mixture in two additions, adding the liquids very gradually to avoid splashing, and scraping the bowl with a rubber spatula after each addition. Be sure to beat until smooth after each addition, especially after the last. It will be a thin mixture.

continues ↘

Pour the batter into the prepared pan. Rotate the pan a bit briskly, first in one direction, then in the other, to level the top. (In a mini Bundt pan the batter will almost reach the top of the pan, but it is OK — it will not run over, and you will have a beautifully high cake.)

Bake for 1 hour and 10 or 15 minutes. Test by inserting a cake tester into the middle of the cake and bake only until the tester comes out clean and dry.

Cool in the pan for about 15 minutes. Then cover with a rack and invert. Remove the pan, sprinkle the cake with a bit of additional bourbon if you like, and leave the cake upside down on the rack to cool.

Before serving, if you wish, sprinkle the top with confectioners' sugar through a fine strainer.

This is a simple, no-icing cake, wonderful as is. Or with a spoonful of vanilla- or bourbon-flavored whipped cream.

TEXAS CHOCOLATE MUFFINS

12 muffins These are not muffins; they are my idea of brownies baked like cupcakes. But in Texas for some reason they call them muffins. They have two kinds of chocolate plus cocoa. They are dense, rich, and very chocolaty. Especially beautiful — totally plain. They are quickly and easily mixed in a saucepan.

NOTE

To toast pecans, place them in a shallow pan in the middle of a preheated 350-degree oven for 12 to 15 minutes.

1 cup *sifted* all-purpose flour

Pinch of salt

3 tablespoons unsweetened cocoa powder

8 ounces (2 sticks) unsalted butter

2 ounces unsweetened chocolate

2 ounces semisweet chocolate

1½ cups sugar

4 large eggs

1 teaspoon vanilla extract

¼ teaspoon almond extract

7 ounces (2 cups) toasted pecans (see Note), broken into large pieces

Adjust a rack one-third up from the bottom of the oven and preheat the oven to 350 degrees. Line the cups of a 12-cup standard muffin pan with paper liners (or butter them even if they are nonstick). Set aside.

Sift together the flour, salt, and cocoa and set aside.

Place the butter and both of the chocolates in a heavy 2½- to 3-quart saucepan over moderately low heat; stir frequently with a wooden spoon until melted and smooth.

Remove the pan from the heat. Stir in the sugar, the eggs one at a time, the vanilla and almond extracts, and then the sifted dry ingredients. After the dry ingredients

are moistened, stir briskly until smooth. If necessary, whisk with a firm wire whisk. Then stir in the nuts.

This is a thick and gooey mixture and I find it clumsy to spoon into the prepared muffin cups. Instead, I pour it, one part at a time, into a 2-cup measuring cup with a spout (which is wide and easy to pour from). Then, with the help of a teaspoon, I pour it into the cups. This is a large amount of batter for 12 muffins; the cups will be filled to the tops. It is OK. The muffins will mound high during baking but they will not run over. They might run into one another a bit on the sides, but they will not stick to each other.

Bake for 33 to 35 minutes, rotating the pan front to back once during baking. To test

continues ⌟

for doneness, insert a toothpick into the middle of a muffin; it should come out just barely or almost dry and clean. A bit of moist batter may cling to the toothpick. Do not overbake. During baking, these will rise with inch-high, perfectly rounded tops that have a gorgeous crackly texture.

Remove the muffins from the pan and cool them on a rack. As they cool, they will develop a hard and crunchy crust that is delicious.

BLACK AND WHITE CAKE

NOTE

You can substitute 1 tablespoon orange zest and 2 teaspoons orange juice for the lemon zest and juice.

12 generous portions This is a marble cake in which the black and white batters form a dramatically beautiful swirling pattern. Whereas most marble cakes have more white batter than dark, this one deliciously has more dark than white. And the dark is very dark.

2 teaspoons instant coffee powder

¼ cup boiling water

⅓ cup strained unsweetened cocoa powder (preferably Dutch-process)

2½ cups *sifted* all-purpose flour

2 teaspoons baking powder

Finely grated zest of 1 small lemon (see Note)

2 teaspoons lemon juice (see Note)

8 ounces (2 sticks) unsalted butter

1 teaspoon vanilla extract

1½ cups sugar

4 large eggs, separated

⅔ cup milk

½ teaspoon almond extract

Generous pinch of salt

OPTIONAL: **confectioners' sugar (to be used after the cake is baked)**

Adjust rack one-third up from the bottom of the oven and preheat oven to 375 degrees. Use a 9-inch Bundt pan (called a mini Bundt, with a 10-cup capacity) or a 9 x 3½-inch tube pan. Or you can use a 10-inch Bundt pan, but the cake will not be as high. (In the 9-inch Bundt pan the cake will rise high and make a cute, fat little cake that is adorable.) Butter the pan (even if it is a nonstick pan), dust it thoroughly with fine, dry bread crumbs, and invert over paper to shake out excess crumbs. Set aside.

In a small mixing bowl, dissolve the coffee in the boiling water. Add the cocoa and stir until smooth; remove small lumps by stirring and pressing against the lumps with a rubber spatula. Set aside to cool slightly.

Sift the flour with the baking powder and set aside. Mix the grated lemon zest with the lemon juice and set aside.

In the large bowl of an electric mixer, cream the butter. Mix in the vanilla and 1¼ cups of the sugar (reserve ¼ cup). Beat to mix thoroughly. Then add the yolks all at once and beat well. On low speed, add the sifted dry ingredients in three additions, alternating with the milk in two additions. Scrape the bowl with a rubber spatula and beat only until each addition is incorporated.

Remove 2 cups of the batter and transfer to a medium or large bowl. This will be the white batter. Stir in the lemon zest and juice and set aside.

To the batter remaining in the mixer bowl, add the almond extract and cocoa mixture and mix until smooth. Set aside.

In the small bowl of the electric mixer with clean beaters, add the salt to the egg

continues ↘

whites and beat until they hold a soft peak. On moderate speed, gradually add the reserved ¼ cup sugar, then increase the speed to high and beat until the whites hold a shape — but they must not be too stiff or dry; stop beating just before they are stiff.

Stir about ½ cup of the meringue into each of the batters to lighten them a bit. Then alternately fold a generous ½ cup into each of the batters until it is all used.

You will have more chocolate batter than white. Use a tablespoon for spooning the chocolate and a teaspoon for the white. Place about five well-rounded large spoonfuls of the chocolate batter in the bottom of the pan, leaving a small space between the spoonfuls. Then place a well-rounded smaller spoonful of the white batter in each empty space. Use large portions; they will make a bolder dramatic pattern. For the second layer, place white on chocolate and vice versa. Continue until you have used all of both batters. (Do not cut through as with most marble cakes.)

Briskly rotate the pan first in one direction and then the other to level the top.

Bake for about 1 hour, or until a cake tester gently inserted into the middle of the cake comes out dry. If the top of the cake becomes too dark, cover it loosely with aluminum foil.

Let the cake cool in the pan for 10 to 15 minutes. Then cover it with a rack and invert the pan and the rack. Remove the pan and let the cake cool upside down. If you have baked it in a smooth tube pan, cover it with another rack and invert again to let the cake cool right side up.

This does not need any icing. If you wish, sprinkle a bit of confectioners' sugar over the top, shaking it through a fine strainer held over the cake.

Cut into thin slices, two or three to a serving.

ORANGE CHOCOLATE LOAF CAKE FROM FLORIDA

About 12 portions This recipe came from a magnificent orange grove in central Florida where the cake is a specialty of the house. When we visited there, large trays of the sliced cake were served along with extra-tall glasses of ice-cold, sweet-and-tart just-squeezed orange juice.

The cake, made with whipped cream instead of butter, is a deliciously plain, moist, coal-black loaf flavored with orange zest and steeped in orange juice after it is baked. The recipe may easily be doubled and baked in two pans.

1¼ cups *sifted* all-purpose flour

2 teaspoons baking powder

¼ teaspoon salt

½ cup unsweetened cocoa powder (preferably Dutch-process)

1 cup sugar

1 cup heavy cream

1 teaspoon vanilla extract

2 large eggs

Finely grated zest of 1 large, deep-colored orange

GLAZE

⅓ cup orange juice

3 tablespoons sugar

Adjust rack one-third up from the bottom of the oven and preheat oven to 350 degrees. You will need a loaf pan measuring about 8½ x 4½ x 2¾ inches, or one with about a 6-cup capacity. Butter the pan and dust it all over lightly with fine, dry bread crumbs, shake out excess crumbs, and set the pan aside.

Sift together the flour, baking powder, salt, cocoa, and sugar and set aside.

Beat the cream and vanilla in the small bowl of an electric mixer until the cream holds a definite shape. On low speed, add the eggs, one at a time, scraping the bowl with a rubber spatula and beating only until the egg is incorporated after each addition. (The eggs will thin the cream slightly.)

Transfer to the large bowl of the mixer and gradually, on low speed, add the sifted dry ingredients, scraping the bowl and beating only until smooth. Remove from the mixer and stir in the grated zest. That's all there is to it.

continues ↘

Turn the batter into the prepared pan and smooth the top. Bake for about 1 hour and 5 minutes, until the top springs back when lightly pressed with a fingertip.

For the Glaze

As soon as the cake goes into the oven, mix the orange juice with the sugar and let it stand while the cake is baking.

After you remove the cake from the oven, let it cool for 5 minutes. Then, a little at a time, brush the orange juice–sugar mixture all over the cake; encourage most of it to run down the sides between the cake and the pan, but thoroughly wet the top also. The cake will absorb it all.

Let the cake stand in the pan until it is completely cool. Then cover the pan loosely with a piece of wax paper. Invert the cake into the palm of your hand — easy does it — remove the pan, cover the cake with a rack, and invert again, leaving the cake right side up.

OLD-FASHIONED CHOCOLATE LOAF CAKE

NOTE

Because of the long, slow baking called for in recipes for old-fashioned pound cakes, these cakes develop a crumbly top crust. To soften the crust slightly, steam it. That is, cover the cake loosely with a cotton towel or napkin as soon as it is removed from the oven, and then again when it is removed from the pan.

8 to 10 portions This is a plain, fine-grained cake similar to a pound cake. It slices beautifully, keeps well if wrapped airtight, and makes a great gift. Serve it with tea or coffee, with cold milk, or as a dessert with ice cream and hot fudge sauce. It is best to let it (and all pound cakes) stand overnight before slicing. This recipe calls for long, slow baking.

- 2 cups *sifted* all-purpose flour
- ½ teaspoon baking powder
- ½ teaspoon salt

- 2 ounces unsweetened chocolate
- 4 ounces semisweet chocolate

- 8 ounces (2 sticks) unsalted butter
- 2 teaspoons vanilla extract
- 1¼ cups sugar
- 5 large eggs, separated

Adjust rack one-third up from the bottom of the oven and preheat oven to 300 degrees. You will need a loaf pan with an 8-cup capacity. I have made this in many different pans. Since there is no conformity among manufacturers as to pan sizes, you will have to check the pan's volume with measuring cups of water.

Butter the pan and dust it with fine, dry bread crumbs; invert and tap the pan to shake out excess. Or line the pan with buttered foil, buttered side up (in which case the crumbs are not necessary). Set aside.

Sift together the flour, baking powder, and salt and set aside.

Place both chocolates in the top of a small double boiler over hot water on moderate heat. Stir occasionally until the chocolate is melted and smooth. Remove the top of the double boiler and set aside to cool the chocolate slightly.

In the large bowl of an electric mixer, cream the butter. Add the vanilla and then 1 cup of the sugar (reserve remaining ¼ cup) and beat to mix thoroughly. Add the egg yolks all at once and beat well, scraping the bowl with a rubber spatula. Add the chocolate and beat until blended. On low speed, gradually add the sifted dry ingredients and beat, scraping the bowl with the spatula, only until they are smoothly incorporated.

In the small bowl of the mixer (with clean beaters), beat the egg whites on moderately high speed until the whites hold a soft shape. Gradually add the reserved ¼ cup sugar and continue to beat until the whites hold a firm shape and are stiff but not dry.

To fold the whites into the thick chocolate mixture: If you have a large rubber spatula use that, or start the folding with a large wooden spatula and then change to a standard-size rubber spatula. Fold in one-third of the whites, then another third, and finally fold in the remainder — with the first two additions do not fold completely (a bit of white may remain), but after the last addition fold until no white remains.

Turn the mixture into the prepared pan and smooth the top. Bake until a cake tester inserted in the center of the cake comes out clean and dry. A 14 x 4¼ x 2¾-inch pan will take about 1 hour and 40 minutes. (A long, thin pan will take less time than a short, wide one.) While it bakes, the cake will crack along the top, as do most pound cakes.

Let the cake cool in the pan for about 15 minutes. Then very gently invert the cake onto a rack and remove the pan. With your hands, carefully turn the cake right side up and let it stand until cool.

Wrap the cake in plastic wrap and let it stand at room temperature (preferably overnight) before serving.

Pound cake should be sliced rather thin. Use a long, thin, sharp knife and cut with a sawing motion.

Since pan sizes vary so much, I can't tell you what size cake you will have. But it will be 2¼ pounds.

CHOCOLATE SOUFFLÉ CAKE

NOTE

↓

When cutting this cake, it will crumble a bit as you cut through the bottom (previously the top) crisp crust. (It did at Fay and Allen's, too.) Don't try to cut thin slices.

`10 portions` At one time, one of the most talked-about chocolate cakes in New York City was the Chocolate Soufflé Cake from Fay and Allen's Foodworks (a fancy food store on the Upper East Side). I had heard raves about it. It was described as a soft, moist, rich, dark chocolate mixture with a crisp, brownie-like crust.

In September 1980, my husband and I were on a tour to promote my chocolate book, and were in New York for only a few hectic days. As we were checking out of our hotel I suddenly remembered the Chocolate Soufflé Cake. With the taxi waiting, I rushed to the phone to call Fay and Allen's, and to my surprise and joy, within a few minutes I had the recipe. I spoke to Mr. Mark Allen, the man who bakes the cakes and the son of the owner. He could not have been nicer or more agreeable. He told me that he got the recipe when he attended the Culinary Institute of America.

It is a flourless mixture similar to a rich chocolate mousse, baked in a large Bundt pan. During baking, a crisp crust forms on the outside; the inside stays moist.

The recipe calls for long, slow baking. It is best to serve it hot, right out of the oven. It is even better if you serve a few fresh raspberries and/or strawberries with each portion.

8 ounces semisweet chocolate (you can use any chocolate labeled semisweet, bittersweet, or extra-bittersweet — the less sweet the better)

8 ounces (2 sticks) unsalted butter

2 tablespoons vegetable oil

8 large eggs, separated

1 cup granulated sugar

1 teaspoon vanilla extract

¼ teaspoon salt

Confectioners' sugar or Whipped Cream (page 56)

Adjust a rack one-third up from the bottom of the oven and preheat the oven to 300 degrees. You will need a 10-inch Bundt pan or any other fancy-shaped tube pan with a 12-cup capacity. Butter the pan (even if it has a nonstick lining); the best way is to use room-temperature butter and brush it on with a pastry brush. Then sprinkle granulated sugar all over the pan; in order to get the sugar on the tube, sprinkle it on with your fingertips. Shake the pan to coat it all with sugar, and then invert it over a piece of paper and tap to shake out excess. Set the pan aside.

continues ⌄

Break up or coarsely chop the chocolate and place it in the top of a large double boiler over hot water on moderate heat. Cut up the butter and add it, and the oil, to the chocolate. Cover and let cook until almost completely melted. Then stir, or whisk with a wire whisk, until completely melted and smooth. Remove from the hot water.

In a mixing bowl, stir the yolks a bit with a wire whisk just to mix. Then, gradually, in a few additions, whisk in about half of the hot chocolate mixture. Then, off the heat, add the yolks to the remaining hot chocolate mixture and mix together (the mixture will thicken a bit as the heat of the chocolate cooks the eggs). Add the granulated sugar and vanilla and stir to mix. Set aside.

In the large bowl of an electric mixer, add the salt to the egg whites and beat until the whites hold a point when the beaters are raised but not until they are stiff or dry.

Fold a few large spoonfuls of the whites into the chocolate mixture. Then add the remaining whites and fold together gently only until incorporated.

Gently turn the mixture into the prepared pan.

Bake for 2¼ hours. During baking the cake will rise and then sink; it will sink more in the middle than on the edges. That is as it should be. It is OK. Remove from the oven and let stand in the pan for about 5 minutes.

Cover the cake with an inverted serving plate. Hold the pan and the plate firmly together and turn them over. The sugar coating in the pan forms a crust and the cake will slide out of the pan easily.

Serve while still hot. If you wish, cover the top of the cake generously with confectioners' sugar, sprinkling it on through a fine strainer held over the cake. Brush excess sugar off the plate. Or serve with whipped cream, spooning a generous amount over and alongside each portion.

(On a later trip to New York I went to Fay and Allen's just to eat this cake there. I was thrilled to see that it was precisely the same as the ones I had made. They served it quite warm, just out of the oven, with a generous topping of icy cold whipped cream.)

Whipped Cream

2 cups heavy cream

¼ cup confectioners' sugar

1½ teaspoons vanilla extract

In a chilled bowl with chilled beaters, whip the ingredients only until the cream holds a shape; it is more delicious if it is not really stiff. (If you whip the cream ahead of time and refrigerate it, it will separate slightly as it stands; just whisk it a bit with a wire whisk before serving.)

OLD-FASHIONED FUDGE CAKE

NOTE

`12 to 16 portions` An old recipe for a large two-layer cake — dark-colored, light-textured, and delicate, with a thick layer of bittersweet chocolate filling and icing that stays soft and creamy. This is a delicious cake, and easy. So easy, in fact, that after I recommended the recipe to a young girl as her first experience in cake baking, she not only proudly brought me a slice, but started making it for friends and relatives. She was eleven years old.

Although I told an eleven-year-old to do the following when measuring the vinegar, it is advisable for everyone. I do it myself. Pour the vinegar out into a small cup first, then scoop it out with the measuring spoon. If you pour a clear liquid into a measuring spoon held over the mixing bowl, it is possible to easily splash in more than you mean to.

3 ounces unsweetened chocolate

1¾ cups *sifted* cake flour

1 teaspoon baking powder

1 teaspoon baking soda

½ teaspoon salt

4 ounces (1 stick) unsweetened butter

1½ cups granulated sugar

2 large eggs

2 tablespoons plus 1½ teaspoons white vinegar (see Note)

1 teaspoon vanilla extract

1 cup milk

WHIPPED CHOCOLATE ICING

6 ounces unsweetened chocolate

4 ounces (1 stick) unsalted butter

2¼ cups confectioners' sugar

2 large eggs

3 tablespoons hot water

½ teaspoon vanilla extract

Adjust rack to center of the oven and preheat oven to 350 degrees. Butter two 9-inch round layer-cake pans and line the bottoms with baking parchment or wax paper cut to fit. Butter the paper, dust with flour, then invert over a piece of paper and tap lightly to shake out excess. Set aside.

Place the chocolate in the top of a small double boiler over hot water on moderate heat. Cover until partially melted, then uncover and stir until completely melted. Remove from the hot water and set aside, uncovered, to cool slightly.

Sift together the cake flour, baking powder, baking soda, and salt and set aside.

In the large bowl of an electric mixer, cream the butter. Add the granulated sugar and beat to mix well. Add the eggs one at a time, beating until the egg is thoroughly incorporated after each addition. Mix in the vinegar and vanilla. The mixture will look curdled — it is OK. Add the melted chocolate and beat only until smooth.

On low speed, add the sifted dry ingredients in three additions, alternating

continues ↘

with the milk in two additions. Scrape the bowl with a rubber spatula and beat only until smooth after each addition.

Place half of the mixture in each prepared pan and smooth the tops.

Bake for 35 to 40 minutes, until the layers begin to come away from the sides of the pans and the tops spring back when lightly pressed with a fingertip.

With a small, sharp knife, cut around the insides of the pans to release. Then let the layers stand in the pans for 5 minutes. Cover each layer with a rack, invert, remove the pan, peel off the paper lining, cover with another rack, and invert again, leaving the layer right side up to cool.

Prepare a large, flat cake plate by lining the sides with four strips of wax paper. Place one layer upside down on the plate, checking to be sure that the papers touch the layer all around. If you have a cake-decorating turntable or a lazy Susan, place the plate on it.

For the Icing

Place the chocolate and butter in the top of a small double boiler over hot water on moderate heat. Cover until partially

melted, then uncover and stir until completely melted.

Meanwhile, place all the remaining ingredients in the small bowl of an electric mixer. Beat briefly only to mix. Set the small bowl in a large bowl and fill the empty space left in the large bowl with ice and water, filling to about three-quarters the depth of the large bowl. (If you are using an electric mixer on a stand, use the large mixer bowl for the ice and water but adjust the stand for "small bowl.")

Add the melted chocolate and butter and beat until the mixture thickens slightly. Remove both bowls (together) from the mixer. With a rubber spatula stir the icing over the ice and water until it thickens to the consistency of thick mayonnaise.

Spread a scant third of the icing about ¼ inch thick over the bottom layer of cake. Cover with the other layer, placing it right side up (both bottoms meet in the middle). Spread the sides and the top with the remaining icing. It may either be spread smoothly with a long, narrow metal spatula, or it may be formed into swirls.

Remove the strips of wax paper by gently pulling each one out toward a narrow end.

MARBLE LOAF CAKE

8 to 10 portions This is a striking and delicious cake baked in a loaf pan. When cut, it reveals beautiful swirls of light and dark batter. Topped with a delicious semisweet chocolate glaze, it is a wonderful treat for company, or to have with a cup of coffee.

NOTE

This recipe may also be made in two smaller pans, each 8 x 4 x 2½ inches (1-quart capacity). The baking time should then be reduced to 50 minutes.

1½ ounces unsweetened chocolate

2½ cups *sifted* cake flour

½ teaspoon salt

1 tablespoon baking powder

4 ounces (1 stick) unsalted butter

1 teaspoon vanilla extract

1 teaspoon almond extract

1½ cups sugar

3 large eggs

¾ cup milk

1 tablespoon instant coffee powder

THICK CHOCOLATE GLAZE

6 ounces semisweet chocolate

1 tablespoon unsalted butter

3 tablespoons light corn syrup

2 tablespoons milk

Adjust rack one-third up from bottom of oven and preheat to 375 degrees. Butter an 11 x 5 x 3-inch loaf pan (see Note) or similar shape with an 8- to 9-cup capacity. Dust all over lightly with fine, dry bread crumbs.

Melt the chocolate in a small heatproof cup set in a pan of shallow hot water on moderately low heat. Set aside to cool.

Sift together the flour, salt, and baking powder and set aside.

In large bowl of electric mixer, beat the butter to soften it a bit. Add the vanilla and almond extracts and then the sugar. Beat for a minute or two. Add the eggs one at a time and beat at high speed for 2 minutes, scraping the bowl occasionally with rubber spatula.

On lowest speed, alternately add the sifted dry ingredients in three additions and the

milk in two additions, scraping the bowl with the rubber spatula as necessary and beating only until smooth after each addition.

Remove from mixer. Transfer one-third of the batter to small bowl of electric mixer. Add the melted chocolate and instant coffee and, with the same beaters on low speed, beat only until mixed. Remove from mixer.

Alternately place spoonfuls of both batters in the prepared pan. With a small metal spatula or a knife, cut zigzag through the batter, cutting in one direction first and then the other — do not overdo it.

Bake for 1 hour, or until the top springs back when lightly touched and a cake tester comes out dry.

continues ⌄

Cool in pan for 10 minutes. Cover with a rack, invert, and remove the pan. Cover with another rack and invert again to cool on the rack, right side up.

For the Glaze

In the top of a small double boiler over hot water on moderate heat, melt the chocolate and the butter. With a small wire whisk, beat in the corn syrup and milk,

beating until smooth. Remove from heat. Cool slightly, stirring occasionally.

Place a large piece of wax paper under the cake on the rack. While glaze is still warm, pour it thickly over the top of the cake. Smooth it over the top only. If a bit runs down the sides, just leave it. Transfer cake to a platter or cake board.

Let stand for a few hours to allow the glaze to set.

SOUR CHERRY CHOCOLATE TORTE

`10 portions` Chocolate and cherries is a marriage made in heaven. This is a shallow, single-layer chocolate cake without icing, but with a hidden layer of sour cherries baked into the middle. It is not only an intriguing taste combination, but the cherries keep the cake marvelously moist. It is a chic, sophisticated little cake for a dinner party. Extremely quick and easy, it can be made a few hours ahead and served while it is still slightly warm, or made early in the day and served at room temperature.

NOTE

That small amount (1 tablespoon) of kirsch in the whipped cream will barely be detectable, but to me it is just enough. Kirsch, cherries, chocolate, and whipped cream is one of the world's greatest taste combinations. If you would like a more noticeable kirsch taste, add another tablespoon. Or, if you wish, use ½ teaspoon of vanilla extract in place of the kirsch. And if you love whipped cream, double the amounts.

- 1 (1-pound) can red sour pitted cherries packed in water
- 6 ounces semisweet chocolate
- 2½ ounces (½ cup) almonds, blanched or unblanched
- 6 ounces (1½ sticks) unsalted butter
- 1 teaspoon vanilla extract
- ¼ teaspoon almond extract
- ⅔ cup granulated sugar
- 3 large eggs
- ⅔ cup *sifted* all-purpose flour

OPTIONAL: Whipped Cream (page 62)

Adjust rack one-third up from bottom of the oven and preheat oven to 350 degrees. Butter a 9-inch springform pan and dust it with fine, dry bread crumbs. Invert over a piece of paper and tap to shake out extra crumbs. Set the pan aside.

Drain all the liquid from the cherries (you should have a scant 2 cups of drained cherries). Spread them in a single layer on several thicknesses of paper towels and let stand.

Place the chocolate in the top of a small double boiler over hot water on moderate heat. Cover until partially melted, then uncover and stir until completely melted and smooth. Remove the top of the double boiler and set aside uncovered to cool slightly.

The almonds must be ground to a fine powder; do this in a food processor, blender, or nut grinder and set aside.

Cream the butter in the large bowl of an electric mixer. Add the vanilla and almond extracts and then the sugar and beat well. Add the eggs one at a time, scraping the bowl with a rubber spatula and beating

continues ↘

after each addition until thoroughly mixed. On low speed, add the chocolate and beat until mixed; add the ground almonds and beat to mix, then the flour and beat, scraping the bowl with a rubber spatula, only until incorporated.

Place about half or slightly more of the batter in the prepared pan and spread it to make a smooth layer about ¾ inch thick. With your fingers pick up the cherries one at a time and place them, almost touching one another, in a single layer all over the batter (they may touch the sides of the pan). Spoon the remaining batter over the cherries and spread it to make a thin, smooth layer.

Bake for 50 minutes. The cake will be dry and crusty on top, and a toothpick inserted in the center will come out clean.

Cool in the pan on a rack for 15 minutes. Remove the sides of the pan and let the cake stand on the bottom of the pan, still on the rack, until it is almost completely cool. (If you want to serve it slightly warm, let it stand for about half an hour or a bit longer — just until it is firm enough to handle.)

Cover with a rack and invert. Remove the bottom of the pan. Cover with a flat cake plate or a serving board and invert again, leaving the cake right side up.

If you'd like to serve the torte with whipped cream, place a large spoonful alongside each portion of cake.

Whipped Cream

The cherry torte is delicious as it is (to me it is irresistible), but I serve it with whipped cream and I have had guests comment that it *must* be served with whipped cream. The combination is perfect!

1 cup heavy cream

2 tablespoons granulated or confectioners' sugar

1 tablespoon kirsch (see Note)

In a small, chilled bowl with chilled beaters, whip all the ingredients only until the cream holds a soft shape. (If you whip the cream ahead of time, refrigerate it in the whipping bowl. It will probably separate slightly as it stands. Just before serving, beat it a bit with a small wire whisk until it goes together again and has the correct thickness.)

CHOCOLATE ANGEL FOOD CAKE

8 to 12 portions This is a light, airy, moist beauty that stands 4 inches high. It can be made with (thawed) egg whites that have been left over from other desserts and frozen. Angel food may be made a day before it is to be served or early in the day to be served that night. But don't freeze angel food — freezing toughens it. This is quite quick and easy, but you must be careful with all the folding in.

1 cup less 2 tablespoons *sifted* cake flour

1½ cups *sifted* confectioners' sugar

½ cup less 1 tablespoon unsweetened cocoa powder (preferably Dutch-process)

1 tablespoon powdered (not granular) instant coffee or espresso

1½ cups egg whites (from 10 to 12 large eggs), at room temperature (they should be removed from the refrigerator at least 1 hour ahead)

½ teaspoon salt

1½ teaspoons cream of tartar

1 cup granulated sugar

OPTIONAL: Serving suggestions (page 65) or 7-Minute Icing (page 65)

Adjust rack one-third up from the bottom of the oven and preheat oven to 375 degrees. You will need an angel-food tube pan measuring 10 inches across the top and 4 inches in depth. (The tube and the bottom of the pan are in one piece; the side rim is a separate piece. The pan should be aluminum, not Teflon.) Do *not* butter or line the pan.

Sift together three times the flour, confectioners' sugar, cocoa, and powdered instant coffee. (Even if you are using a triple-sifter — three layers of wire mesh — which I think is the best kind, sift three times.) Set aside.

Place the egg whites and salt in the large bowl of an electric mixer. Beat briefly until foamy. Place the cream of tartar in a small, fine strainer and, while beating, strain the cream of tartar onto the whites.

Continue to beat at high speed until the whites hold a firm shape or are stiff but not dry; test by lifting a large portion of the beaten whites with a rubber spatula — they should mound high on the spatula without sliding off.

Now the granulated sugar and then the sifted flour mixture are folded into the whites. It is important not to dump the dry ingredients into one spot; they should be sprinkled lightly all over the top of the whites. If you use a wider bowl you will have more surface to sprinkle over. (I use one that measures 13 inches across the top.) Or the folding may be done on a large, deep turkey platter. So, if you have a wider, larger bowl or a turkey platter, transfer the whites to it.

To fold in the sugar: Place the granulated sugar in a strainer or a sifter (or sprinkle it

continues ↘

on carefully with a large spoon), about ¼ cup at a time, and distribute it lightly all over the surface of the egg whites. After each addition, very gently fold the sugar in, using the largest rubber spatula you can find.

After all the sugar is folded in, place the sifted flour mixture in the strainer or sifter and sift about ¼ cup of it all over the surface. Fold it in. Continue until all of the flour mixture has been folded in.

At no time should you fold in, or handle the mixture, any more than necessary.

Pour the batter evenly into the ungreased pan. With a long, narrow metal spatula or a table knife, cut through the mixture in widening circles to cut through any large air bubbles. Smooth the top. (The pan will be slightly more than one-half full.)

Bake for about 40 minutes, or until the cake just barely springs back when lightly pressed with a fingertip.

Now the pan has to be inverted to "hang" until the cake is cool. Even if the pan has three little legs for this purpose, they don't really raise the cake enough. Place the tube of the inverted pan over a narrow-necked bottle, or an upside-down metal funnel. Let the cake "hang" until cool — at least 1 hour.

Turn the pan right side up. With a knife that has a firm, sharp blade about 6 inches long, cut around the outside edge of the cake, pressing the blade firmly against the pan, and then cut around the tube in the middle. Push up the bottom of the pan to

remove the sides. Insert the knife between the bottom of the cake and the pan; press the blade firmly against the pan and cut all around to release the cake.

Place a cake plate over the cake and invert the plate and the cake. Lift off the bottom of the pan. Leave the cake upside down. Cover it, top and sides, with plastic wrap. It is best to let angel food stand at room temperature for several hours or overnight before serving.

Serve warm with any of the suggestions below or with the 7-Minute Icing.

To ice the cake (if you like): It is best to ice the cake early in the day for that night. With a long, narrow metal spatula, spread a very thin layer of the icing over the entire cake, including the center hole made by the tube, in order to seal any loose crumbs. Then spread the remaining icing to make a thick layer over the sides first and then the top. The icing may be spread smoothly (which is easiest to do by using a long, narrow metal spatula and working on a cake-decorating turntable), or pull it up into peaks and/or stripes by using the back of a large spoon. Either way, do it quickly; if you work over the icing too much it will lose its fine shiny quality.

To serve, cut the cake gently with a serrated bread knife, using a sawing motion — do not press down on the cake or it will squash. Or cut with a special tool called a cake rake, which is meant for cutting angel food. Or use two long-pronged forks, back to back, to separate into portions.

Angel food may be served as is, or with confectioners' sugar sprinkled through a fine strainer over the top. Or it may be completely covered with whipped cream. Or serve it with ice cream and chocolate sauce. Or serve it with fresh fruit and whipped cream (raspberries, either fresh or frozen, thawed and drained — or bananas, sliced just before serving and sprinkled with kirsch). Or try canned black Bing cherries, plain or brandied, drained. Or to make this plain cake a special occasion dessert, cover it with the 7-Minute Icing.

7-Minute Icing

½ cup egg whites (from 3 to 4 large eggs; you may use whites which have been left over from other desserts and frozen, but thaw completely before using)

1½ cups sugar

¼ cup plus 1 tablespoon cold water

1 teaspoon cream of tartar

⅛ teaspoon salt

1½ teaspoons vanilla extract

Place everything except the vanilla in the top of a large double boiler with at least an 8- to 10-cup capacity. Place over hot water on moderate heat.

Beat with an electric mixer at high speed for 4 to 5 minutes, until the mixture stands in peaks when the beaters are raised. Or beat with an egg beater for about 7 minutes.

Immediately, in order to stop the cooking, transfer the mixture to the large bowl of the electric mixer. Add the vanilla and beat at high speed very briefly, only until the mixture is smooth and barely firm enough to spread. Do not overbeat or the icing will become too stiff. Use immediately!

CHOCOLATE PUMPKIN CAKE

12 to 16 portions Moist, mildly spiced, not too sweet, very dark and chocolaty, plain (no icing), beautiful-looking (made in a fancy-shaped pan). Don't shy away from this because of pumpkin with chocolate; the pumpkin is only to keep it moist and doesn't give much taste to the cake. It is a perfect cake for the holiday season, or to wrap as a gift. A perfect cake for any time with tea or coffee. Wonderful to have on hand for any occasion. Everyone loves it. And it is easy to make and keeps well.

You will need a Bundt pan or kugelhopf with a 3-quart capacity.

2¾ cups *sifted* all-purpose flour

2 teaspoons baking powder

1 teaspoon baking soda

½ teaspoon salt

1½ teaspoons ground cinnamon

½ teaspoon ground ginger

¼ teaspoon ground cloves

¼ teaspoon ground nutmeg

¾ cup unsweetened cocoa powder (preferably Dutch-process)

8 ounces (2 sticks) unsalted butter

1½ teaspoons vanilla extract

2 cups granulated sugar

4 large eggs

16 ounces (scant 2 cups) canned solid-pack pumpkin (not the can labeled "pumpkin pie filling")

6 ounces (1½ cups) walnuts, cut or broken into medium-size pieces

OPTIONAL: confectioners' sugar (to be used after the cake is baked)

Adjust rack one-third up from the bottom of the oven and preheat oven to 325 degrees. Butter a 10-inch Bundt pan or any fancy-shaped tube pan with a 3-quart capacity. It is best to do this with very soft but not melted butter, applying it with a pastry brush. Then dust the whole pan, including the tube, with fine, dry bread crumbs. Invert the pan over paper and tap lightly to shake out excess. Set the prepared pan aside.

Sift together the flour, baking powder, baking soda, salt, cinnamon, ginger, cloves, nutmeg, and cocoa. Set aside.

In the large bowl of an electric mixer, cream the butter. Add the vanilla and sugar and beat to mix well. Add the eggs one at a time, scraping the bowl with a rubber spatula and beating after each addition until it is incorporated. On low speed, add half of the sifted dry ingredients, then the pumpkin, and finally the remaining dry ingredients, scraping the bowl with the spatula and beating after each addition only until it is incorporated. Stir in the nuts.

Turn the batter into the prepared pan. Smooth the top. Bake for 1½ hours, or until a cake tester gently inserted into the middle of the cake comes out clean and dry. Let it stand for about 15 minutes.

Cover with a rack and carefully invert. Remove the pan and let the cake cool on the rack. Then let it stand for several hours or overnight before serving.

If you like, just before serving, cover the top generously with confectioners' sugar, sprinkling it through a fine strainer held over the cake.

OREO COOKIE CAKE

16 portions A Washington-based reporter from *USA Today* called me to say she was doing a story on store-bought chocolate cookies and asked if I ever buy any. (Yes, I do. Especially chocolate-covered graham crackers.) During our conversation she told me that Oreo cookies are the most popular commercial cookies in the world: More Oreo cookies are sold than any other. (I would have guessed chocolate chip cookies.)

The conversation inspired me to add Oreo cookies to a white sour cream cake I had been making when the reporter called. As a matter of fact, as you will see, part of the batter was in the pan already when the phone rang. And when I baked it, it was so good, I wrote the recipe that way.

See if anyone can guess before you tell them what this cake is. No one could when I served it. It is similar to a pound cake but more moist; it has a divine flavor, a delicious crust — and Oreo cookies.

14 to 15 Oreo sandwich cookies	1 teaspoon baking soda	1½ cups sugar
2¾ cups *sifted* all-purpose flour	8 ounces (2 sticks) unsalted butter	3 large eggs
½ teaspoon salt	1 teaspoon vanilla extract	1 cup sour cream
	¼ teaspoon almond extract	OPTIONAL: confectioners' sugar or Glaze (page 69)

Adjust a rack one-third up from the bottom of the oven and preheat the oven to 350 degrees. You will need a tube pan with a 10- to 12-cup capacity, preferably one with a rounded bottom and a fancy design (this is especially beautiful made in the swirl-patterned pan with a 12-cup capacity). Butter the pan well (even if it has a nonstick finish) and dust all over with fine, dry bread crumbs. Invert it over paper and tap out excess crumbs. Set the pan aside.

Place the cookies on a cutting board. With a sharp, heavy knife, cut them one at a time into quarters; at least, that should be what you have in mind — they will actually crumble and only a few will remain in quarters. Set aside.

Sift together the flour, salt, and baking soda and set aside.

In the large bowl of an electric mixer, beat the butter until soft. Add the vanilla and almond extracts and the sugar and beat to mix well. Then add the eggs one at a time, beating until thoroughly incorporated after each addition. On low speed, add the dry ingredients in three additions alternately with the sour cream in two additions, scraping the bowl as necessary with a rubber spatula and beating only until incorporated after each addition.

continues ⌄

Place about 1½ cups of the batter by heaping spoonfuls in the bottom of the pan. Smooth with the bottom of a teaspoon and then, with the bottom of the spoon, form a rather shallow trench in the mixture.

Now add the cut-up Oreo cookies to the remaining batter and fold them in very gently, folding as little as possible just to mix them with the batter.

With a spoon, place the mixture by heaping spoonfuls into the pan over the plain batter. With the bottom of the spoon, smooth the top. This is going to be the bottom of the cake, but the cake doesn't know that and it rises in a round dome shape. To prevent that a bit, spread the batter slightly up on the sides of the pan, leaving a depression in the middle. It will not fix it completely, but it will help.

Bake for 1 hour, until a cake tester inserted gently into the cake comes out clean and dry. When done, the top will feel slightly springy to the touch. During baking the cake will form a crack around its surface and the crack will remain pale — that is as it should be.

Cool in the pan for 15 minutes. Then cover the pan with a rack and turn the pan and rack over. Remove the pan. Let the cake cool.

The cake can be served as it is, plain (plain, but moist and wonderful) or with confectioners' sugar sprinkled through a fine strainer over the top, or with the gorgeous, thick, dark chocolate, candylike glaze just poured unevenly over the top.

To glaze, place the cake on a rack over a large piece of wax paper or aluminum foil. Pour the glaze around and around over the top of the cake, letting it run down unevenly in places. Let the cake stand until the glaze has set and then transfer to a cake plate.

Glaze

6 ounces semisweet chocolate

2 ounces (½ stick) unsalted butter

About 1 tablespoon heavy cream

Break up the chocolate and place it in the top of a small double boiler over warm water on low heat. Cover with a folded paper towel (to absorb steam) and then with the top cover and let cook until barely melted. Remove the top of the double boiler and stir the chocolate until completely smooth.

Cut the butter into small pieces and add it to the chocolate, stirring until melted and smooth. Then stir in the cream very gradually (different chocolates use different amounts of cream); the mixture should be thick, just barely thin enough to flow slowly and heavily.

BUENA VISTA LOAF CAKE

1 (9-inch) loaf cake This won first prize at several county fairs in Colorado and California. It is a plain and wonderful chocolate loaf loaded with fruit, nuts, and chocolate chips — almost a fruitcake but not as sweet. It is easy to wrap and makes a marvelous gift.

2 cups *sifted* all-purpose flour

½ teaspoon salt

1 teaspoon baking soda

1 teaspoon ground cinnamon

3 tablespoons unsweetened cocoa powder (preferably Dutch-process)

4 ounces (1 stick) unsalted butter

1 teaspoon vanilla extract

1 teaspoon instant espresso or other powdered (not granular) instant coffee

1 cup sugar

2 large eggs

½ cup milk

8 ounces (1 cup, packed) dates, cut in half

3 ounces (⅔ cup) raisins

7 ounces (2 cups) walnut and/or pecan halves or large pieces

6 ounces (1 cup) semisweet chocolate morsels

Adjust rack one-third up from the bottom of the oven and preheat oven to 350 degrees. Butter a 9 x 5 x 3-inch loaf pan (8-cup capacity) and dust it with fine, dry bread crumbs. Invert to shake out excess and set aside.

Sift together the flour, salt, baking soda, cinnamon, and cocoa and set aside. In the large bowl of an electric mixer, cream the butter. Add the vanilla, instant espresso, and sugar and beat to mix well. Beat in the eggs one at a time. On low speed, add about half of the sifted dry ingredients, scraping the bowl with a rubber spatula and beating only until incorporated. Then gradually beat in the milk, and finally the remaining dry ingredients, again scraping

the bowl and beating only until incorporated. Remove from the mixer.

Add the dates and stir to mix well, then stir in the raisins, nuts, and chocolate morsels.

Turn into the prepared pan and smooth the top. Bake for about 1½ hours, or until a cake tester inserted into the middle comes out clean and dry.

Let the cake stand in the pan for about 10 minutes. Then cover with a rack and invert pan and rack. Remove the pan and then carefully turn the cake right side up and let it stand until it is cool.

The crust will be very crisp and crunchy; slice with a serrated knife.

BIG DADDY'S CAKE

12 portions A big, gorgeous cake baked in a large Bundt pan, topped with a dark, thick chocolate glaze that runs down the sides unevenly. When you cut into the cake, you will find a moist, tender white cake, studded with pecans and containing a tunnel of soft and gooey chocolate sauce. Most delicious. And a total mystery, to me at least. The white batter is poured into the pan, then topped with a chocolate sauce. During baking they change places; the chocolate sauce goes down to the bottom of the white batter, without leaving a trace of chocolate on the white. Ah, sweet mystery...

If you can serve this before the icing and the surprise chocolate tunnel inside become firm, it is best. I have made this cake late in the morning and after dinner the icing and the chocolate tunnel were still properly soft and moist. Longer than that and they became firm.

NOTE

⤓

To toast pecans, place them in a shallow pan in the middle of a preheated 350-degree oven for 12 to 15 minutes.

- 7 ounces (2 cups) toasted pecans (see Note)
- 4 cups *sifted* all-purpose flour
- 2 teaspoons baking powder
- 1 teaspoon salt
- 6 ounces semisweet chocolate
- 3 tablespoons hot water or strong coffee (2 to 3 teaspoons instant coffee in 3 tablespoons water)
- 3 tablespoons heavy cream
- 12 ounces (3 sticks) unsalted butter
- 1½ teaspoons vanilla extract
- ¼ teaspoon almond extract
- 2¼ cups sugar
- 6 large eggs
- 1¼ cups milk

BIG DADDY'S GLAZE

- 6 ounces semisweet chocolate
- 2 teaspoons solid vegetable shortening (e.g., Crisco)

Adjust a rack one-third up from the bottom of the oven and preheat the oven to 350 degrees. Generously butter a 10-inch Bundt pan or any other fancy tube pan with a 12- to 14-cup capacity (do this even if it has a nonstick finish).

Coarsely break up half the pecans and set them aside to sprinkle on the batter just before baking. Chop the remaining cup of pecans finely. (I do it on a large board with a long, heavy chef's knife — the pieces will be uneven, but aim for pieces about the size of rice.)

Place the finely chopped pecans in the buttered pan, turn the pan and shake it from side to side to coat it completely with

continues ⌄

the nuts. Invert the pan over paper and allow loose nuts to fall out. Then, with your fingers, sprinkle those loose nuts into the bottom of the pan and set aside.

Sift together the flour, baking powder, and salt and set aside.

Break up or chop the chocolate coarsely and place it in the top of a small double boiler over hot water on moderate heat. Add the water or coffee. Cover the pan and cook until the chocolate is melted. Remove the top of the double boiler from the heat and stir the chocolate briskly with a small wire whisk until smooth. Add the cream and whisk again until smooth. Set aside.

Beat the butter in the large bowl of an electric mixer until soft and smooth, then beat in the vanilla and almond extracts and the sugar and continue to beat for about 2 minutes. Add the eggs one at a time, scraping the bowl as necessary, and beating until thoroughly incorporated after each addition. On low speed, gradually add the sifted dry ingredients in three additions alternately with the milk in two additions. (After adding the milk, and even after adding the dry ingredients, the mixture will appear curdled — it is OK.)

Turn the batter into the prepared pan and smooth the top. With the bottom of a large spoon, form a trench around the middle of the top of the cake (about ½ inch deep and 1½ inches wide). Stir the prepared chocolate mixture and spoon it into the trench, keeping away from the sides of the

pan. With your fingertips, sprinkle the reserved coarsely broken pecans all over the top of the batter (they should touch the sides of the pan).

Bake for 50 to 55 minutes, then cover the top of the pan loosely with foil to prevent overbrowning. Continue to bake for 15 to 20 minutes (total baking time is 1 hour and 5 to 15 minutes), until a cake tester inserted gently in the middle of the cake comes out clean. (During baking the top will form a deep crack — it is all right.)

Let the cake cool in the pan for 20 minutes. Then cover it with a wide, flat cake plate and, holding the pan and the plate firmly together, turn them both over. Be careful while doing this — the cake is very heavy. Get a good secure grip on the cake pan with a pot holder; the other hand should be over the middle of the plate with your fingers spread apart for support. Remove the pan. Let the cake stand until cool.

For the Glaze

Break up or coarsely chop the chocolate and place it with the shortening in the top of a small double boiler, uncovered, over hot water on moderate heat. Stir occasionally until melted and smooth.

Pour the glaze over the top of the cake. Then smooth the top a bit, allowing a small amount of the glaze to run down into the grooves of the cake. Let stand at room temperature and serve at room temperature.

GRANDMA HERMALIN'S CHOCOLATE CAKE SQUARES

NOTE

⬇

If you like bittersweet chocolate, substitute 1 ounce of unsweetened chocolate for 1 ounce of the semisweet chocolate in the icing.

9 portions This is a simple but very delicious cake, a bit like devil's food, with a rich and fudgy chocolate icing. Cutting the cake into squares makes it a perfect finger food for a barbecue or another casual party.

1 cup *sifted* all-purpose flour

1 teaspoon baking soda

½ teaspoon baking powder

⅛ teaspoon salt

4 ounces (1 stick) unsalted butter

1 teaspoon vanilla extract

1 cup sugar

1 large egg

½ cup unsweetened cocoa powder

½ cup milk

1 tablespoon instant coffee powder

½ cup boiling water

ICING

4 ounces semisweet chocolate (see Note)

2 ounces (½ stick) butter, cut in 4 pieces

Adjust oven rack one-third up from the bottom of the oven. Preheat oven to 350 degrees. Butter a 9-inch square cake pan and dust the bottom only, very lightly, with fine, dry bread crumbs.

Sift together the flour, baking soda, baking powder, and salt. Set aside.

In small bowl of electric mixer, beat the butter a bit to soften. Add the vanilla and sugar and beat for a minute or two. Beat in the egg. On lowest speed, add the cocoa. Then, in this order, gradually add one-half of the milk, one-half of the dry ingredients, remaining milk, and remaining dry ingredients, scraping bowl frequently with a rubber spatula all during mixing. Mix only until smooth after each addition.

Dissolve the instant coffee in the boiling water. While it is still hot, add it very gradually on lowest speed to the chocolate mixture. Beat only until smooth. Batter will be thin.

Turn the batter into the prepared pan. Bake for 40 minutes, or until the top springs back when lightly touched. Cool in the pan on a rack for about 10 minutes. Cover with a rack and invert. Remove pan. Cover with another rack and invert again to finish cooling right side up.

For the Icing

In the top of a small double boiler over hot water on moderate heat, melt the chocolate. Remove the top of the double boiler. With a small wire whisk, beat in the butter, one piece at a time, beating until each piece is thoroughly incorporated before adding the next.

This icing may be used immediately, or, if it is too thin, place the pan into ice water and stir constantly until icing thickens very slightly, but watch it closely to see that it doesn't harden. It should still be fluid when used.

Pour the icing over the cake and smooth with a long, narrow, metal spatula.

WILLIAMS-SONOMA CHOCOLATE CAKE

8 portions Offhand, I can't think of any great chocolate recipes that include wine in the ingredients. Cognac, rum, bourbon, even Scotch whisky, and most liqueurs — but not wine. Some foods scream out "Where's the wine?" but chocolate does not.

Once when I was in San Francisco, Wes Halbruner (the book buyer for Williams-Sonoma) gave me this wonderful chocolate recipe that uses port wine (I was told to use Ficklin brand). It is an extraordinary cake, a taste thrill, a rare treat. Wes said I should use Callebaut chocolate (which surely is divine), but I have made this with other delicious semisweet chocolates as well and the cake was always wonderful.

The recipe, as I received it, said that the cake must be served hot, right from the oven. Hot is fantastic, but I love it at any temperature — even frozen. Serve it plain. Or with whipped cream and fresh raspberries or strawberries. And/or Chocolate Sauce (page 267).

4 ounces (1 stick) unsalted butter	4 ounces semisweet chocolate	¾ cup *sifted* all-purpose flour
½ cup port wine	1 cup sugar	⅛ teaspoon salt
	3 large eggs, separated	

Adjust a rack to the center of the oven and preheat the oven to 325 degrees. Butter a 10-inch springform pan (which may be 2 to 3 inches deep), line the bottom with parchment or wax paper cut to fit, butter the paper, dust all over with flour, and then invert the pan and tap out excess. Set aside.

Place the butter, port, and chocolate in a small, heavy pan over rather low heat and stir occasionally until the butter and chocolate are melted.

Meanwhile, remove and reserve 2 tablespoons of the sugar. Add the remaining sugar to the egg yolks in the small bowl of an electric mixer and beat at high speed for a few minutes until very pale. On low speed, gradually add the warm melted chocolate mixture (I suggest that you pour your mixture into a pitcher first to make it easier to add), and beat until smooth. Then beat in the flour. Remove the bowl from the mixer.

In a clean small bowl with clean beaters, beat the egg whites and salt until the whites hold a soft shape. Gradually add the reserved 2 tablespoons sugar and beat until the whites hold a definite shape but are not stiff or dry.

Fold about one-third of the beaten whites into the chocolate mixture. Then transfer

continues ⬂

both the remaining chocolate mixture and the egg-white mixture to a larger bowl and fold them together only until just incorporated. Do not handle any more than necessary. Pour the batter into the prepared pan.

Bake for 30 minutes, until a toothpick inserted near the middle comes out clean but not dry.

Remove the cake from the oven and let stand for 5 minutes. Then, gently cut around the sides of the cake with a table knife to release it from the pan and remove the sides of the pan. Cover the cake with a plate and turn the plate and cake over. Remove the bottom of the pan and the paper lining. Serve upside down. The cake will be only 1 inch high.

Serve as soon as possible (or later). Be prepared for a custard-like quality if you serve the cake right away.

SPECIAL-OCCASION CAKES

SEPTEMBER 7TH CAKE

Makes 12 portions I named this fabulous flourless cake for my birthday so I was sure to have it on my special day. Two thin, lightweight, dark layers are filled with white whipped cream and are thickly covered with a wonderful dark coffee-chocolate whipped cream. The cake has no flour; it is really a fluffy chocolate omelet that settles down like a hot soufflé when it cools. This may be made a day before or early in the day for that night, or the layers may be frozen before they are filled and iced.

CAKE

- 6 extra-large eggs, separated
- ¾ cup granulated sugar
- ¼ cup plus 1 tablespoon strained unsweetened cocoa powder (preferably Dutch-process)
- ¼ teaspoon salt

FILLING

- ¾ teaspoon unflavored gelatin
- 1½ tablespoons cold water
- 1½ cups heavy cream
- ⅓ cup confectioners' sugar
- ¾ teaspoon vanilla extract

ICING

- 8 ounces semisweet chocolate
- 2 ounces (½ stick) unsalted butter
- 1 tablespoon instant coffee powder
- ¼ cup boiling water
- 2 cups heavy cream
- ¼ cup confectioners' sugar
- 1 teaspoon vanilla extract

Adjust rack one-third up from bottom of the oven and preheat oven to 375 degrees. Butter two 9-inch round layer-cake pans. Line the bottoms with rounds of wax paper or baking parchment cut to fit. Butter the paper, dust the inside of the pan all over with flour, and invert the pans and tap to shake out excess flour.

For the Cake

In the small bowl of an electric mixer, beat the egg yolks at high speed for 5 minutes, until they are light lemon-colored. Add about half (6 tablespoons) of the granulated sugar (reserve the remaining half) and continue to beat at high speed for 5 minutes more, until the mixture is very thick and forms a wide ribbon when the beaters are lifted.

Add the cocoa and beat on lowest speed, scraping the bowl with a rubber spatula, and beating only until the cocoa is completely mixed in. Remove from the mixer and set aside.

Add the salt to the egg whites in the large bowl of the electric mixer. With clean beaters, beat at high speed until the whites increase in volume and barely hold a soft shape. Reduce the speed to moderate while gradually adding the reserved granulated sugar. Increase the speed to high again and continue to beat until the whites hold a definite shape when the beaters are raised or when some of the mixture is lifted on a rubber spatula — they should not be stiff or dry.

In several additions, small at first (about a large spoonful), fold half of the beaten whites into the chocolate mixture. Then fold the chocolate mixture into the remaining whites. Do not handle any more than necessary.

Turn half of the mixture into each of the prepared pans. Gently smooth each layer.

Bake for 30 to 35 minutes, until the layers spring back when lightly pressed with a fingertip and begin to come away from the sides of the pans.

Remove from the oven. With a small, sharp knife, carefully cut around the sides of the layers to release them. Cover each layer with a rack, invert pan and rack, remove pan, and peel off the paper lining. Cover layer with another rack and invert again to let the layers cool right side up.

While they are cooling the layers will sink and the sides will buckle and look uneven but don't worry. That is to be expected in the recipe. The filling and icing will cover them and they will be light, moist, and delicious.

When the layers are completely cool, prepare a flat cake plate as follows: Cut four strips of wax paper, each one about 10 x 3 inches. Place them around the outer edges of the plate.

Place one cake layer upside down on the plate and see that the wax paper touches all the edges of the cake.

For the Filling

Sprinkle the gelatin over the water in a small, heatproof cup. Let stand for 5 minutes. Place the cup in a small pan containing about an inch of hot water. Set over moderate heat and let stand until the gelatin dissolves, then remove from the hot water and set aside.

Reserve 2 or 3 tablespoons of the cream and place the remainder in the small bowl of an electric mixer (if the room is warm the bowl and beaters should be chilled). Add the confectioners' sugar and vanilla. Beat only until the cream has increased in volume and holds a soft shape. Then quickly stir the reserved tablespoons of cream into the warm dissolved gelatin and, with the mixer going, pour the gelatin all at once into the slightly whipped cream and continue to beat. The cream should be beaten until it is firm enough to hold a shape.

Place the whipped cream on the bottom cake layer. Carefully spread it evenly. Cover it with the other layer, placing the top layer right side up. Place in the refrigerator and prepare the icing.

For the Icing

Break up or coarsely chop the chocolate and place it in the top of a small double boiler over hot water on moderate heat. Add the butter. In a large cup, dissolve the coffee in the boiling water and pour it over the chocolate. Stir with a rubber spatula until the mixture is melted and smooth. Remove it from the hot water and transfer it to a medium mixing bowl.

Now the chocolate must cool to room temperature. You can let it stand or, if you are very careful not to overdo it, stir it briefly over ice and water—but not long enough for the chocolate to harden. In any event, the chocolate must cool to room temperature—test it on the inside of your wrist.

continues ⌄

When the chocolate has cooled, place the cream, confectioners' sugar, and vanilla in the small bowl of the electric mixer. Beat only until the cream holds a soft shape. It is very important that you do not whip the cream until it holds a definite shape, that would be too stiff for this recipe and would not only cause the icing to be too heavy but would also give it a slightly curdled appearance. Everything about this cake should be light and airy, and the chocolate will stiffen the cream a bit more.

In two or three additions, fold about half of the cream into the chocolate and then fold the chocolate into the remaining cream.

To ice the cake: Remove the cake from the refrigerator.

If you have a turntable for decorating cakes or a lazy Susan, place the cake plate on it.

Use as much of the icing as you need to fill in any hollows on the sides of the cake — use a spoon or a metal offset spatula — and then smooth the icing around the sides. If you are working on a turntable, rotate it while you hold a small metal offset spatula against the sides to smooth the icing.

Now the cake can be finished in one of two ways (depending on whether or not you want to use a pastry bag). You can either use all of the icing to cover the top very thickly, or you can spread it very thinly and reserve about 3 cups of the icing and decorate the top with a pastry bag and a star-shaped tube.

Place the icing on the top and spread it smoothly. Then spread the sides again to make them neat.

To decorate the top, which will be completely covered with rippled lines of icing, fit a 15-inch pastry bag with a #6 star tube and fold down a deep cuff on the outside of the bag. Place the icing in the bag. Unfold the cuff. Close the top of the bag. To form the icing lines, begin at the edge of the cake furthest from you. Squeeze an inch or two of icing out of the tube in a line coming toward you. Continue to squeeze and without stopping the flow of the icing, move the tube back away from you over about half the line you have just formed, making another layer of icing on the first. Still without stopping the flow of the icing, bring the tube toward you again and make another 1- to 2-inch line, then double back over half of the distance again. Continue across the whole diameter of the cake. The finished line will be along the middle of the cake. Make another, similar line to one side of the first, touching it. I find it easier to work from the middle — one side all the way and then the other side all the way to entirely cover the top of the cake with these wavy lines.

Remove the strips of wax paper by pulling each one out toward a narrow end.

Refrigerate for at least 6 hours or overnight and serve cold. To slice this cake without squashing it, insert the point of a sharp knife in the center of the cake. Then cut with an up-and-down sawing motion.

ORIENT EXPRESS CHOCOLATE TORTE

12 portions This was served on the Orient Express during its heyday — when it was renowned for luxurious food and service. It is a wonderfully not-too-sweet flourless sponge cake made with ground almonds and ground chocolate that give it a speckled tweedy appearance and a light, dry, crunchy texture — enhanced by a smooth, rich, chocolate buttercream filling and icing. The iced cake may be frozen.

- 3 ounces unsweetened chocolate
- 7½ ounces (1½ cups) unblanched almonds
- 5 large eggs, separated, plus 2 egg yolks
- ¾ cup sugar
- Pinch of salt

BUTTERCREAM

- 3 ounces (¾ stick) unsalted butter
- ½ teaspoon vanilla extract
- ½ cup sugar
- 2 large eggs
- 3 ounces (3 squares) unsweetened chocolate

NOTE

When this was served on the Orient Express, the top was covered with toasted sliced almonds and confectioners' sugar and the rim was decorated elaborately with mocha buttercream. I don't think it needs any decoration but it lends itself to almost anything you might like to design for it — chocolate leaves, cones, curls, etc. Or cover the top with Chocolate Curls (page 240) or chocolate shavings and sprinkle with confectioners' sugar. Or form a circle of whole toasted blanched almonds around the rim.

Adjust rack one-third up from bottom of the oven and preheat oven to 300 degrees. Butter a 9 x 3-inch springform pan or a one-piece 9 x 2½-inch or 9 x 3-inch cake pan and line the bottom with baking parchment or wax paper cut to fit. Butter the paper and dust all over with fine, dry bread crumbs. Invert to shake out excess and set the pan aside.

The chocolate and almonds must be finely ground. First chop the chocolate coarsely and then grind it with the almonds in a food processor fitted with the steel blade or grind in a blender. Or they may be ground in a nut grinder. Set aside.

Place the 7 egg yolks in the small bowl of an electric mixer. Add the sugar and beat until the yolks are pale lemon-colored but not until thick.

Add the ground chocolate and almonds and beat until mixed. Transfer to a larger mixing bowl.

Add the salt to the 5 egg whites and beat (with clean beaters) until they hold a definite shape but not until they are stiff or dry.

Add the beaten whites to the chocolate mixture and fold together only until incorporated.

Turn into the prepared pan and rotate the pan a bit briskly first in one direction, then the other, to level the batter.

Bake for about 65 minutes, until the top barely springs back when lightly pressed with a fingertip.

Remove from the oven and immediately, with a small, sharp knife, cut around the sides to release. Let the cake cool in the pan for 10 to 15 minutes.

Cover with a rack and invert cake pan and rack, remove the pan, and peel off the paper slowly. Carefully, cover with another rack and invert again, leaving the cake right side up to cool on the rack.

The cake will be cut to make two layers. (It is a delicate and fragile cake so if you freeze it first it will be easier to cut and safer to handle.

For the Buttercream

This takes a lot of beating and some chilling and more beating to dissolve the sugar and achieve its silken, smooth texture.

In the small bowl of an electric mixer, cream the butter with the vanilla. Add the sugar and beat for 3 to 4 minutes. Add the eggs one at a time and beat at high speed for a few minutes after each addition.

Meanwhile, place the chocolate in the top of a small double boiler over hot water on moderate heat. Cover until partially melted, then uncover and stir until completely melted.

Add the warm melted chocolate to the buttercream and beat again for several minutes. Now, place the bowl of buttercream and the beaters in the freezer or the refrigerator until the mixture is quite firm.

When you are ready to fill and ice the cake, prepare a cake plate by placing four strips of wax paper around the outer edges.

Using a serrated bread knife, cut the cake horizontally to make two even layers.

Place the bottom layer of the cake, cut side up, on the plate, checking to see that the wax paper touches the cake all around.

continues ⌄

If you have a cake-decorating turntable or a lazy Susan, place the cake plate on it.

To finish the buttercream, remove it from the freezer or refrigerator and beat again for several minutes. It should be beaten until it is soft enough to spread easily, light in color, and as smooth as honey. Don't be afraid of overbeating now.

Spread about one-third of the buttercream over the bottom layer, cover with the top layer, placing it cut side down, and spread the remaining buttercream smoothly over the sides and top.

Remove the wax paper strips by pulling each one out toward a narrow end.

Serve at room temperature.

DEVILISH CAKE

12 portions This is a dark, two-layer sour-cream cake with a thin layer of deliciously bittersweet chocolate filling and icing. It is a very old recipe from New England, where it has been made by a Maine sail-making family for generations.

½ cup strained unsweetened cocoa powder (preferably Dutch-process)

¾ cup boiling water

4 ounces (1 stick) unsalted butter

1 teaspoon vanilla extract

½ teaspoon salt

1½ cups granulated sugar

2 large eggs

1 teaspoon baking soda

1 cup sour cream

2 cups *sifted* all-purpose flour

CHOCOLATE ICING

4 ounces unsweetened chocolate

2 tablespoons unsalted butter

½ cup minus 1 tablespoon milk

1 cup strained confectioners' sugar

1 large egg

½ teaspoon vanilla extract

Pinch of salt

Adjust rack to the center of the oven and preheat oven to 350 degrees. Butter two 9-inch round layer-cake pans. Dust them with flour, invert over a piece of paper, and tap to shake out excess. Set pans aside.

In a small bowl, mix the cocoa and boiling water until smooth. Set aside.

In the large bowl of an electric mixer, cream the butter. Add the vanilla, salt, and granulated sugar and beat to mix well. Add the eggs one at a time, beating until smooth after each addition.

In a small bowl, stir the baking soda into the sour cream. On low speed, add the flour to the egg mixture in three additions alternating with the sour cream in two additions, scraping the bowl with a rubber spatula and beating only until smooth after each addition. Then add the cocoa mixture and beat only until smooth.

Pour the batter into the prepared pans. Shake the pans a bit and rotate them slightly to level the tops.

Bake for 30 minutes, until the layers barely begin to come away from the sides of the pan, or the tops barely leave an impression when lightly pressed with a fingertip. Do not overbake or the cake will be dry.

Cool in the pans for 15 minutes.

Cover each layer with a rack and invert, remove pans, cover with another rack, and invert again, leaving the layers right side up on the racks to cool.

Place four strips of wax paper around the outer edges of a cake plate. Place one layer of cake upside down on the plate; check to see that the papers touch the cake all around. If you have a cake-decorating

continues ❯

turntable or a lazy Susan, place the plate on it.

For the Icing

Place the chocolate in the top of a large double boiler over hot water on moderate heat. Cover until the chocolate is melted. Add the butter, milk, and confectioners' sugar and stir until the butter is melted. Cook, stirring, for 3 minutes.

Beat the egg in a small bowl only to mix. Very gradually, a few spoonfuls at a time, stir the hot chocolate into the egg. Stir constantly until you have added about one-third to one-half of the chocolate. Then stir the egg into the remaining hot chocolate. Add the vanilla and salt.

Transfer the mixture to the small bowl of an electric mixer. Place the small bowl in the larger mixer bowl. Fill the remaining empty space between the two bowls about halfway with ice and water. (If you are using a mixer on a stand it should be adjusted to the setting for the small bowl.)

Beat at high speed, scraping the bowl constantly with a rubber spatula, for only 1 to 2 minutes, until the icing thickens very slightly — do not let it harden.

Pour about one-third of the icing over the bottom cake layer and spread it smoothly — it will be a very thin layer.

Cover with the second layer of cake, placing it right side up so that both bottoms meet in the center. Pour the remaining icing over the top. Spread it over the top and sides.

Remove the wax paper strips by slowly pulling each one toward a narrow end.

ROBERT REDFORD CAKE

16 portions *Chocolate News,* a food publication, once printed a photo of Robert Redford along with a recipe for a chocolate honey cake which, they said, he had enjoyed at the Hisae restaurant in New York City.

I broke the 4-minute mile getting to the kitchen to try the recipe, and it was a delicious cake.

Soon after that my husband and I were in New York and went to Hisae. With the first bite I knew the cake was different from the one I had made. This one had less of a honey taste, but it was a sweeter cake. The management was extremely generous about sharing the recipe. (The fact that it is very different from the one in *Chocolate News* is a mystery I am not trying to solve.)

This is the recipe from the restaurant. It is closely related — like a big sister — to Queen Mother's Cake (page 95). This has honey instead of sugar, it has fewer nuts, and it is a larger cake and makes more portions. It is super-dense, compact, moist and rich, and not too sweet. And it really should be served with whipped cream and, if possible, berries.

If it weren't for Redford's picture, I probably would not have noticed the recipe to begin with. So thank you, Robert Redford; you are a gentleman and a scholar and a man of good taste indeed.

NOTE

⌄

This cake, along with my Queen Mother's Cake (page 95) and the Orient Express Chocolate Torte (page 86) is perfect for Passover. Many people write me to say that they make them with kosher chocolate, matzo meal instead of bread crumbs, and pareve margarine. And they say, "It was the hit of the seder."

Fine, dry bread crumbs (see Note)

6½ ounces (1¼ cups) blanched hazelnuts or blanched almonds (see page 22)

12 ounces semisweet chocolate

6 ounces (1½ sticks) unsalted butter

½ cup honey

10 large eggs, separated

¼ teaspoon salt

ICING

¾ cup heavy cream

12 ounces semisweet chocolate

OPTIONAL: fresh berries

WHIPPED CREAM

Heavy cream

Confectioners' sugar, granulated sugar, or honey

Vanilla extract

continues ↘

Adjust a rack one-third up from the bottom of oven and preheat the oven to 375 degrees. Butter a 10 x 3-inch round cake pan or springform pan. Line the bottom with a round of wax paper or baking parchment cut to fit, butter the paper, and dust all over with fine, dry bread crumbs. Tap to shake out excess crumbs over a piece of paper; set the pan aside.

The blanched hazelnuts or almonds must be ground to a fine powder; it can be done in a food processor, blender, or nut grinder. Set the ground nuts aside.

Break up or coarsely chop the chocolate and place in the top of a large double boiler over shallow, warm water on moderate heat. Cover with a folded paper napkin or paper towel (to absorb condensation) and with the pot cover. Let stand until partly melted, then uncover and stir until completely melted. Remove the top of the double boiler, carefully dry the bottom (a drop of moisture in the chocolate would make it "tighten"), and transfer the chocolate to a bowl (to stop the cooking). Stir occasionally until tepid or cooled to room temperature.

Meanwhile, in the large bowl of an electric mixer, beat the butter until it is soft. Gradually add the honey and beat until smooth. Then add the egg yolks, two or three at a time, beating until smooth after each addition. (The mixture will look curdled now, it is OK.) Beat only until mixed.

Add the chocolate and beat, scraping the bowl with a rubber spatula and beating only until mixed. (The curdled look will go away now.)

Add the ground nuts and beat only to mix.

Now, to beat the egg whites, you will either need the same bowl and beaters you used for the chocolate mixture (in which case, transfer the chocolate mixture to another large bowl, and thoroughly wash the bowl and beaters), or if you have an additional large bowl for your mixer and an extra set of beaters, use those, or beat the eggs in a large copper bowl with a large, balloon-shaped wire whisk. Either way, add the salt to the whites and beat only until the whites just barely stand up straight when the beater or whisk is raised, or when some of the whites are lifted on a rubber spatula.

With a large rubber spatula, fold about one-quarter of the whites into the chocolate mixture. Then fold in another quarter.

Now, if you have a larger mixing bowl (I use an 8-quart one), transfer the folded mixture to the larger bowl, add the remaining whites, and fold together gently only until the mixtures are blended. If you do not have a larger bowl to finish the folding, it can be done in the large mixer bowl, but not quite as easily — it is a large amount of batter.

Turn the mixture into the prepared pan. Bake at 375 degrees for 20 minutes, then reduce the temperature to 350 degrees and bake for 50 minutes more (total baking time is 1 hour and 10 minutes), until a cake tester comes out clean. Turn the oven off, open the oven door, and let the cake cool in the oven for about 15 minutes. Then remove it from the oven and let it stand at room temperature until completely cool.

During the cooling, the cake will sink more in the center than along the rim; that is what it should do.

When the cake is completely cool, cover it with a rack and turn over the pan and rack. Remove the pan and the paper lining. Cover the cake with another rack and invert again, leaving the cake right side up.

Now the top of the cake must be cut with a long, thin, sharp knife to make it level. (It is easiest to do this if you place the cake on a cake-decorating turntable.)

The cake may be iced either side up; if the sides taper in toward the top (which happens sometimes), it is best to ice it right side up, but if the sides are straight it is best to ice it upside down. Place the cake carefully on a large cake platter or a serving board.

To protect the plate while you ice the cake, you will need four 10 x 3-inch strips of wax paper. Use a wide metal spatula to gently raise one side of the cake and slide a strip of the paper partly under the cake. Repeat with the remaining papers, and check to be sure that the papers touch the cake all around.

If you have a cake-decorating turntable or a lazy Susan, place the cake platter or serving board on it.

For the Icing

In a heavy saucepan over moderate heat, cook the cream until it forms a wrinkled skin on the top. Meanwhile, break up or coarsely chop the chocolate. When the cream is ready, add the chocolate, reduce the heat to low, and stir with a small wire whisk until the mixture is perfectly smooth. Transfer it to a bowl to stop the cooking. Stir occasionally until cool and very slightly thickened.

Pour the cooled icing over the top of the cake. Carefully spread it to allow only a small amount of it to run down the sides of the cake. With a long, narrow metal spatula, spread the top very smoothly (easy if you are working on a cake-decorating turntable) and then with a small, narrow metal spatula, smooth the sides. (The icing on the sides might run down a bit onto the wax papers on the plate; if so, it might be necessary to use a rubber spatula to scoop it up and replace it on the sides, and then to smooth it again.)

Remove the wax-paper strips by pulling each one out toward a narrow end, pulling them slowly and gently.

The cake may be served soon while the icing is soft, or it may wait overnight at room temperature. (If you make the cake ahead of time it may be frozen. Thaw and ice it the day it is to be served, or a day ahead.)

For the Whipped Cream

This cake really is just not complete without whipped cream. The amount of whipped cream to prepare depends on the number of portions you will serve. Plan on 1 cup of heavy cream for each 4 or 5 portions. For each cup of cream,

continues ↘

add 2 tablespoons of confectioners' or granulated sugar (or 1 tablespoon of honey), and ½ teaspoon of vanilla extract. In a chilled bowl with chilled beaters, whip all the ingredients only until the cream holds a soft shape; it should not be stiff. If you whip the cream early in the day for that evening, refrigerate it; it will separate a bit—just whip it a bit with a small wire whisk before serving.

Fresh raspberries or strawberries are also a part of the recipe. (If you do not have fresh berries, do not serve any.) Serve the cream and the berries separately; spoon a generous amount of each alongside each portion, cream on one side of the cake and berries on the other side.

QUEEN MOTHER'S CAKE

NOTE
⬇
If the room is too cold or the chocolate stands too long, it might not curl or it could crack when you form the cigarettes.

Makes 12 portions This is one of the most popular recipes in all of my books and is the one cake I make more often than any other. I originally got the recipe in 1962 from a food column by Clementine Paddleford in the *New York Herald Tribune*.

Jan Smeterlin, the eminent pianist, picked up the recipe on a concert tour in Austria. When the Queen Mother was invited to tea at the home of some friends of the Smeterlins', the hostess baked the cake according to Smeterlin's recipe. The Queen Mother loved it and asked for the recipe. Then — as the story goes — she served it often at her royal parties.

It is a flourless chocolate cake that is nothing like the flourless chocolate cakes that have become so popular. It is not as heavy or dense. This has ground almonds and the texture is almost light, although it is rich and moist. It is divine.

The cake may be frozen before or after it is iced, but while the icing is fresh it has a beautiful shine, which becomes dull if the cake stands overnight or if it is frozen. So to enjoy this at its very best, ice the cake during the day for the night. But I know several people who always have an un-iced Queen Mother's Cake in the freezer.

6 ounces (scant 1½ cups) blanched (skinned) or unblanched whole almonds

6 ounces semisweet chocolate, chopped into small pieces

¾ cup sugar

6 ounces (1½ sticks) unsalted butter

6 large eggs, separated

⅛ teaspoon salt

1 teaspoon lemon juice

ICING

½ cup heavy cream

2 teaspoons instant espresso or coffee powder

8 ounces semisweet chocolate, chopped into small pieces

OPTIONAL, FOR SERVING: Chocolate Cigarettes (page 97) or sweetened whipped cream and raspberries

First toast the almonds in a single layer in a shallow pan in a 350-degree oven for 12 to 15 minutes, shaking the pan a few times, until the almonds are lightly colored and have a delicious smell of toasted almonds when you open the oven door. Set aside to cool.

continues ↘

Adjust a rack one-third up in the oven and preheat oven to 375 degrees. Butter the bottom and sides of a 9 x 3-inch springform pan and line the bottom with a round of baking parchment cut to fit. Butter the paper. Dust the pan all over with fine, dry bread crumbs, invert over paper, and tap lightly to shake out excess. Set the prepared pan aside.

Place the chocolate in the top of a small double boiler over hot water on moderate heat. Cover until partially melted, then uncover and stir until just melted and smooth. Remove the top of the double boiler and set it aside until tepid or room temperature.

Place the almonds and ¼ cup of the sugar (reserve remaining ½ cup sugar) in a food processor fitted with a metal chopping blade. Process very well, until the nuts are fine and powdery. Stop the machine once or twice, scrape down the sides, and continue to process for at least a full minute. I have recently realized that the finer the nuts are, the better the cake will be. Set aside the ground nuts.

In the large bowl of an electric mixer, beat the butter a bit until soft. Add ¼ cup of the sugar (reserve remaining ¼ cup sugar) and beat to mix. Add the egg yolks one at a time, beating and scraping the sides of the bowl as necessary until smooth. On low speed, add the chocolate and beat until mixed. Then add the processed almonds and beat, scraping the bowl, until incorporated.

Now the whites should be beaten in the large bowl of the mixer. If you don't have an additional large bowl for the mixer, transfer the chocolate mixture to any other large bowl.

In the large bowl of the mixer, with clean beaters, beat the egg whites with the salt and lemon juice, starting on low speed and increasing it gradually. When the whites barely hold a soft shape, reduce the speed a bit and gradually add the remaining ¼ cup sugar. Then, on high speed, continue to beat until the whites just barely hold a straight point when the beaters are slowly raised. Do not overbeat.

Stir a large spoonful of the whites into the chocolate mixture to soften it a bit.

Then, in three additions, fold in the remaining whites. Do not fold thoroughly until the last addition and do not handle any more than necessary.

Turn the mixture into the prepared pan. Rotate the pan a bit briskly from left to right in order to level the batter.

Bake for 20 minutes at 375 degrees and then reduce the temperature to 350 degrees and continue to bake for an additional 50 minutes (total baking time is 1 hour and 10 minutes). Do not overbake; the cake should remain soft and moist in the center. (The top might crack a bit — it's OK.)

The following direction was in the original recipe, and although I do not understand why, I always do it. Wet and slightly wring out a folded towel and place it on a smooth surface. Remove the cake pan from the oven and place it on the wet towel. Let stand until tepid, 50 to 60 minutes.

Release and remove the sides of the pan (do not cut around the sides with a knife — it will make the rim of the cake messy). Now let the cake stand until it is completely cool, or longer if you wish.

The cake will sink a little in the middle; the sides will be a little higher. Use a long, thin, sharp knife to cut the top level. Brush away loose crumbs.

Place a rack or a small board over the cake and carefully invert. Remove the bottom of the pan and the paper lining. The cake is now upside down; this is the way it will be iced. Place four strips of baking parchment (each about 12 x 3 inches) around the edges of a cake plate. With a large, wide spatula, carefully transfer the cake to the plate; check to be sure that the cake is touching the papers all around (in order to keep the icing off the plate when you ice the cake).

If you have a cake-decorating turntable or a lazy Susan, place the cake plate on it.

For the Icing

Scald the cream in a 5- to 6-cup saucepan over moderate heat until it begins to form small bubbles around the edges or a thin skin on top. Add the espresso or coffee powder and whisk to dissolve. Add the chocolate and stir occasionally over heat for 1 minute. Then remove the pan from the heat and whisk or stir until the chocolate is all melted and the mixture is smooth.

Let the icing stand at room temperature, stirring occasionally, for about 15 minutes or a little longer, until the icing barely begins to thicken.

Then, stir it to mix and pour slowly over the top of the cake, pouring it onto the middle. Use a long, narrow metal offset spatula to smooth the top and spread the icing so that a little of it runs down the sides (not too much—the icing on the sides should be a much thinner layer than on the top). With a small, narrow metal offset spatula, smooth the sides.

Remove the strips of paper by pulling each one out by a narrow end.

Decorate the cake or individual portions with the Chocolate Cigarettes. Or place a mound of whipped cream (lightly sweetened with confectioners' sugar and lightly flavored with vanilla extract) on one side of each portion on individual dessert plates, and a few raspberries on the other side of each portion.

Chocolate Cigarettes

These are long, thin, shaved curls of chocolate that are used as a decoration. They look very professional. You can find compound or coating chocolate at kitchen supply stores, or online.

To make a very generous amount of curls (you can make much less), coarsely chop about 8 ounces of compound chocolate (see page 18). Melt the chocolate slowly in

continues ⌄

the top of a double boiler over hot water on moderate heat. When partially melted, remove from the water and stir until completely melted. Pour onto a marble work surface (such as a large marble cheese board), forming a ribbon 3 to 4 inches wide and 10 inches long. The chocolate should be about ¼ to ⅜ inch thick. Let cool at room temperature until it is no longer soft or sticky.

To make the curls, use a long, heavy knife — I use a Sabatier chef's knife with a 12-inch blade. Hold it at a 45-degree angle across the width and right near the end of the chocolate. Cut down slowly and firmly. The chocolate will roll around itself as it is cut. Repeat, each time placing the blade very close to the cut end — the curls should be paper thin. Transfer them with a wide metal offset spatula to a shallow tray. Cover with plastic wrap and store either at room temperature, if it is not too warm, or in the refrigerator or freezer.

ST. LOUIS CHOCOLATE LAYER CAKE

12 portions This is a prized heirloom recipe that has been kept secret for many years. It is a two-layer devil's food cake with a wonderful fluffy white marshmallow filling and icing. (Do not freeze this cake after it has been iced.)

NOTE

To measure ⅔ teaspoon, measure 1 teaspoon and, with a small metal spatula or a table knife, mark it into thirds. Then cut away one-third and return it to the box.

- 1¾ cups *sifted* all-purpose flour
- 2 teaspoons baking powder
- ⅛ teaspoon salt
- 2 ounces unsweetened chocolate
- ⅓ cup water
- 6 ounces (1½ sticks) unsalted butter
- 1½ cups sugar
- 3 large eggs, separated
- ¾ cup milk

MARSHMALLOW ICING

- 1½ cups sugar
- ⅔ teaspoon cream of tartar (see Note)
- ⅔ cup water
- ⅛ teaspoon salt
- ⅔ cup egg whites (from 4 to 5 large eggs; you can use whites that have been left over from other recipes, frozen, and then thawed)
- 1¼ teaspoons vanilla extract

Adjust rack to center of the oven and preheat oven to 375 degrees. Butter two 9-inch round layer-cake pans and dust all over with flour. Invert over paper and tap to shake out excess flour. Set the prepared pans aside.

Sift together the flour, baking powder, and salt and set aside.

Place the chocolate and water in a small saucepan over low heat and stir until the chocolate is melted and the mixture is smooth. Set aside to cool slightly.

In the large bowl of an electric mixer, cream the butter. Add the sugar and beat well. Add the egg yolks all at once and beat, scraping the bowl with a rubber spatula, until well mixed. Add the chocolate and beat to mix.

On low speed, add the sifted dry ingredients in three additions, alternating with the milk in two additions, scraping the bowl with the spatula and beating until smooth after each addition. Remove from the mixer and set aside.

In the small bowl of the electric mixer with clean beaters, beat the egg whites until they hold a firm shape but are not dry. Fold the whites into the chocolate mixture. Divide the batter between the two pans and smooth the tops.

Bake for 25 to 30 minutes, until the tops barely spring back when lightly pressed with a fingertip. (The cakes are soft and will not spring back as sharply as most cakes do. Do not overbake or the cake will be dry.) Let the layers cool in the pans for 10 to 15 minutes.

With a small, sharp knife, cut around the cake sides to release. Cover each layer with a rack, invert, and remove pan. Cover with another rack and invert again, leaving the layers right side up to cool on the racks. Cool completely.

Prepare a flat cake plate or serving board by placing four strips of wax paper around the outer edges.

These layers are tender and delicate and must be completely cool and handled with care. Place one layer upside down on the cake plate, checking to be sure that the wax paper touches the cake all around.

If you have a cake-decorating turntable or a lazy Susan, place the cake plate on it.

Spread one-third of the icing over the bottom layer about ⅓ to ½ inch thick. Cover with the top layer, placing it right side up so that both layer bottoms meet in the middle.

With a long, narrow metal spatula, spread the remaining icing around the sides and on the top and spread it smoothly. Or form it into loose swirls and high peaks — these will stay just where you put them. It is the most agreeable and cooperative icing I have ever used with a pastry bag. If you like to use a pastry bag, spread the icing more thinly and reserve a generous amount for decorating. Fit the bag with a large star-shaped tube and you will have great fun with rosettes and curlicues of all kinds.

Remove the wax paper strips by pulling each one out toward a narrow end.

Let the cake stand uncovered at room temperature for several hours before serving.

For the Icing

Place the sugar, cream of tartar, and water in a 6-cup saucepan (preferably one that is tall and narrow — in a wide one, the mixture will be too low to reach the bulb of the candy thermometer). With a wooden spatula, stir over moderate heat until the sugar is dissolved and the mixture begins to boil. Cover and let boil for 3 minutes. (This keeps the steam in the pot and dissolves any sugar crystals that cling to the sides. However, if you still see any granules when you remove the cover, dip a pastry brush in cold water and use it to wipe the sides.)

Uncover and insert a candy thermometer. Raise the heat to high and let boil without stirring until the thermometer registers 242 degrees.

Shortly before the sugar syrup is done (or when the thermometer registers about 236 degrees — soft-ball stage), add the salt to the egg whites in the large bowl of an electric mixer. Beat until the whites are stiff. (If the sugar syrup is not ready, turn the beater to the lowest speed and let beat slowly until

continues ↘

the syrup is ready. Or you can let the whites stand, but no longer than necessary.)

When the syrup is ready (242 degrees — medium-ball stage), put the mixer on high speed and gradually add the syrup to the beaten whites in a thin stream. Then beat at high speed, scraping the bowl occasionally with a rubber spatula, for about 5 minutes, or until the icing is quite thick and stiff. Mix in the vanilla. If necessary beat some more. The icing may still be warm when it is used.

DIONE'S CHOCOLATE ROLL

10 portions The first cooking programs I remember on American television featured Dione Lucas. She was a sensational cook, entertainer, and teacher. When she opened an omelet restaurant in New York City called the Egg Basket, I think I was one of the first customers. The restaurant had a counter where you could watch while Dione prepared omelets for everyone. I had the first stool, and I had the time of my life. She was a magician with omelets.

The restaurant served only one dessert, Dione Lucas's famous Chocolate Roll.

Some time later, I considered myself extremely lucky to be able to attend cooking classes at Ms. Lucas's cooking school in the basement of a brownstone in New York City. There were about seven people in each class, and everyone cooked—all at once. We were allowed to choose whatever we wanted to cook. I chose this chocolate roll at my first class.

You will need an 18 x 12-inch (across the top) rimmed baking sheet. This is larger than the usual size. It is available at kitchen shops.

- 8 ounces semisweet chocolate
- ½ cup boiling water
- 8 large eggs, separated
- 1 cup sugar
- Pinch of salt
- ¼ cup unsweetened cocoa powder (preferably Dutch-process, to be
- used after the cake is baked), plus more if needed
- Whipped Cream Filling (page 105)

Adjust a rack to the middle of the oven and preheat the oven to 350 degrees. Now you must line an 18 x 12 x 1-inch rimmed baking sheet with aluminum foil. Heavy-duty foil, which is wide enough for this, is too stiff. Regular lighter-weight foil is not wide enough; therefore you have to use two lengths. Tear off two 21-inch lengths of regular foil. Turn the pan upside down. Place one length of foil over the pan, shiny side against the pan, placing it off to one side so that when it is pressed into place there will be about ½ inch of foil extending above the rim of one long side and the two short sides of the pan. Place the second length of foil so that it partly covers the first and will extend above the other long side of the pan. With your hands, fold down the sides and corners of the foil, shaping it to fit the pan. Remove the foil. Turn the pan right side up. Place the shaped foil in the pan and press it into place.

To butter the foil, place a piece of butter in the pan and set the pan in the oven to melt the butter, then spread it with a pastry

continues ↘

brush or piece of crumpled wax paper over the bottom and sides. Set aside.

Break up the chocolate and place it and the boiling water in the top of a double boiler over warm water on moderate heat. Cover until the chocolate is almost melted. Then stir until completely melted and smooth. Remove the top of the double boiler. If the mixture is not completely smooth, beat it with a beater or an electric mixer, and then let stand to cool until tepid or room temperature.

Place the egg yolks in the small bowl of an electric mixer and add ¾ cup of the sugar (reserve the remaining ¼ cup). Beat at high speed for 5 minutes, until almost white. In a larger bowl, fold together the cooled chocolate and the yolk mixture until smoothly colored. Set aside.

Place the egg whites and salt in the clean large bowl of the electric mixer. With clean beaters, beat until the whites hold a soft shape. Reduce the speed to moderate and gradually add the remaining ¼ cup of sugar. Increase the speed to high again and continue to beat only until the whites just barely hold a straight point when the beaters are raised — not so long that they become stiff or dry.

With a large rubber spatula, fold about one-third of the whites into the chocolate mixture without being thorough. Fold in another third just briefly. Then add all the remaining whites and carefully fold together until no whites show. (It was at this point that Ms. Lucas took the spatula from my hand and said, "When there are just one or two areas of white, and they rise to the top of the chocolate, smooth over them gently with the spatula, like this — instead of folding too much.")

Turn into the prepared pan. In order not to handle this any more than necessary, it is

better to place it in large mounds all over the pan—instead of in one mound. Gently smooth it into the corners and level the top.

Bake for 17 minutes.

Meanwhile, wet a large linen or smooth cotton towel with cold water and wring it out.

While the cake is baking, make the Whipped Cream Filling (below).

When the cake is removed from the oven it should remain in the pan for 20 minutes, covered with the damp towel. And, to keep the steam and moisture in the cake, the damp towel should be covered with one or two layers of dry linen or cotton towel, or with foil or plastic wrap.

After 20 minutes, remove the towels from the top of the cake.

Through a fine strainer held over the top, dust the ¼ cup of cocoa all over the cake, including the edges.

Cover the cake with two overlapping lengths of wax paper and cover the wax paper with a large cookie sheet (or a tray or board or what have you). Holding the

pan and the cookie sheet together firmly, turn them over. Remove the pan. Slowly remove the foil (it will come off easily).

Cover the cake with plastic wrap or wax paper to prevent drying out and let the cake cool completely while you prepare the whipped cream.

Uncover the cake and place the whipped cream by large spoonfuls all over it. With a long, narrow metal spatula, spread the cream evenly up to the edge on three sides of the cake; stop the cream about 1 inch short of one long side.

Using the wax paper to help, roll the cake the long way toward the long side that has the 1-inch border.

As you finish rolling the cake, the final turn should deposit the cake seam down onto a chocolate roll board or any long, narrow serving platter.

There will be a few cracks on the surface of the cake—it is to be expected. If you wish, you can sift additional cocoa over the cracks to hide them a bit.

Refrigerate, and serve cold.

Whipped Cream Filling

Whipped cream for filling a cake roll should be just as stiff as is possible without curdling. Chilling the bowl and the beaters helps it to whip stiffly with less chance of trouble.

(Dione Lucas had her own way of doing it. She placed the cream in a large bowl, and that into a larger bowl partly filled with ice and water. And she beat with a large

continues ⌄

balloon whisk. Sometime in my youth I must have whipped too long, making butter instead of whipped cream. That must be why I have always been gun-shy of overwhipping. During that first class with Dione Lucas, I whipped the cream in a bowl set over ice and I whipped with the balloon whisk as I was told. Every time my whisking slowed down, because I thought the cream was stiff enough, no matter where she was in the room and no matter what she was doing (fluting mushrooms or decorating a ballotine), she called out, "More — it's not stiff enough." I did what she said. It became the stiffest whipped cream I had ever made and it was not butter. The ice-cold bowl was the secret.)

1½ cups heavy cream

3 tablespoons confectioners' sugar

1 teaspoon vanilla extract

In a chilled bowl, with chilled beaters or a large whisk, whip the cream with the sugar and vanilla until the cream is firm. Set aside.

COUNTY-FAIR CHOCOLATE LAYER CAKE

12 generous portions A dark and tender two-layer cocoa cake with a luscious dark chocolate filling and icing that stays rather soft and creamy. It is over 4 inches high and is quite easy for such an impressive and delicious cake.

COCOA CAKE LAYERS

2 cups *sifted* cake flour

1 teaspoon baking soda

½ teaspoon salt

6 tablespoons strained unsweetened cocoa powder (preferably Dutch-process)

4 ounces (1 stick) unsalted butter

1 teaspoon vanilla extract

1¼ cups sugar

2 large eggs

1 cup milk

CHOCOLATE ICING

5 ounces unsweetened chocolate

1 cup heavy cream

1¼ cups sugar

4 ounces (1 stick) unsalted butter, cut into 1-inch pieces

1 teaspoon vanilla extract

Adjust rack to center of the oven and preheat oven to 350 degrees. Butter two 8-inch round layer-cake pans, dust them with flour, invert, and tap lightly to shake out excess, and then set aside.

Sift together the flour, baking soda, salt, and cocoa and set aside.

In the large bowl of an electric mixer, cream the butter. Add the vanilla and then the sugar and beat well. Beat in the eggs one at a time, scraping the bowl with a rubber spatula and beating well after each addition.

On low speed, add the sifted dry ingredients in three additions alternating with the milk in two additions. Scrape the bowl with the spatula and beat only until smooth after each addition.

Divide the batter between the prepared pans and spread smoothly.

Bake for 35 to 40 minutes, until the layers just begin to come away from the sides of the pans.

Cool the layers in the pans for 5 to 6 minutes. Then, with a small, sharp knife, cut around the sides to release. Cover each layer with a rack, invert, remove the pan, cover with another rack and invert again, leaving the layers right side up to finish cooling.

Prepare a flat cake plate or serving board by placing four strips of wax paper around the outer edges of the plate. Place one cooled cake layer upside down on the plate, checking to see that the papers touch the cake all around.

continues ⌐

If you have a cake-decorating turntable or a lazy Susan, place the cake plate on it.

For the Icing

Chop the chocolate into small pieces — it is all right for them to be uneven — and set aside.

In a heavy 2½- to 3-quart saucepan, stir the cream and sugar to mix. With a wooden or rubber spatula, stir over moderate heat until the mixture comes to a boil. Then reduce the heat and let simmer for exactly 6 minutes.

Remove from the heat, add the chocolate, and stir until it is melted. Add the butter and stir until it is melted. Add the vanilla and stir.

Partially fill a large bowl with ice and water. Place the saucepan of icing in the bowl of ice water and stir frequently until completely cool. Then stir constantly until the mixture begins to thicken. When the icing begins to thicken, remove it from the ice water and stir/beat briskly with a rubber or wooden spatula until it becomes smooth and thick enough to spread — or about like a very heavy mayonnaise. It should take only a few seconds or maybe a minute or so of stirring/beating. If the icing remains too soft, return it to the ice water briefly, then remove and stir/beat again.

When the icing is thick enough, quickly spread it about ⅓ inch thick over the cake on the plate. Cover with the second layer, placing it right side up (both flat sides meet in the middle). Pour the remaining icing over the cake and, with a long, narrow metal spatula, spread it over the top and sides of the cake. If you wish, form large swirls on the top, using the spatula to indent the icing from the outer rim toward the center in a rather abstract daisy shape.

Remove the wax paper strips by pulling each one toward a narrow end.

SPONGE ROLL WITH BITTERSWEET CHOCOLATE FILLING AND ICING

8 to 10 portions This recipe is from a little patisserie on the French Riviera. I asked the owner if I could watch him make éclairs and he said, "Certainly, come in at four o'clock tomorrow morning." I was there and for the first few hours I watched him make bread and croissants and brioche and kugelhopf and then I watched the creation of napoleons and palmiers and then fruit tarts and petits fours and layer cakes and — this delicate, extremely light sponge roll with bittersweet filling and icing. I didn't see a single éclair, but I thanked him profusely, he gave me a little bag of petits fours, and we shook hands and bid each other *au revoir*.

This is a lovely and elegant cake roll — very French. It can be made a few hours before serving or the day before, or it can be frozen (thaw it wrapped). It is quite simple to make and great fun, beautifully professional looking — festive and delicious.

SPONGE LAYER

- ¼ cup granulated sugar
- 4 large eggs, separated
- 3 tablespoons *sifted* all-purpose flour
- Pinch of salt
- About 3 tablespoons confectioners' sugar (to be used after the cake is baked)

BITTERSWEET CHOCOLATE ICING AND FILLING

- 6 ounces semisweet chocolate
- 1 ounce unsweetened chocolate
- 3 tablespoons prepared coffee (normal strength or stronger), or water
- 3 tablespoons unsalted butter, at room temperature (or if cold, cut into small pieces)
- 2 tablespoons light or dark rum or Cognac
- ½ to 1 cup chocolate shavings (must be made ahead of time and ready to use before the icing hardens)
- Confectioners' sugar

Adjust oven rack one-third up from bottom of the oven and preheat oven to 350 degrees. Butter a 15½ x 10½ x 1-inch rimmed baking sheet. Line it all, bottom and sides, with one long piece of aluminum foil and butter the foil. Set the prepared pan aside.

In the small bowl of an electric mixer, add 3 tablespoons of the sugar (reserve 1 tablespoon) to the egg yolks and beat at

continues ↘

high speed for 5 to 7 minutes, until the yolks are cream-colored (the French *patissier* called it white). Add the flour and beat on low speed, scraping the bowl with a rubber spatula, only until incorporated. Remove from the mixer.

If you do not have another small bowl and an extra set of beaters for the mixer, transfer the yolk mixture to a second bowl and wash and dry the first bowl and the beaters. (Or beat the whites with an egg beater or a wire whisk.)

Add the salt to the whites in the small bowl of the electric mixer and beat until they increase in volume and begin to thicken. Gradually add the reserved 1 tablespoon sugar and continue to beat only until the whites hold a definite shape when the beaters are raised or when some of the whites are lifted with a spatula — they should not be beaten until stiff and dry.

Fold one-third of the whites into the yolks, then fold in a second third, and then the final third — do not handle any more than necessary.

Turn the batter into the prepared pan and gently spread it — it should be reasonably smooth and it will stay just where you put it, it will not run — check the corners. But don't waste any time before putting it into the oven.

Bake for about 18 minutes, or until the top springs back when lightly pressed with a fingertip — it will be a pale golden color — do not overbake.

When the cake is done, sprinkle the confectioners' sugar through a fine strainer generously over the top. Quickly cover the cake with a piece of wax paper several inches longer than the cake pan (the confectioners' sugar will keep it from sticking). Cover the paper with a cookie sheet, invert the pan and cookie sheet (holding them firmly together), remove the pan, and quickly and carefully peel off the foil. Then quickly roll the cake and the wax paper together, rolling from a narrow end — don't squash the cake but roll firmly and compactly.

Let stand until cool.

For the Icing and Filling

Place both chocolates and the coffee in a small, heavy saucepan over low heat. Stir frequently until the chocolate is melted and the mixture is smooth. Add the butter and stir until smooth. Remove from the heat and stir in the rum or Cognac. If the icing was made while the cake was baking, just set it aside and let stand at room temperature.

When the cake is cool and ready to be filled and iced, place some ice and water in a mixing bowl that is large enough to hold the saucepan of icing.

Place the pan of icing in the ice water and stir constantly until the icing thickens slightly — it should not harden but it should be thick enough so that it does not run out of the cake when the cake is rolled. (Lift the pan from the ice water occasionally and stir well to be sure it is not thickening too much on the bottom or sides.)

When it has thickened to the consistency of a very soft mayonnaise, remove it from the ice water and work quickly as it will continue to thicken now.

Remove and reserve ⅓ cup, which will be used to cover the outside of the roll. Unroll the cake, loosen it from the wax paper, spread the icing evenly to the edge on three sides of the cake — stop it a little short of the farther narrow end — then reroll the cake firmly. With a pastry brush, brush excess sugar off the top of the cake and, with a narrow metal spatula, spread the reserved icing over the top and sides — then quickly, before the icing hardens, with a spoon sprinkle the chocolate shavings over the top and as much of the sides as possible.

The cake roll should still be on the wax paper on one end of the cookie sheet; transfer it to the refrigerator for about half an hour or until the glaze is firm.

Then, through a small fine-mesh strainer, sprinkle confectioners' sugar generously over the top.

With a wide metal spatula (or the flat side of a cookie sheet) transfer the cake to a serving platter and let stand at room temperature. It may stand all day or overnight. It should be served at room temperature unless the room is too warm, in which case it should be refrigerated as necessary — but it is best if the chocolate is not too firm.

Cut into 1- to 1¼-inch slices.

F.B.I. CHOCOLATE LAYER CAKE

10 to 12 portions When J. Edgar Hoover came to dinner at my parents' home, this is the cake my mother served for dessert. Mr. Hoover liked it so much he threatened an F.B.I. investigation if he didn't get the recipe. I was assigned to deliver it by hand the following morning.

It is two dark and delicious chocolate layers, quite easy to make, filled and covered with whipped cream.

1¾ cups *sifted* all-purpose flour

1 teaspoon baking powder

½ teaspoon baking soda

¼ teaspoon salt

½ cup unsweetened cocoa powder (preferably Dutch-process)

4 ounces (1 stick) unsalted butter

1 teaspoon vanilla extract

1¾ cups granulated sugar

4 large eggs, separated

1¼ cups milk

WHIPPED CREAM

2 cups heavy cream

1 teaspoon vanilla extract

¼ cup strained confectioners' sugar

My mother made this, as I do, in two 10-inch layer-cake pans. They are not generally available at hardware stores but they are at specialty kitchen equipment shops or online, and they do make a beautiful cake. If you do not have that size, it may be made in two 9-inch pans.

If you are using 10-inch pans, adjust two racks to divide the oven into thirds. For 9-inch pans, adjust one rack to the center of the oven. Preheat oven to 325 degrees. Butter the pans and line the bottoms with baking parchment or wax paper cut to fit. Butter the paper, dust all over with flour, invert, and tap lightly to shake out excess. Set the prepared pans aside.

Sift together the flour, baking powder, baking soda, salt, and cocoa and set aside.

In the large bowl of an electric mixer, cream the butter. Add the vanilla and sugar and beat to mix well. Add the egg yolks and beat to mix well. On low speed, add the dry ingredients in three additions, alternating with the milk in two additions. (Use a smaller amount for the first dry addition.) Add the milk very gradually, scraping the bowl with a rubber spatula while adding, and beat only until each addition is incorporated. Remove from the mixer.

In a small, clean bowl with clean beaters, beat the egg whites until they hold a definite shape but not until they are stiff or dry. Add the whites to the chocolate mixture and fold together only until they are incorporated.

Pour half of the batter into each of the prepared pans and smooth the tops.

If you have used 10-inch pans, place one pan on each rack, staggering the pans so one is not directly over the other. If you have used 9-inch pans, they may both fit on the one rack in the center. (However, if your oven is small, you may have to use two racks even for 9-inch pans.)

Bake until the layers begin to come away from the sides of the pans; it will take about 45 minutes in 10-inch pans, a little longer in 9-inch pans.

As soon as the layers are removed from the oven, with a small, sharp knife, cut around the sides to release. Let stand for 4 or 5 minutes. Cover each layer with a rack, invert, remove pan and paper lining, cover with another rack and invert again, leaving the layers right side up to cool.

Prepare a large, flat plate by placing four strips of wax paper around the outer edges. Place one layer upside down on the plate, checking to be sure that the papers touch it all around.

If you have a cake-decorating turntable or a lazy Susan, place the cake plate on it.

For the Whipped Cream

In a large, chilled bowl with chilled beaters, whip the ingredients until the cream is firm enough to hold its shape.

Spread about one-third of the whipped cream about ½ inch thick over the cake layer on the plate. Carefully place the other layer right side up (the two flat sides meet in the middle) on the whipped cream. Spread the remaining cream over the sides and top of the cake; it may be spread smoothly or lifted into swirls and peaks.

continues ⌄

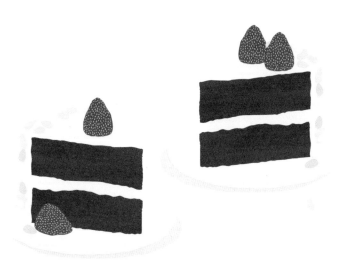

Remove the four strips of wax paper by pulling each one out toward a narrow end.

Refrigerate for a few hours before serving.

Toasted Almond Decoration

This cake does not need any decoration but it lends itself to whatever. It is especially attractive and delicious if the cream is spread smoothly and the sides are coated with toasted sliced almonds as follows.

To toast the almonds: Place about 1 cup of thinly sliced almonds in a shallow pan in a 350-degree oven and stir occasionally for 10 minutes or so, until the almonds are golden brown. Cool completely.

Place a few spoonfuls of the almonds in the palm of your hand; turn your hand close to the sides of the cake, leaving the almonds on the whipped cream. Many of them will fall down onto the plate — OK. They may be lifted with a small metal spatula or a table knife and replaced on the cream.

Or use more almonds and sprinkle them on the top, too.

VARIATION

Strawberry Chocolate Layer Cake: My mother always used the almonds (see box), and she either made the following strawberry version or served strawberries on the side. The strawberries, if they were served on the side, were sliced thick and sprinkled with just a bit of granulated sugar and kirsch. (The strawberries should be prepared about an hour or so before serving to absorb the flavors and give off a bit of their juice.)

Quickly wash and then hull 1 or 2 pints of strawberries and drain them thoroughly on paper towels. Reserve the largest berries for the top of the cake. For the filling, cut some berries in halves, or quarters if they are very large. Press them down into the filling; if necessary, cover with a bit more cream so they are barely covered. Place the reserved large berries, pointed ends up, in the whipped cream, either in a circle around the rim of the cake or all over the top.

HUNGARIAN SEVEN-LAYER CAKE

12 portions This is fun, and a wonderful cake that is a first cousin to Dobosh Torte — it is seven thin layers of a classic white sponge cake, filled and covered with a deliciously bittersweet dark chocolate buttercream.

You will need 8-inch layer-cake pans and, since you will bake seven separate layers, it will go a little faster if you have many pans. However, the layers bake quickly, so even with only a few pans this is not a tremendous chore (although it does take more patience than baking a one- or two-layer cake). The cake may be refrigerated for a day or two, or it may be frozen.

NOTES

For a sweeter filling and icing, substitute semisweet chocolate for all or part of the unsweetened chocolate.

If you freeze this, chill it until the icing is firm before wrapping; then thaw overnight or for several hours in the refrigerator before unwrapping.

Before serving, the top may be covered with small chocolate shavings which may, if you wish, be coated with a sprinkling of sweetened or unsweetened cocoa powder.

6 large eggs, separated

¾ cup granulated sugar

1 cup *sifted* all-purpose flour

¼ teaspoon salt

BITTERSWEET CHOCOLATE FILLING AND ICING

5 ounces unsweetened chocolate (see Notes)

¼ cup water

½ cup sugar

1 tablespoon instant coffee powder

4 large egg yolks

4 ounces (1 stick) unsalted butter, cut into ½-inch pieces

If you have only two or three 8-inch pans, and if they will fit on the same rack, adjust the rack to the lowest position in the oven. If you have more pans than will fit on one rack, adjust two racks, one to the lowest position and the other closer to the middle. Preheat oven to 350 degrees.

Cut seven circles of wax paper to fit the 8-inch pans. Butter as many pans as you have, line them with the papers and butter the papers. Set the prepared pans aside and reserve the extra circles of wax paper.

In the small bowl of an electric mixer, beat the egg yolks and about half of the sugar at high speed for about 5 minutes, until very pale and thick. On low speed, gradually add the flour and beat, scraping the bowl with a rubber spatula and beating only until the flour is incorporated. The mixture will be very thick. Remove it from the mixer (use

continues ↘

your index finger to scrape the beaters clean).

Add the salt to the egg whites in the large bowl of the electric mixer. With clean beaters, beat until the whites hold a soft shape. Reduce the speed to moderate, gradually add the remaining sugar, then increase the speed again and beat until the whites hold a firm shape.

Add about ½ cup of the beaten whites to the yolk mixture and stir it in. Then stir in another ½ cup. Then, adding about ½ cup at a time, fold in all but about 2 cups of the whites. Fold the yolk mixture into the remaining whites.

You will have about 6½ cups of batter to make seven layers, therefore each layer should use a scant 1 cup of batter. It is not necessary to measure the amount — you can approximate it. Spread the batter smoothly all the way to the edge of each prepared pan — it must touch the sides of the pan all the way around, and it should be smooth.

The layers should bake about 15 minutes. If you are using more than one rack, the pans must be reversed top to bottom once during baking; each layer should spend some time on the lowest rack so that the bottom bakes well. When done, the tops will be barely colored, and the layers may show signs of beginning to come away from the pans at the edges.

Spread out a large, smooth (not terrycloth) cotton or linen towel. When the layers are done, cut around the sides to release and then invert the layers onto the towel. Remove the pans and peel off the papers.

If the bottoms are baked dry enough the papers will peel off in one piece; if they don't, it is all right to tear the papers off, one section at a time. (The bottoms should be a little darker than the tops.) With your hands, immediately turn the layers right side up — the tops of the layers are sticky and would stick to the towel. Let stand until cool.

The remaining batter may wait uncovered at room temperature, but don't waste any time getting it all baked. Wash the pans, prepare them as before, and bake the remaining layers.

Prepare a flat cake plate by lining the sides with four strips of wax paper. Place one layer right side up on the plate, checking to be sure that the papers touch the cake all around.

If you have a cake-decorating turntable or a lazy Susan, place the cake plate on it.

For the Filling and Icing

Place the chocolate in the top of a small double boiler over hot water on moderate heat. Cover until partially melted, then uncover and stir until completely melted.

Meanwhile, in a small saucepan, mix the water with the sugar and instant coffee. Place over moderate heat and stir until the sugar is dissolved and the mixture comes to a boil.

Also meanwhile, in the small bowl of an electric mixer, beat the egg yolks at high speed until they are pale lemon-colored.

When the sugar/coffee syrup is ready, turn the mixer speed to low and very slowly, in a

continues ⩗

thin stream, beat the syrup into the yolks. Then add the warm melted chocolate and beat only until smooth — it will be very thick.

Now, beating slowly, add the butter, one or two pieces at a time, and beat well until completely blended.

With a long, narrow metal spatula, spread a very thin layer of the buttercream over the cake, spreading it smoothly all the way to the edges. The layers of filling must be thin or there will not be enough to cover the top and sides — this amount is just right if you spread it thin enough.

All the layers should be placed right side up except the top one, which should be upside down to ensure a perfectly flat top.

After filling all the layers, cover the top and sides. But just before spreading the icing on the top and sides of the cake, if the icing is not silken smooth, and if you have a food processor, process the icing (use the metal blade) for a few seconds and like magic it will become completely smooth. Then, with a long, narrow metal spatula, spread the icing smooth.

Remove the wax paper strips by pulling each one out toward a narrow end.

Refrigerate for several hours to set the icing. The cake may be cold when it is served or at room temperature. It should be cut with a sharp, heavy knife.

CHOCOLATE CUPCAKES

24 cupcakes These cupcakes and Brownies (page 183) are the desserts I usually make when I am asked to make something for a cake sale.

2 cups *sifted* all-purpose flour

1 teaspoon baking soda

¼ teaspoon salt

½ cup unsweetened cocoa powder (preferably Dutch-process)

5⅓ ounces (10⅔ tablespoons) unsalted butter

1 teaspoon vanilla extract

1½ cups sugar

3 large, extra-large, or jumbo eggs

1 cup milk

CHOCOLATE ICING

6 ounces semisweet chocolate

⅓ cup heavy cream

1 tablespoon sugar

1½ tablespoons unsalted butter

NOTES

When baking cupcakes, if you have only one pan with 12 cups, reserve the remaining batter and bake additional cupcakes after the first panful. If you bake only one pan at a time, bake it in the center of the oven.

Lining the pans with papers is a convenience and a timesaver. The cupcakes take on a better shape, they rise higher, and they stay fresh longer.

To freeze frosted cupcakes, let them stand until the icing is no longer sticky. Place them on a pan or tray in the freezer until they are frozen firm. Then cover them with a large piece of plastic wrap, turning it down securely on the sides and under the bottom, and return the pan or tray to the freezer. To thaw, let stand at room temperature until thawed before removing the wrapping.

Adjust two racks to divide the oven into thirds and preheat oven to 350 degrees. You'll need two 12-cup cupcake pans with cups measuring about 2¾ inches in diameter (see Notes). Butter the cups, sift a bit of flour over the pans, invert, and tap to shake out excess. Or line the cups with cupcake-liner papers (see Notes). Set aside.

Sift together the flour, baking soda, salt, and cocoa, and set aside.

In the large bowl of an electric mixer, cream the butter. Add the vanilla and sugar and beat to mix. Add the eggs one at a time, beating until smooth after each addition and scraping the bowl with a rubber spatula as necessary to keep the mixture smooth. On the lowest speed, alternately add the sifted dry ingredients in three additions with the milk in two additions. Continue to scrape the bowl with the rubber spatula and beat only until smooth. Do not overbeat.

continues ↘

Spoon the batter into the prepared pans, filling the cups only two-thirds to three-quarters full. There is no need to smooth the tops — the batter will level itself.

Bake for 25 minutes, or until the tops spring back when lightly pressed with a fingertip. Do not overbake. Cool in the pans for 2 to 3 minutes before removing to a rack to finish cooling.

For the Icing

Place all the ingredients in a small, heavy saucepan over moderate heat. Cook, stirring occasionally, until the chocolate is partially melted. Remove from the heat and stir constantly until the chocolate is completely melted and the mixture is smooth. Transfer to a small, shallow bowl. Let stand, stirring occasionally, until the icing reaches room temperature.

Hold a cupcake upside down and dip the top into the icing; twirl the cake slightly, and then continue to hold it upside down for a few seconds for excess icing to drip off. Repeat with all of the cakes. Then, after dipping them all, dip each one a second time. If there is still some icing left, the cakes may be dipped a third time. When the icing gets low, transfer it to a custard cup, or a coffee or teacup, but don't try to use up the last bit — the cupcakes won't look as smooth.

MONTANA MOUNTAIN CAKE

10 portions A high three-layer chocolate cake filled and iced with Caramel Coffee 7-Minute Icing.

3 ounces unsweetened chocolate

3 cups *sifted* cake flour

1½ teaspoons baking soda

½ teaspoon salt

6 ounces (1½ sticks) unsalted butter

1½ teaspoons vanilla extract

2¼ cups sugar

3 large eggs

1½ cups ice water

Caramel Coffee 7-Minute Icing (page 123)

NOTES

If you use 8-inch pans, the finished cake will be about 6 to 7 inches high — startling! You will need large plates for serving.

Since 7-Minute Icing does not freeze well, it is best to ice the cake the day you are going to serve it.

For 8-inch pans, adjust rack to center of oven. For 9-inch pans, adjust two racks to divide oven in thirds. Preheat oven to 375 degrees. Butter three 8- or 9-inch round layer-cake pans and dust them lightly with fine, dry bread crumbs.

Melt the chocolate in top of small double boiler over hot water on moderate heat. Set aside.

Sift together the flour, baking soda, and salt and set aside.

In a large bowl of an electric mixer, beat the butter to soften a bit. Add the vanilla and sugar and beat for a minute or two. Beat in the eggs one at a time, scraping the bowl with a rubber spatula as necessary to keep the mixture well blended. Continue to beat for 2 to 3 minutes. Beat in the chocolate. On lowest speed, alternately add the sifted dry ingredients in three additions and the ice water in two additions, continuing to scrape the bowl as necessary with the spatula and beating only until smooth after each addition.

Divide the batter between the prepared pans. Spread the tops level and then push the batter up on the sides a bit so that the centers are slightly lower.

Bake for 25 to 30 minutes, or until tops spring back when lightly touched and cakes begin to come away from the sides of the pans.

Cool in the pans for about 5 minutes. Cover with racks or cookie sheets and invert. Remove pans. Cover with racks and invert again to finish cooling right side up.

Place four strips of wax paper or baking parchment around the edges of a cake plate. Place one layer on the plate, right side up.

With a long, narrow, metal spatula, spread icing over the layer. Cover with second layer, right side up, and spread with icing. Top with third layer, also right side up. Spread icing on sides and top.

continues ⌄

With the spatula or the back of a spoon, quickly pull the icing up in definite peaks all over the cake.

Remove wax paper strips by pulling each one out by a narrow end.

Caramel Coffee 7-Minute Icing

This is the classic 7-Minute Icing (page 65) with a few adaptations.

½ cup egg whites (from 3 to 4 large eggs; you may use whites that have been left over from other desserts and frozen, but thaw completely before using)

1½ cups light brown sugar (or 1 cup dark brown sugar and ½ cup granulated sugar)

¼ cup plus 1 tablespoon strong black coffee (or about 1 tablespoon instant coffee dissolved in ¼ cup plus 1 tablespoon hot water)

1 teaspoon cream of tartar

⅛ teaspoon salt

1½ teaspoons vanilla extract

Place everything except the vanilla in the top of a large double boiler with at least an 8- to 10-cup capacity. Place over hot water on moderate heat.

Beat with an electric mixer at high speed for 4 to 5 minutes, until the mixture stands in peaks when the beaters are raised. Or beat with an egg beater for about 7 minutes.

Immediately, in order to stop the cooking, transfer the mixture to the large bowl of the electric mixer. Add the vanilla and beat at high speed very briefly, only until the mixture is smooth and barely firm enough to spread. Do not overbeat or the icing will become too stiff. Use immediately!

CRAIG CLAIBORNE'S RUM CHOCOLATE DESSERT

NOTE

⬇

I think this cake is best at room temperature. Therefore it should be covered with the whipped cream immediately before serving. But if that is too much of a hassle, put the whipped cream on ahead of time and refrigerate the cake until serving time. (It is really divine either way.)

8 to 10 portions Many years ago, when Craig printed this recipe in the *New York Times,* he wrote the following introduction for it: "Food cravings encompass everything from such mundane fare as peanuts, pickles and watermelon to the more sophisticated delights of oysters, caviar and champagne. Of all the foods on earth, however, it may be true that a craving for chocolate is the most universal. This rich, whipped-cream-topped chocolate pudding goes a long way to explain why."

I don't know why Craig called this a pudding. I call it a cake. Maybe the best of all. It slices beautifully. Serve it at your finest party, or make it just for yourself. Make it during the day for that night. Or make it the day before and ice it shortly before serving. Also, it can be frozen before it is iced — if so, thaw at room temperature for several hours.

4½ tablespoons *unsifted* all-purpose flour

¾ cup sugar

5 ounces semisweet chocolate

1 teaspoon instant coffee powder

2 tablespoons boiling water

6 ounces (1½ sticks) unsalted butter

¼ cup dark rum

6 large eggs, separated

¼ teaspoon salt

WHIPPED CREAM

1 cup heavy cream

2 tablespoons strained confectioners' sugar

½ teaspoon vanilla extract

Chocolate Cigarettes (page 97) or candied violets or rose petals

Adjust rack one-third up from bottom of the oven and preheat oven to 350 degrees. You will need a round cake pan 8 inches in diameter and 3 inches deep (you can use an 8 x 3-inch cheesecake pan or an 8 x 3½-inch (2½-quart) soufflé dish. Cut a round of wax paper to fit the bottom. Butter the sides of the pan or dish and one side of the paper. Place the paper, buttered side up, in the pan. Shake a bit of flour into the pan, tap it around to coat all surfaces, then invert the pan to remove excess. Set pan aside.

Sift the flour and sugar together and set aside.

Place the chocolate in the top of a large double boiler over hot water on moderate heat. Dissolve the coffee in the boiling water and pour over the chocolate. Cover the pot and leave until the chocolate is melted. Remove the top of the double boiler and stir well with a wire whisk until smooth. With the whisk, gradually stir in the butter, adding about a ½-inch slice at a time and whisking until smooth after each addition. Gradually whisk in the dry ingredients and then the rum.

Place the egg yolks in a large mixing bowl and stir them lightly with the whisk just to mix. Gradually add the warm chocolate mixture, stirring well to mix.

Add the salt to the egg whites and beat until they just hold a shape or are stiff but not dry. In two or three additions, fold the whites into the chocolate.

Pour the mixture into the prepared cake pan or soufflé dish. Smooth the top. Place in a larger but not deeper pan, and pour in hot water to reach about halfway up the sides of the cake pan or soufflé dish.

Bake for 1 hour and 10 minutes. Remove the smaller pan from the hot water and place on a rack to cool to room temperature (it will take 1 hour or more but it may stand overnight). The cake will shrink as it cools — don't worry. (The cooled cake will be about 1½ inches high.)

With a small, sharp knife, cut around the sides to release. Cover with a flat cake plate or a serving board, centering the plate evenly over the cake. Invert the plate and the cake pan. (If it doesn't lift off easily, bang the plate and the pan gently against a table or countertop.) Remove the pan and peel off the paper lining.

For the Whipped Cream

Whip all the ingredients until they are stiff enough to hold a shape when spread over the cake. With a small metal spatula, first cover the sides of the cake and then the top. The cream may be spread smoothly or swirled into peaks.

The whipped cream may be left as is or decorated with Chocolate Cigarettes (page 97) or with candied violets or rose petals. (The violets or rose petals should be put on at the last minute or they might discolor the cream.)

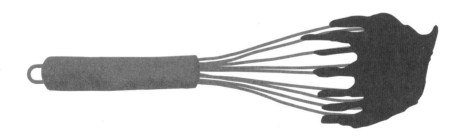

KANSAS CITY CHOCOLATE DREAM

8 or 9 portions Variations of this recipe pop up in many areas of the country under many different names: Chocolate Upside-Down Cake, Chocolate Sauce Pudding, Chocolate Pudding Cake, Hot Fudge Sauce Cake, to name a few. Whatever the name, you will usually have a square pan of chocolate cake floating in a rather thin, dark chocolate syrup; both the cake and the syrup are spooned out together and served like a pudding with a sauce.

This Missouri recipe is similar, but is something else. It is a small, shallow square upside-down cake which, when turned onto a cake plate, covers itself with a thick layer of dark chocolate topping that resembles nothing else I can think of. The topping is as dark and shiny as black patent leather, as tender and semi-firm as a pot de crème, and as mocha-chocolate flavored as you might weave dreams about.

The topping and the cake are baked together. Sensationally quick/easy/foolproof. This is wonderful just as soon as it has barely cooled, or it can wait hours, or it can be frozen.

CAKE

- 1 cup *sifted* all-purpose flour
- 2 teaspoons baking powder
- ¼ teaspoon salt
- 2 tablespoons unsweetened cocoa powder (preferably Dutch-process)
- ⅔ cup granulated sugar
- ¾ cup milk
- 1 teaspoon vanilla extract
- 2 tablespoons unsalted butter, melted
- ½ cup walnuts, broken into medium-size pieces

TOPPING

- ½ cup firmly packed dark brown sugar
- ⅓ cup granulated sugar
- 6 tablespoons unsweetened cocoa powder (preferably Dutch-process)
- 2 teaspoons granular instant coffee
- 1 cup water

Adjust a rack one-third up from the bottom of the oven and preheat the oven to 350 degrees. Butter a shallow 8-inch square cake pan and set aside.

For the Cake

Into the small bowl of an electric mixer, sift together the flour, baking powder, salt, cocoa, and sugar. Add the milk, vanilla, and melted butter and beat until smooth and slightly pale in color. Remove the bowl from the mixer. Stir in the nuts. Turn into the buttered pan and smooth the top. Let stand.

For the Topping

In a small, heavy saucepan, combine all the ingredients. Stir over rather high heat until the sugars melt and the mixture comes to a full boil.

Gently ladle the boiling hot mixture all over the cake batter.

Bake for 40 minutes, until a toothpick inserted gently into the cake comes out clean. (During baking, the topping will sink to the bottom.) Set aside to cool in the pan.

When the cake has cooled, cover with a square or oblong serving plate or a cutting board. Holding them firmly together, turn the pan and the plate over. If the cake does not slide out of the pan easily (and it probably will not), hold the plate and the pan firmly together upside down and tap them on the work surface. Now the cake will come out, and it will be covered with the topping, some of which will still be in the pan; use a rubber spatula to remove it all and put it on the cake. Smooth the top gently or pull the topping up into uneven peaks.

Serve immediately or let stand all day or freeze. (If you freeze this, do not cover with plastic wrap; the topping never does freeze hard and plastic wrap will stick to it. Just cover the whole thing with an inverted box deep enough so it doesn't touch the cake.) Freezing diminishes the flavor of all foods, especially this. Although this can be served frozen, it has more flavor if it is brought to room temperature.

This cake does not need a thing but a plate and fork. However, if you are serving it for a birthday party or some other festivity, ice cream is wonderful with it.

CHOCOLATE MERRY-GO-ROUND

12 portions This is just a delicious white sponge cake with a wonderful rich, dark chocolate buttercream, but the method of putting the two together is most unusual — it will be an eight-layer cake but the layers will go vertically instead of horizontally. Although I think that all baking is an art, this one is a little more artsy-craftsy than the usual — but not difficult.

This should be made very early in the day of the night you plan to serve it, or made the day before — it must be served very cold. It may be frozen.

SPONGE CAKES

- 1 cup *sifted* all-purpose flour
- ½ teaspoon baking powder
- 2 tablespoons orange juice
- 2 tablespoons vegetable oil
- 5 large eggs, separated
- ½ teaspoon vanilla extract
- 1 cup sugar
- ⅛ teaspoon salt

CHOCOLATE BUTTERCREAM

- 6 ounces (6 squares) unsweetened chocolate
- 1 cup plus 2 tablespoons sugar
- 3 tablespoons plus 2 teaspoons water
- 12 ounces (3 sticks) unsalted butter
- ½ teaspoon vanilla extract
- 2 tablespoons unsweetened cocoa powder (preferably Dutch-process)
- 3 large eggs

Adjust two racks to divide the oven into thirds and preheat oven to 350 degrees. Butter two 15½ x 10½ x 1-inch rimmed baking sheets. Line each pan with a large piece of wax paper to cover the bottoms and the sides. Butter the paper and set aside.

For the Cakes

Sift together the flour and baking powder and set aside.

Measure the orange juice and vegetable oil into a glass measuring cup (you should have ¼ cup) and set aside.

Place the egg yolks, vanilla, and ½ cup of the sugar (reserve the remaining ½ cup) in the small bowl of an electric mixer. Beat at high speed until the yolks are pale lemon-colored. On low speed, add half of the dry ingredients, then the juice mixture, and then the remaining dry ingredients, scraping the bowl with a rubber spatula and beating only until smooth after each addition. Transfer to a larger mixing bowl.

Place the egg whites and the salt in a clean small electric mixer bowl. With clean beaters, beat at high speed until the whites hold a very soft shape. Reduce the speed to moderate and gradually add the reserved ½ cup sugar. Then increase the speed again and beat only until the whites hold a definite shape, but not until they are stiff or dry.

Fold two or three large spoonfuls of the whites into the yolk mixture. Fold in two or three more spoonfuls. Then add all the remaining whites and fold in.

It is important for the layers to be the same thickness; measure 3 cups (which is half) of the batter into each pan. The batters must be spread as smoothly as possible; watch the corners — be careful they aren't thinner — and there should be no hollows in the middles. The layers will be very thin.

Bake for 10 minutes. Then quickly reverse the pans top to bottom and front to back to ensure even baking. Bake for 3 to 5 minutes more (total baking time 13 to 15 minutes), until the tops of the cakes spring back when lightly pressed with a fingertip. They will be a pale golden color when done. They should not be overbaked.

While the cakes are baking, spread out two smooth linen or cotton towels — not terrycloth.

As soon as the layers are done, invert them onto the towels. Quickly remove the pans, peel off the paper linings (the layers will be ½ inch thick), and cover each layer loosely with a second smooth linen or cotton towel. Let stand until cool.

For the Buttercream

Chop the chocolate into rather fine pieces and set aside on a piece of wax paper.

Place the sugar and water in a small saucepan over moderate heat. Stir constantly with a wooden spatula until the sugar is dissolved and the mixture comes to a fast boil. Dip a pastry brush in water and wash down the sides to remove any undissolved granules of sugar.

Add the chopped chocolate and stir over heat until the chocolate is melted and the mixture is smooth. Remove from the heat and let stand, stirring occasionally, for 5 minutes.

Meanwhile, in the small bowl of an electric mixer, cream the butter. Add the vanilla and cocoa and beat well. Then add the eggs one at a time, scraping the bowl with a rubber spatula and beating after each addition until it is incorporated.

On low speed, gradually add the chocolate mixture (which will still be warm), scraping the bowl with a rubber spatula and beating only until smooth. (The warm chocolate will thin the buttercream.) Remove from the mixer and set aside.

Now you will invert the cooled cakes onto a large cutting surface. Remove the top towels and then lift the remaining towels with the layers on them, invert onto the surface, and remove the towels, leaving the cakes right side up.

Partially fill a large bowl with ice and water. Place the bowl of buttercream in the bowl of ice and water and stir constantly with a

continues ↘

rubber spatula until the mixture is as thick as mayonnaise. While it is chilling it will thicken unevenly (the coldest part will thicken sooner); when that happens remove the bowl of buttercream and stir it well with the spatula until it smooths out, then return it to the ice and continue to stir.

When the mixture is thick enough, remove and set aside 2 cups for the icing. With a long, narrow metal spatula, spread half of the remaining buttercream (¾ cup) on each sponge sheet. Spread very smoothly all the way to all the edges.

Now each cake will be cut into four strips the long way. It is important that the strips are all cut exactly the same width; use a ruler and toothpicks to mark both of the narrow ends of each cake into quarters.

With a long, sharp knife, cut the strips.

To Form the Cake

Roll one of the strips (with the chocolate to the inside) into a tight spiral, like a jelly roll. Place another strip next to the end of the rolled strip, extending it, and continue to roll.

Place the rolled strips (which will be the middle of the cake) on a flat side so the spiral pattern is up, in the center of a large, flat cake plate. Carefully pick up another strip, place a narrow end of it against and touching the end of the rolled strips, and roll it around the cake. Continue this way with the remaining strips, being careful not to leave a gap where the ends of the strips come together.

When all of the strips are rolled around in a spiral, you will have a cake 9 inches in diameter and 2½ inches high.

If you have a cake-decorating turntable or a lazy Susan, place the cake plate on it.

Briskly stir the reserved 2 cups buttercream to soften it slightly. Spread it over the top and sides of the cake, spreading it smoothly with a long, narrow metal spatula.

Wipe the cake plate if any icing is on it.

Refrigerate the cake overnight, or freeze it for several hours or longer. (Freeze until the icing is firm before wrapping. Thaw for several hours or overnight in the refrigerator before unwrapping.) It must be cold when it is served or it will not slice well.

THE NEWEST CHEESECAKE

10 to 16 portions My favorite cheesecake recipe came from Craig Claiborne. I made it every day for ten years for restaurants my husband owned. Sometime during those years I made up a black-and-white version. And Craig made a hazelnut version. (All three are in my dessert book.) This is an exciting combination of the three cakes.

It is formed into three layers before baking, one white, one nut, and one chocolate. None of these cakes individually takes very much time to put together—but this combination one takes longer since the two bottom layers must be frozen before the next one is put on or they will run into each other.

You will need a special cheesecake pan (they are deep and do not have removable bottoms) which used to be difficult to find. But since the cheesecakes in the dessert book became so popular, the pan is now generally available at specialty kitchen equipment shops all around the country (or online).

This may be made early in the day for that night (it must be refrigerated at least 5 to 6 hours before serving), or it can be made a day or two before, or it may be frozen (cheesecakes freeze wonderfully) and thawed before serving.

3¾ ounces (¾ cup) blanched hazelnuts; or almonds, walnuts, or pecans (see Notes)

2 pounds cream cheese, at room temperature

1 teaspoon vanilla extract

1¾ cups sugar

4 large eggs

⅛ teaspoon almond extract

2 ounces unsweetened chocolate

⅓ cup graham-cracker crumbs (to be used after cake is baked)

NOTES

Hazelnuts usually come with brown skins which must be removed (see directions for blanching, page 22). Or, if you buy them already skinned but not toasted, toast them to bring out their flavor. (To toast, place them in a shallow baking pan in a 350-degree oven. Shake the pan occasionally until the nuts are only lightly colored.) Hazelnuts are difficult to find. I buy them unblanched at a health food store, or blanched but not toasted from a wholesale nut dealer.

If you use almonds they should be blanched (see page 22) and toasted as above.

If you use walnuts or pecans they should not be toasted. But if they are ground in a processor or a blender you must be very careful (especially with walnuts). Stop the machine while they are still in small pieces, or they will become oily and pasty—they should remain in little pieces and should not become a nut butter.

Use an 8-inch round one-piece cheesecake pan 3 inches deep. Butter it lightly all over the bottom, up to the rim, and around the inside of the rim or the cake will stick and will not rise evenly. Any unbuttered spots will prevent the finished cake from sliding out of the pan easily. Set the buttered pan aside.

The nuts must be finely chopped or ground. This may be done in a nut grinder, food processor, or blender. If there are a few uneven or larger pieces, it is all right (it is even better with some large pieces). Set the ground nuts aside.

In the large bowl of an electric mixer, beat the cheese, scraping the bowl frequently with a rubber spatula until it is very smooth. Beat in the vanilla and then the sugar very well, and then add the eggs one at a time, scraping the bowl with the spatula and beating only until smooth after each addition. After adding the eggs, do not beat any more than necessary — this cheesecake should not be airy.

Remove 2 cups of the mixture and transfer to a mixing bowl. (The remaining batter should be left at room temperature while the layers are being frozen.) Add the ground nuts and the almond extract to the 2 cups and stir to mix.

This will be the first layer. Pour it carefully into the middle of the pan. Very gently shake the pan to make the cheese mixture as smooth and level as you can. Keep the edges clean and straight.

Place the pan in the freezer for 1 hour or a bit longer, until the layer is firm enough to be covered with the next layer without losing its shape.

Remove and set aside 2 more cups of the basic batter for the top layer.

Place the chocolate in the top of a small double boiler over hot water on moderate heat. Cover until melted. Then uncover and remove the top of the double boiler. Mix the chocolate into the batter that is remaining in the mixer bowl.

Place the chocolate batter carefully by rounded spoonfuls all over the cold nut layer and very gently shake the pan to level the chocolate mixture — keep the edge as straight and neat as you can.

Return the cake to the freezer. The chocolate layer will need only about 15 or 20 minutes to become firm.

Adjust a rack to the lowest position in the oven and preheat the oven to 350 degrees.

When the chocolate layer is firm enough, spoon or pour the white layer carefully and evenly over it. Level the top by briskly rotating the pan a bit first in one direction and then another.

Place the cheesecake pan inside a larger pan. The larger pan must not touch the sides of the cake pan and it must not be deeper than the cake pan. Pour hot water into the larger pan to a little more than halfway up the side of the cake pan. (If the large pan is aluminum, adding about ½ teaspoon cream of tartar to the hot water will keep the pan from discoloring. You don't have to mix it — just put it in.)

Bake for 1 hour and 50 minutes. (This takes more baking than the other cheesecakes because it is partially frozen when it goes into the oven.) The top of the cake will be a rich golden brown and feel dry to the

continues ⌄

touch, but the cake will still be soft inside. (The cake will rise to or above the rim of the pan while it is baking, but it will sink below the rim as it cools.)

Lift the cake pan out of the water and place it on a rack for about 2 hours until it is completely cool. Do not chill the cake in the refrigerator or the butter will harden and the cake will stick to the pan.

Let stand until the bottom of the cake pan has reached room temperature. Then, to facilitate removing the cake from the pan, dip the pan for a few seconds into a large container of deep hot water (it can be boiling hot). Dry the pan. Place a flat plate or board over the top of the pan and invert. Remove the cake pan.

Sprinkle the bottom of the cake evenly with the graham-cracker crumbs. (If you are going to freeze the cake, place a round of wax paper on top of the crumbs so that

you will be able to lift the frozen cake from the plate and wrap it in plastic wrap.) Now, very gently place another flat plate or board (it should not be too heavy) on top of the crumbs (or on top of the round of wax paper). Hold it all with one hand underneath and one hand on top, with the fingers of both hands spread out. Very carefully and quickly turn everything over so the cake is right side up (once you start to turn it over do not hesitate — it should be an even and smooth motion). Do this without pressing too hard or you will squash the cake, which is still soft.

Refrigerate for at least 5 to 6 hours or overnight. Or freeze it. (Wrap after freezing and thaw before unwrapping.)

Serve at room temperature — it is more delicate and creamy at room temperature. But some people love it very cold. I'm wild about it either way.

NEW YORK CITY CHOCOLATE CHEESECAKE

12 to 16 portions This is a thick, dense, heavy, and rich chocolate cheesecake in a chocolate-cookie-crumb crust. It is a big-party dessert. It may be made a day or two before serving, or it may be made way ahead and frozen.

CRUST

- 8 ounces chocolate wafers (The store-bought ones are sometimes called icebox wafers. Better yet, make your own Chocolate Wafers, page 151.)
- 3 ounces (¾ stick) unsalted butter

FILLING

- 12 ounces semisweet chocolate (2 cups morsels or 12 squares, coarsely chopped)
- 24 ounces (three 8-ounce packages) cream cheese, at room temperature
- 1 teaspoon vanilla extract
- ⅛ teaspoon salt
- 1 cup sugar
- 3 large eggs
- 1 cup sour cream

Adjust rack one-third up from the bottom of the oven and preheat oven to 375 degrees. Separate the bottom from the sides of a 9 x 3-inch springform pan; butter the sides only (if you butter the bottom the crust will stick to the bottom and it will be difficult to serve). Replace the bottom in the pan and set aside.

For the Crust

Crumble the cookies coarsely and place them in a food processor or a blender and make fine crumbs (or place them in a plastic bag and pound and roll them with a rolling pin); you should have 2 cups of crumbs. Place in a mixing bowl. Melt the butter and stir it into the crumbs until thoroughly mixed.

Pour about two-thirds of the mixture into the prepared pan.

To form a thin layer of crumbs on the sides of the pan, tilt the pan at about a 45-degree angle and, with your fingertips, press a layer of the crumbs against the sides. Press from the bottom up toward the top of the pan and leave a rim of uncrumbed pan ¾ of an inch deep around the top. Rotate the pan gradually as you press on the crumbs. Then turn the pan upright on its bottom, pour in the remaining crumbs and, with your fingertips, distribute them evenly around the bottom of the pan. Then press them firmly to make a compact layer.

For the Filling

Place the chocolate in the top of a small double boiler over hot water on low heat. Cover until partially melted, then uncover and stir until completely melted and smooth. Remove from the hot water and set aside to cool slightly.

In the large bowl of an electric mixer, cream the cream cheese until it is very smooth. Add the vanilla, salt, and sugar and beat well, scraping the sides with a rubber spatula, until very smooth. Add the chocolate and beat to mix. Add the eggs one at a time, scraping the bowl with the spatula and beating until thoroughly blended after each addition. Add the sour cream and beat until smooth.

Pour the filling into the crumb crust (it will not quite reach the top of the crumbs) and rotate the pan briskly first in one direction, then in the other, to smooth the top. (It might also be necessary to smooth the top a bit with a spatula.)

Bake for 1 hour. (It will still seem quite soft.)

Let stand on a rack until completely cool. Cover the top of the pan with aluminum foil and refrigerate overnight.

The cheesecake may be removed from the pan just before serving or days before. With a firm, sharp, heavy knife, cut around the sides of the crust, pressing the knife blade firmly against the pan as you cut. Then release and remove the sides of the pan. Now use a firm (not flexible) metal spatula (either a wide one or a long narrow one): Insert the spatula gently and carefully under the crust and ease it around to release the cake completely from the bottom of the pan. The cake will be firm and strong and easy to transfer. If you are serving it within a day or two (the cake may be refrigerated a day or two before serving), place it on a large, flat dessert platter; if you are going to freeze it, place it on a large piece of plastic wrap and wrap airtight. Refrigerate or freeze. If you freeze the cake it should thaw completely, overnight in the refrigerator, before it is unwrapped. Serve it cold.

SERVING SUGGESTIONS

This cake is so dense that I like to serve a large bowl of soft whipped cream (page 56) on the side. And a bowl of brandied cherries. Or fresh strawberries or raspberries, or drained, canned Bing cherries. Or peeled and sliced kiwifruit.

Or, if you prefer a more decorated presentation, the rim of the cake may be trimmed with whipped cream applied through a pastry bag fitted with a large star-shaped tube. Either make large rosettes touching one another, or C- or S-shaped patterns, also touching. And the border of whipped cream may be topped with chopped green pistachio nuts, chocolate shavings, or with candied violets or rose petals (which should be put on just before serving — they may run into the cream if they stand).

To decorate the border, use 1 cup of cream, 2 tablespoons confectioners' sugar, and a scant ½ teaspoon of vanilla extract. Whip until the cream holds a definite shape.

If you are going to serve a lot of people, serve the whipped cream separately and use 3 cups of cream and three times the amount of sugar and vanilla. Whip only until the cream holds a soft shape. If you whip it ahead of time, refrigerate it, and then stir it with a wire whisk before serving.

This cake is very rich and should be served in small portions.

MOCHA VELVET

12 to 14 portions My friend Lora Brody, a caterer and chocolate-dessert-and-cookie expert from West Newton, Massachusetts, has had a special reputation for her cheesecakes since her original recipes for Ginger Cheesecake and Main Course Cheesecakes were printed in the *New York Times*. This is Lora's recipe for a chocolate cheesecake. It is a large, beautiful, delicious refrigerator cake (the filling is not baked) with an unusually mellow and exotic flavor that comes from a combination of ricotta cheese, coffee, and chocolate.

It is best to make this a day ahead. You will need a 10-inch springform pan.

NOTE
↓

Amaretti are extremely crisp Italian macaroons — I prefer the kind with an apricot flavor, though any will do. Or you could use 8 ounces of any well-dried almond macaroons.

CRUST

- 8 ounces Amaretti (see Note)
- ½ cup graham-cracker crumbs
- 4 ounces (1 stick) unsalted butter, melted

FILLING

- 1 tablespoon plus 1½ teaspoons (1½ envelopes) unflavored gelatin
- 3 tablespoons plus 1 teaspoon cold water
- 8 ounces semisweet chocolate
- ⅓ cup instant espresso or other dry instant coffee powder
- 1 cup boiling water
- ½ cup sugar
- 32 ounces (2 pounds) whole-milk ricotta cheese
- 1 teaspoon vanilla extract
- 1 cup heavy cream

TOPPING

- 1 cup heavy cream
- 1 tablespoon granulated or confectioners' sugar
- ½ teaspoon vanilla extract
- About ¼ cup toasted almonds, blanched or unblanched, thinly sliced (toast by baking in a 350-degree oven for 10 to 15 minutes, until lightly browned)

Adjust rack one-third up from the bottom of the oven and preheat oven to 400 degrees. Butter the sides only (not the bottom) of a 10 x 3-inch springform pan.

For the Crust

The Amaretti must be ground into fine crumbs. Grind them in a food processor fitted with the steel blade, or in two or three batches in a blender, or place them in a strong bag and pound them with a rolling pin. You will have 2 cups of crumbs. Set aside and reserve ½ cup.

Place the remaining 1½ cups in a mixing bowl. Stir in the graham-cracker crumbs and then add the melted butter and mix well.

Turn the crumb mixture into the pan. With your fingertips, press some of the crumbs against the sides of the pan, but leave a rim of uncrumbed pan about 1½ inches wide around the top of the pan. The crust should be 1½ inches high. Don't worry about the top edge of the crumbs being a perfectly straight line. Press the remaining crumbs firmly against the bottom of the pan. (Try not to concentrate the crumbs too heavily where the sides and the bottom of the pan meet.)

Bake the crust for 5 minutes, then let it cool completely.

For the Filling

Sprinkle the gelatin over the cold water in a small cup and set aside to soften.

Break up the chocolate and place it in a heavy 2- to 3-quart saucepan.

Dissolve the espresso powder in the boiling water and pour it over the chocolate. Place over low heat and stir frequently until the chocolate is melted. Then stir with a wire whisk until smooth. Add the softened gelatin and the sugar and stir over low heat for a few minutes to dissolve. Remove from the heat and set aside, stirring occasionally, until cool.

In the large bowl of an electric mixer, beat the ricotta cheese well. Add the vanilla and the chocolate mixture and beat until thoroughly mixed. Remove from the mixer.

continues ⌄

Whip the cream until it holds a shape but not until it is stiff. Fold into the chocolate mixture.

Pour about half of the filling into the cooled crumb crust. Sprinkle the reserved ½ cup of ground Amaretti evenly over the filling. Cover with the remaining filling. Spread the top smoothly, or form a neat design with the back of a spoon (I make parallel ridges). Cover with aluminum foil and refrigerate overnight.

Several hours before serving, remove the sides of the pan as follows: Insert a sharp, heavy knife between the crust and the pan. Pressing firmly against the pan, cut all the way around the crust, then release and remove the sides.

The cake may be removed from the bottom of the pan if you wish. If so, it should be done now. Use a firm (not flexible) metal spatula (either a wide one or a long, narrow one). Insert it gently and carefully under the bottom crust and ease it around to release the cake completely. Use two wide metal spatulas, or a small, flat cookie sheet, or the removable bottom of a quiche pan or layer-cake pan to transfer the cake to a platter.

For the Topping

In a small, chilled bowl with chilled beaters, whip the cream with the sugar and vanilla until it holds a shape and is firm enough to be used with a pastry bag.

Fit a pastry bag with a star-shaped tube, place the cream in the bag, and form a decorative border with the cream around the rim of the cake. Or place it by spoonfuls around the rim.

Crumble the toasted almonds slightly and sprinkle them over the whipped cream.

Refrigerate.

COOKIES
AND BARS

POSITIVELY-THE-ABSOLUTELY-BEST-CHOCOLATE-CHIP COOKIES

About 50 (3-inch) cookies A poll taken among food editors at newspapers and magazines found that chocolate chip cookies were the number one favorite of all homemade cookies in America. (That's not news.)

Well, this recipe is the mother of all chocolate chip cookie recipes.

It's closely based on the original Toll House recipe. But I make a few changes: I use 2 teaspoons vanilla instead of 1. And I use 16 ounces of chocolate instead of 12. Also, instead of using morsels, I use semisweet or bittersweet chocolate bars, cut into pieces.

Do not sift the flour before measuring it! Just stir it a bit to aerate it.

8 ounces (2 sticks) unsalted butter

1 teaspoon salt

2 teaspoons vanilla extract

¾ cup granulated sugar

¾ cup firmly packed light brown sugar

2 large eggs

2¼ cups *unsifted* all-purpose flour

1 teaspoon baking soda

1 teaspoon hot water

8 ounces (2 generous cups) walnuts, cut or broken into medium-size pieces

16 ounces (2 cups) semisweet or bittersweet chocolate bars, chopped into pieces

Adjust two racks to divide the oven into thirds and preheat oven to 375 degrees. Line cookie sheets with baking parchment or with aluminum foil, shiny side up.

In the large bowl of an electric mixer, beat the butter until soft. Add the salt, vanilla, and both sugars and beat to mix. Add the eggs and beat well. On low speed, add about half of the flour and, scraping the bowl with a rubber spatula, beat only until incorporated.

In a small cup, stir the baking soda into the hot water to dissolve it (see Notes), then mix it into the dough. Add the remaining flour and beat only to mix. Remove the bowl from the mixer. Stir in the walnuts and the chocolate.

Spread out a large piece of aluminum foil next to the sink. Use a rounded large spoonful of the dough for each cookie and place the mounds any which way on the foil. Wet your hands with cold water and shake off excess, but do not dry your hands. Pick up a mound of dough and roll it between your wet hands into a ball, then press it between your hands to flatten to about a ½-inch thickness.

Place the cookies on the lined sheets about 2 inches apart.

Bake two sheets at a time, reversing the sheets top to bottom and front to back as necessary to ensure even browning. (If you bake one sheet alone, bake it on the upper rack). Bake for about 12 minutes, until the cookies are browned all over. The cookies must be crisp; do not underbake.

Let the cookies stand a few seconds, then transfer with a metal spatula to racks to cool.

Store in an airtight container.

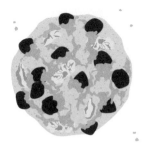

VARIATIONS

Cooks have varied the above recipe in just about every way possible. Some use whole-wheat flour for all or half of the flour, or less flour to make thinner cookies, or more flour to make thicker cookies. Or more sugar. Some add 2 cups of raisins or chopped dates, or coconut, either with or in place of the nuts. Some cooks add grated orange zest or chopped candied orange peel. Or chopped candied ginger. Or pumpkin seeds and/or wheat germ. Or 1 teaspoon cinnamon. Some add about 1 cup of peanut butter to the basic recipe and use peanuts in place of walnuts. (If you use salted peanuts, shake them vigorously in a large strainer to remove as much salt as possible; then use slightly less salt in the ingredients.) And a popular cookie that I have seen in many places across the country is what appears to be the basic recipe but it probably has more flour; it is formed into extra-large cookies that are 6 to 8 inches in diameter.

The quickest way of shaping and baking the dough is baking it in a pan for bar cookies. Butter a 15½ x 10½ x 1-inch rimmed baking sheet and spread the dough smoothly in the pan. Bake in the middle of a 375-degree oven for 20 minutes. Cool in the pan. Use a small, sharp knife to cut into 35 squares and use a wide metal spatula to remove the cookies.

COCONUT GROVE COOKIES

44 cookies These are chocolate cookies with hidden chunks of chocolate and a baked-on coconut meringue topping.

NOTE

Cake flour (not cake mix and not self-rising flour) is more finely ground than all-purpose flour. One cup sifted cake flour equals 1 cup minus 2 tablespoons sifted all-purpose flour, so in the dough recipe you could substitute 2¼ cups minus 1 tablespoon all-purpose flour if cake flour is unobtainable.

CHOCOLATE DOUGH

- 2½ cups *sifted* cake flour (see Note)
- 1½ teaspoons baking powder
- ¼ teaspoon salt
- 8 ounces semisweet chocolate
- 4 ounces (1 stick) unsalted butter
- 1 teaspoon vanilla extract
- 2 teaspoons instant coffee powder
- ½ cup granulated sugar
- ¼ cup firmly packed dark brown sugar
- 2 large egg yolks (reserve the whites for the meringue topping)
- ⅓ cup milk

MERINGUE TOPPING

- 2 large egg whites
- Pinch of salt
- ½ cup granulated sugar
- Scant ¼ teaspoon almond extract
- 2 tablespoons *sifted* cake flour (see Note)
- 7 ounces (2 packed cups) finely shredded sweetened coconut

Adjust two racks to divide the oven into thirds and preheat oven to 375 degrees. Line cookie sheets with baking parchment.

For the Chocolate Dough

Sift together the flour, baking powder, and salt and set aside.

Place 4 ounces (reserve remaining 4 ounces) of the chocolate in the top of a small double boiler over hot water on moderate heat. Stir occasionally until melted and smooth, then remove from heat and set aside to cool.

To cut the remaining 4 ounces of chocolate, use a heavy knife, work on a cutting board, and cut the chocolate into pieces measuring ¼ to ½ inch across. Set aside.

In the large bowl of an electric mixer, cream the butter. Add the vanilla and instant coffee and then both sugars and beat well. Beat in the egg yolks, scraping the bowl with a rubber spatula. Beat in the melted chocolate. On low speed, gradually add half of the sifted dry ingredients, continuing to scrape the bowl with the spatula. Now gradually add the milk and the remaining dry ingredients and beat only until smooth.

Remove the bowl from the mixer and stir in the cut chocolate pieces. Set the chocolate dough aside at room temperature and prepare the meringue topping.

For the Meringue Topping

In the small bowl of an electric mixer with clean beaters, beat the egg whites with the salt until the whites hold soft peaks. Gradually add the sugar, 1 to 2 spoonfuls at a time, and then beat at high speed until the meringue is very stiff. Toward the end of the beating, beat in the almond extract.

Remove the bowl from the mixer and fold in the flour and then the coconut.

To Form the Cookies

Use a rounded spoonful of the chocolate dough for each cookie and place them 2 inches apart on the cookie sheets. Then top each cookie with a slightly rounded spoonful of the meringue topping. In order to wind up even, use a tiny bit less of the meringue topping than the chocolate dough for each cookie. Try to place the topping carefully so that it won't run off the chocolate cookie while it is baking. A little of it will run off the side of the cookie no matter what, but that's OK; it looks nice anyhow.

Bake 12 to 13 minutes, until the topping is lightly browned. Reverse the cookie sheets top to bottom and front to back once during baking to ensure even browning.

With a wide metal spatula, transfer the cookies to racks to cool.

KEY WEST CHOCOLATE TREASURES

NOTE
⤓
If you store these in a box, place wax paper between the layers.

32 large cookies These are large, semisoft chocolate-coconut cookies with chocolate icing.

2 cups *sifted* all-purpose flour

¼ teaspoon salt

¼ teaspoon baking soda

1 teaspoon instant coffee powder

½ cup boiling water

3 ounces unsweetened chocolate

4 ounces (1 stick) unsalted butter

1 teaspoon vanilla extract

1 cup firmly packed dark brown sugar

1 large egg

⅔ cup sour cream

2 ounces (generous firmly packed ½ cup) shredded sweetened coconut

KEY WEST CHOCOLATE ICING

1½ ounces unsweetened chocolate

1 tablespoon unsalted butter

¼ cup sour cream

½ teaspoon vanilla extract

1½ cups strained confectioners' sugar

Adjust two racks to divide the oven into thirds and preheat oven to 375 degrees. Line cookie sheets with baking parchment.

Sift together the flour, salt, and baking soda and set aside. Dissolve the instant coffee in the boiling water.

Melt the chocolate with the prepared coffee in the top of a small double boiler over hot water on moderate heat. Stir until smooth. Remove the top of the double boiler and set aside.

In the large bowl of an electric mixer, cream the butter. Add the vanilla and brown sugar and beat to mix well. Beat in the egg. Add the chocolate mixture (which may still be slightly warm) and beat until smooth. On low speed, gradually add half of the sifted dry ingredients, then all of the sour cream, and then the remaining dry ingredients, scraping the bowl with a rubber spatula and beating only until smooth after each addition.

Remove the bowl from the mixer and stir in the coconut.

Use a heaping spoonful of dough for each cookie — make these large — and place them 2 inches apart on the sheets.

Bake for 12 to 15 minutes, reversing the sheets top to bottom and front to back once to ensure even baking. The cookies are done if the tops spring back firmly when lightly touched with a fingertip. (If you bake only one sheet at a time use the higher rack.)

With a wide metal spatula, transfer the cookies to racks to cool.

For the Icing

Melt the chocolate with the butter and sour cream in the top of a small double boiler over hot water on moderate heat. Stir until the mixture is smooth. Remove the top of the double boiler and, off the heat, stir in the vanilla; then, gradually stir in the confectioners' sugar.

Use the icing quickly, as it thickens while it stands. With a small metal spatula, a table knife, or the back of a teaspoon, spread the icing over the top of each cookie, but do not spread it all the way to the edges; leave a small margin. Let the cookies stand for about an hour or more until the icing is firm and dry.

DOLLY'S CRISP TOFFEE BARS

32 cookies My friend Dolly (Mrs. Andy) Granatelli is a superb cook and hostess who says that asking her not to cook would be like asking her not to breathe. These cookies are one of her specialties, chocolate chip butter bars, extremely crisp and crunchy, chewy and buttery, quick and easy; they keep well, mail well, and everyone loves them.

8 ounces (2 sticks) unsalted butter

½ teaspoon salt

1 teaspoon vanilla extract

1 cup firmly packed light or dark brown sugar

2 cups *sifted* all-purpose flour

4 ounces (generous 1 cup) walnuts, cut into medium-size pieces

6 ounces (1 cup) semisweet chocolate morsels

Adjust rack to the center of the oven and preheat oven to 350 degrees.

In the large bowl of an electric mixer, cream the butter. Add the salt, vanilla, and sugar and beat well. On low speed, gradually add the flour, scraping the bowl with a rubber spatula and beating until the mixture holds together.

Add the nuts and chocolate morsels and stir until they are evenly distributed.

The dough will be stiff. With a spoon or with your fingers, place small mounds of the dough in an unbuttered 15½ x 10½ x 1-inch rimmed baking sheet. With floured fingertips press the dough firmly to make an even layer — it will be thin.

Bake for 25 minutes, reversing the pan front to back once to ensure even baking. The cake will be golden brown.

Let cool in the pan for only a minute or so. Then, with a small, sharp knife, cut into bars. Let stand in the pan until cool.

With a wide metal spatula, transfer the cookies to paper towels to dry the bottoms.

Wrap them individually in clear cellophane or wax paper or store them in an airtight container.

CHOCOLATE WAFERS

36 (2¾-inch) cookies The dough for these wonderful thin, crisp, plain cookies is rolled out and cut with a cookie cutter. The recipe can easily be doubled if you wish.

2 ounces unsweetened chocolate

1 cup plus 2 tablespoons *sifted* all-purpose flour

¾ teaspoon baking powder

¼ teaspoon baking soda

Pinch of salt

2 ounces (½ stick) unsalted butter

1 teaspoon vanilla extract

½ cup sugar

1½ teaspoons light cream or milk

1 large egg

NOTE
↓

These cookies may be crumbled to make a delicious chocolate-cookie crumb crust, as in New York City Chocolate Cheesecake (page 136), Frozen Chocolate Mousse (page 250), and Salted Almond Chocolate Pie (page 223) If you make them for that purpose, roll out the dough and then just cut it with a long knife into large squares; don't bother to use a cookie cutter.

Place the chocolate in the top of a small double boiler over hot water on moderate heat. Cover until partially melted, then uncover and stir until smooth. Remove from the heat and set aside to cool slightly.

Sift together the flour, baking powder, baking soda, and salt and set aside.

In the large bowl of an electric mixer, cream the butter. Add the vanilla and sugar and beat to mix well. Add the melted chocolate and beat until incorporated. Then add the light cream or milk and the egg and beat to mix well. On low speed, add the sifted dry ingredients, scraping the bowl with a rubber spatula and beating only until incorporated.

Place the dough on a piece of wax paper, fold the sides of the paper over the dough and press down on the paper to flatten the dough to a scant 1-inch thickness. Wrap in the paper and refrigerate for 20 to 30 minutes — no longer or the dough will crack when you roll it out. (However, if you do refrigerate it for longer — even overnight — let it stand at room temperature for about an hour before rolling it out.)

Adjust two racks to divide oven into thirds and preheat oven to 400 degrees. Line cookie sheets with aluminum foil.

Flour a pastry cloth and place the unwrapped dough on it. (If you have doubled the recipe, roll only half of the dough at a time.) With a floured rolling pin — which should be refloured frequently to avoid sticking — roll the dough out until it is only ⅛ inch thick (thin).

I use a round cookie cutter that is 2¾ inches in diameter — use any size you like, and cut the cookies as close to each other as possible.

Place the cookies ½ inch apart on the aluminum foil. (It might be necessary to transfer the cookies from the pastry cloth

continues ⌄

to the foil with a wide metal spatula — handle them carefully in order to keep them perfectly round and flat.)

Leftover pieces of the dough should be pressed together and rerolled.

Bake two sheets at a time, reversing the sheets top to bottom and front to back once to ensure even baking. (If you bake one sheet at a time, bake it on the upper rack.) Bake for 7 to 8 minutes, until the cookies feel almost firm to the touch. These are supposed to be crisp (they will become more crisp as they cool) and they should not be underbaked, but watch them carefully to be sure they do not burn.

With a wide metal spatula, transfer the cookies to racks to cool.

Store airtight.

CHOCOLATE CHIP HONEY COOKIES

32 to 36 cookies These are plain, old-fashioned, homey drop cookies. They are light, soft, full of chocolate chips and nuts, and quick and easy to make — and they keep well in a cookie jar.

1¼ cups *sifted* all-purpose flour

½ teaspoon baking soda

½ teaspoon salt

4 ounces (1 stick) unsalted butter

½ teaspoon vanilla extract

½ cup honey

1 large egg

4 ounces (generous 1 cup) pecans or walnuts, cut into medium-size pieces

6 ounces (1 cup) semisweet chocolate morsels

Adjust two racks to divide the oven into thirds and preheat oven to 375 degrees. Line cookie sheets with aluminum foil.

Sift together the flour, baking soda, and salt and set aside.

In the large bowl of an electric mixer, cream the butter. Add the vanilla and honey and beat to mix. Add the egg and beat to mix; the mixture will look curdled now — it is OK, don't worry.

On low speed, add the sifted dry ingredients and, scraping the bowl with a rubber spatula, beat only until incorporated.

Remove the dough from the mixer and stir in the nuts and chocolate morsels.

Use a slightly rounded spoonful of the dough for each cookie. Place them about 2 inches apart on the foil-lined sheets.

Bake for 13 to 15 minutes, reversing the sheets top to bottom and front to back as necessary during baking to ensure even browning. (If you bake only one sheet at a time, bake it on the higher rack.) Bake until the cookies are nicely colored all over and spring back firmly when lightly pressed with a fingertip.

With a wide metal spatula, transfer the cookies to racks to cool.

When cool, store airtight.

CHOCOLATE CHIP COCONUT MACAROONS

`36 cookies` These are white cookies with chocolate chips and a layer of melted chocolate on the bottom. They are easy to make and keep well.

⅓ cup *sifted* all-purpose flour

¼ teaspoon baking powder

⅛ teaspoon salt

1 tablespoon unsalted butter

¾ cup sugar

2 large eggs

1 teaspoon vanilla extract

10½ ounces (4 loosely packed cups) shredded sweetened coconut

6 ounces (1 cup) semisweet chocolate morsels

6 ounces semisweet chocolate or compound chocolate (see Note)

NOTE

⤓

If you use a compound chocolate (see page 18) for the glaze, it will dry quickly without refrigeration, the finished cookies may stand at room temperature, and the chocolate will not discolor. Otherwise, any real semisweet chocolate may be used, with the directions for refrigerating on the next page.

Adjust two racks to divide the oven into thirds and preheat oven to 325 degrees. Line cookie sheets with aluminum foil.

Sift together the flour, baking powder, and salt and set aside.

Place the butter in a small pan over low heat to melt. Then set it aside to cool but do not let it harden — it must stay liquid.

Meanwhile, in the small bowl of an electric mixer, add the sugar to the eggs and beat at high speed for 5 minutes, until the mixture is almost white. On lowest speed, add the sifted dry ingredients, scraping the bowl with a rubber spatula and beating only until incorporated.

Remove from the mixer, fold in the liquid butter and then the vanilla. Then fold in the coconut and finally the chocolate morsels.

Use a well-rounded spoonful of the mixture for each cookie and place them 1½ inches apart on the aluminum foil.

Bake two sheets at a time, reversing the sheets top to bottom and front to back once during baking to ensure even browning. (If you bake one sheet at a time, bake it on the lower rack.) Bake for about 18 minutes, or until some parts of the tops of the cookies are lightly golden-colored — some parts of the cookies will still be white.

With a wide metal spatula, transfer the cookies to racks to cool.

While the cookies are baking or cooling, prepare the glaze: Break up the semisweet or compound chocolate and place it in the top of a small double boiler over warm water on low heat to melt slowly. Cover until partially melted, then uncover and stir until completely smooth. Remove the top of the double boiler from the hot water.

Cover one or two cookie sheets with wax paper or aluminum foil.

With a small metal spatula, spread some of the chocolate on the bottoms of the cookies, spreading it smoothly all the way to the edges in a rather thin layer. After you spread the chocolate on a cookie, place it chocolate side down on the lined cookie sheet.

Refrigerate until the chocolate is firm and the cookies can be lifted easily. Place them in an airtight box. These are best if they are stored in the refrigerator and served cold if you have used regular semisweet chocolate (see Note).

VIENNESE CHOCOLATE ICEBOX COOKIES

48 cookies Icebox cookies are a particular old-fashioned type of cookie that you may keep in the refrigerator, slice, and bake at a moment's notice. These elegant cookies are fragile, dark, crisp, and delicious.

3 ounces unsweetened chocolate

8 ounces (2 sticks) unsalted butter

1 teaspoon vanilla extract

¼ teaspoon almond extract

⅔ cup sugar

1 large egg

1½ cups *sifted* all-purpose flour

A few teaspoons coarse sugar or sanding sugar; or a few tablespoons blanched almonds, coarsely chopped

Place the chocolate in the top of a small double boiler over hot water on moderate heat. Cover and let stand only until melted. Remove from the hot water and set aside, uncovered, to cool slightly.

In the large bowl of an electric mixer, cream the butter. Add the vanilla and almond extracts and the granulated sugar and beat to mix, then beat in the egg and then the melted chocolate. On low speed, gradually add the flour, scraping the bowl with a rubber spatula and beating only until the mixture is smooth.

Tear off a piece of wax paper about 15 inches long. Place the dough by large spoonfuls down the length of the paper, forming a heavy strip of dough about 12 inches long.

Bring up both long sides of the paper. With your hands press against the paper, forming the dough into a roll about 2 inches in diameter, or a block about 2½ inches by 1 inch–either shape should be about 12 inches long. Wrap the paper

around the dough, smooth the sides and the ends. Slide a cookie sheet under the paper and transfer the dough to the refrigerator and chill at least until it is firm.

This dough may be kept in the refrigerator for a week or two, or it may be frozen. But it must be sliced at refrigerator temperature — it will crack if you slice it frozen.

When ready to bake, adjust two racks to divide the oven into thirds and preheat oven to 375 degrees. Line cookie sheets with aluminum foil.

Place the dough on a board, open the top of the paper, and with a sharp, heavy knife cut the dough into ¼-inch slices. (Wipe the blade of the knife whenever any of the dough sticks to it.)

Place the cookies about 1 inch apart on the aluminum foil. Sprinkle the tops of the cookies with the coarse sugar or chopped almonds.

Bake for 10 to 12 minutes, reversing the sheets top to bottom and front to back

continues ⌄

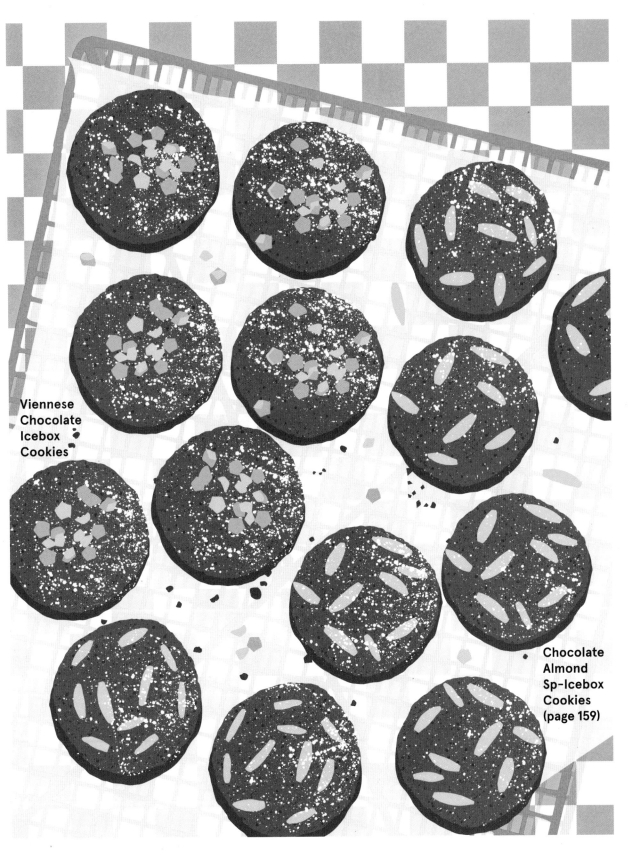

Viennese
Chocolate
Icebox
Cookies

Chocolate
Almond
Sp-Icebox
Cookies
(page 159)

once to ensure even baking. Test by touching the tops with a fingertip — when they just feel firm they are done. Watch them carefully — chocolate burns easily if overbaked.

With a wide metal spatula, transfer the cookies to racks to cool.

Handle with care — these crack easily. Place them in layers on a tray or in a freezer box — not in a cookie jar. Store airtight.

CHOCOLATE ALMOND SP-ICEBOX COOKIES

48 cookies Crisp, dark, bittersweet chocolate spice cookies with slivers of almonds going every which way. Don't be startled by the list of spices — these cookies are not sharp; they have a Christmasy taste, but are superior cookies any time of the year. They may be prepared way ahead of time and frozen until you slice and bake them. A glass jar or a little box of these makes a lovely gift.

1¼ cups *sifted* all-purpose flour

1 teaspoon baking powder

½ teaspoon ground cinnamon

½ teaspoon instant espresso powder or any other powdered (not granular) instant coffee

⅛ teaspoon salt

⅛ teaspoon ground ginger

⅛ teaspoon black pepper

⅛ teaspoon ground cloves

⅛ teaspoon ground allspice

⅛ teaspoon ground nutmeg

⅛ teaspoon dry mustard

3 ounces unsweetened chocolate

4 ounces (1 stick) unsalted butter

⅔ cup sugar

1 large egg

2½ ounces (¾ cup) thinly sliced almonds, blanched or unblanched

Sift together the flour, baking powder, cinnamon, espresso powder, salt, ginger, pepper, cloves, allspice, nutmeg, and dry mustard and set aside.

Place the chocolate in the top of a small double boiler over hot water on low heat, cover until melted, then remove the top of the double boiler and set aside, uncovered, to cool slightly.

In the large bowl of an electric mixer, cream the butter. Add the sugar and beat to mix well. Beat in the egg and then the melted chocolate. On low speed, add the sifted dry ingredients and beat, scraping the bowl with a rubber spatula, only until incorporated. Remove from the mixer and stir in the almonds.

Tear off a piece of wax paper about 14 inches long. Place large spoonfuls of the dough down the length of the paper, forming a strip 12 inches long. Fold the sides of the paper together over the top and, pressing against the paper, form the dough into a smooth cylinder about 2½ inches wide, 1 inch high, and 12 inches long.

Wrap the dough in the paper. Slide a cookie sheet under it and transfer it to the freezer for at least several hours until it is firm, or much longer if you wish. (If it is going to stay frozen for more than a few hours or so, when it is firm wrap the package in aluminum foil for extra protection.)

continues ⬎

When you are ready to bake, adjust two racks to divide the oven into thirds and preheat oven to 375 degrees. Line cookie sheets with aluminum foil. (Or, if you prefer, these may be baked on unlined, unbuttered sheets.)

Unwrap the dough. With a sharp knife, cut it into even slices ¼ inch thick. Place the slices 1 inch apart (these do not spread) on the cookie sheets.

Bake for 10 to 11 minutes, reversing the sheets top to bottom and front to back once to ensure even baking. These should be baked long enough to be crisp when cool (they become crisp as they cool), but watch them carefully so they don't burn. When the cookies are done, they will feel a little resistant to the touch.

With a wide metal spatula, transfer to a rack to cool.

Store airtight.

CHOCOLATE AND PEANUT BUTTER RIPPLES

30 cookies A chocolate dough and a peanut butter dough, baked together, make this a rather thin, crisp, candy-like cookie.

CHOCOLATE DOUGH

- 2 ounces unsweetened chocolate
- 4 ounces (1 stick) unsalted butter
- 1 teaspoon vanilla extract
- ¼ teaspoon salt
- ¾ cup granulated sugar
- 1 large egg
- 1 cup *sifted* unbleached all-purpose flour

PEANUT BUTTER DOUGH

- 2 tablespoons unsalted butter
- ¼ cup smooth (not chunky) peanut butter
- ½ cup firmly packed light brown sugar
- 2 tablespoons *sifted* unbleached all-purpose flour

Adjust two racks to divide the oven into thirds and preheat oven to 325 degrees. Line cookie sheets with baking parchment.

For the Chocolate Dough

Melt the chocolate in the top of a double boiler over hot water on moderate heat. Set the chocolate aside.

In the large bowl of an electric mixer, cream the butter. Add the vanilla, salt, and granulated sugar and beat well. Beat in the egg and then the melted chocolate, scraping the bowl as necessary with a rubber spatula. On low speed, gradually add the flour and mix only until smooth. Transfer the dough to a small, shallow bowl for ease in handling. Set it aside.

For the Peanut Butter Dough

In the small bowl of the electric mixer, cream the butter with the peanut butter.

Beat in the brown sugar until well mixed. Add the flour and beat to mix. Transfer to a small, shallow bowl for ease in handling.

To Shape the Cookies

Divide the chocolate dough in half and set one half aside. By level or barely rounded spoonfuls, drop the remaining half on the cookie sheets, placing the mounds 2 inches apart. You will need two to three cookie sheets and will end up with 30 mounds of the dough.

Top each mound with a scant teaspoon of peanut butter dough. And then top each cookie with another spoonful of the chocolate dough. Don't worry about the doughs being exactly on top of each other. Flatten the cookies slightly with a fork, dipping the fork in granulated sugar as necessary to keep it from sticking.

continues ⬎

Bake for 15 minutes, reversing the cookie sheets top to bottom and front to back once to ensure even baking. (If you bake only one sheet at a time, use the higher rack.) Do not overbake. These cookies will become crisp as they cool.

Let the cookies cool briefly on the sheets, only until they are firm enough to transfer with a wide metal spatula to racks. When cool, handle with care. Store in an airtight container.

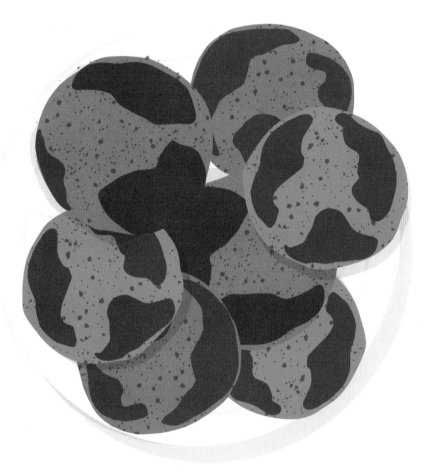

CHOCOLATE SCOTCH SHORTBREAD COOKIES

35 to 40 cookies Traditionally, shortbread is not chocolate. Untraditionally, this is very chocolate. These are thick, dry, crisp cookies that are buttery and plain. They keep well, mail well, and are lovely to package as a gift.

NOTE

↓

If you make this in a food processor, the butter should be firm and cold, right out of the refrigerator. If you make it in an electric mixer, the butter should be removed from the refrigerator 20 or 30 minutes before using.

- 8 ounces (2 sticks) unsalted butter (see Note)
- 1 teaspoon vanilla extract

- 1 cup confectioners' sugar
- ¼ teaspoon salt
- 2 cups *sifted* all-purpose flour

- ½ cup strained unsweetened cocoa powder (preferably Dutch-process)

Adjust two racks to divide the oven into thirds and preheat oven to 300 degrees.

This recipe may be prepared in a food processor (it's a breeze) or in an electric mixer. (I have also made it without either by just mixing all the ingredients together on a board with my bare hands.)

To Use a Processor

Fit it with a steel blade and place the dry ingredients in the bowl. Cut the cold butter into ½-inch slices over the dry ingredients. Add the vanilla. Cover and process until the ingredients hold together.

To Use an Electric Mixer

Cream the butter in the large mixer bowl. Add the vanilla, sugar, and salt and beat to mix. On low speed, add the flour and cocoa, scraping the bowl with a rubber spatula and beating only until the mixture holds together.

If the dough is not perfectly smooth, place it on a board or smooth work surface and knead it briefly with the heel of your hand.

Form the dough into a ball and flatten it slightly.

Flour a pastry cloth, rubbing the flour in well, and a rolling pin. Place the dough on the cloth and turn it over to flour both sides. With the floured rolling pin (reflour it as necessary), roll the dough until it is ½ inch thick (no thinner). It is important to make it the same thickness all over.

continues ↘

Use a plain round cookie cutter 1½ inches in diameter. Before cutting each cookie, dip the cutter in flour and tap it to shake off excess. Cut the cookies as close to each other as possible. Place the cookies 1 inch apart on unbuttered cookie sheets.

Press together leftover scraps of dough, reflour the cloth lightly if necessary, and reroll the dough. Cut out more cookies and place on cookie sheets, discarding any left-over scraps of dough.

Now each cookie should be pierced three times in a vertical row in the middle with the tines of a four-pronged fork, piercing all the way through the cookie each time. If the dough sticks to the fork, or if removing the fork causes the cookies to lose their shape, transfer the sheets of cookies to the refrigerator or freezer and chill only until the dough becomes slightly firm — do not let it freeze or become too firm or the fork will crack the cookies.

Bake for 25 to 30 minutes, or until the cookies are firm to the touch, reversing the sheets top to bottom and front to back once during baking to ensure even baking. Watch these carefully — they could burn and become bitter before you know it

unless you check them often. (If you bake only one sheet, bake it on the higher rack; one sheet will bake in less time.)

With a wide metal spatula transfer the cookies to racks to cool.

VARIATIONS

While working on this recipe I tried many variations and they were all good. Many of our friends like it better with the addition of 1 teaspoon of instant espresso powder or any other powdered (not granular) instant coffee. And it may be made without salt and/or vanilla. Some authorities claim that the chocolate flavor is stronger without vanilla.

Stamped Shortbread: If you have a ceramic or wooden cookie stamp, or a little wooden form for stamping butter, use it to make stamped shortbread cookies. Follow the above recipe up to the direction for piercing the cookies with a fork. Do not pierce these. Instead, press the stamp onto each cookie, pressing firmly enough to imprint the design and, at the same time, to flatten the cookies slightly. Bake as directed.

CHECKERBOARDS

48 cookies A checkerboard cookie must be neat and precise; therefore it is often thought of as a fancy petit four to be ordered from a fancy patisserie, or possibly as a fancy nibble served with the compliments of the chef in a fancy restaurant — not something that the average home cook would play around with. But believe me, you can make them — they are not difficult. Neat and precise, yes — but not difficult. Gorgeous is what they are.

- 8 ounces (2 sticks) unsalted butter
- ½ teaspoon vanilla extract
- ¼ teaspoon almond extract
- ½ cup sugar
- ¼ teaspoon salt
- 2¾ cups *sifted* all-purpose flour
- 2 tablespoons unsweetened cocoa
- powder (preferably Dutch-process)
- 1 large egg, lightly beaten and strained

In the large bowl of an electric mixer, cream the butter. Add the vanilla and almond extracts and then the sugar and salt and beat to mix well. On low speed, gradually add the flour and beat, scraping the bowl with a rubber spatula, for a few minutes. The mixture will be crumbly.

Turn it out onto a large board or smooth work surface, squeeze it between your hands and knead it until it holds together and is smooth. Extra kneading is good — work it well.

Now the dough has to be divided into two exactly equal halves. You have a scant 2½ cups of dough; carefully measure 1¼ cups minus one tablespoon of the dough, pressing it down in the cup (use the metal measuring cups that are made for measuring dry ingredients) and set it aside.

Add the cocoa to the remaining dough. Knead to incorporate the cocoa thoroughly. The mixture must be smooth. With the heel of your hand push off small amounts of the dough, pushing on the board and away from you; re-form the dough and push it off again. Repeat until the mixture is evenly colored. Now, with your hands shape each piece of dough into a flat square.

Place one square on a lightly floured pastry cloth and, with a lightly floured rolling pin, roll it into a square shape that is ½ inch thick and 6 inches square (no smaller); keep the edges straight and the corners as square as you can. The edges may be pressed into a straight line by pushing a ruler or a long, heavy knife against them, or they may be trimmed with a long, heavy knife. Use your fingers to square-off the corners. Carefully, with your hands or with two wide metal spatulas, temporarily transfer the square and roll out the remaining square.

Hold a ruler facing you against the farthest edge of one of the squares and, with the

continues ↘

tip of a small, sharp knife, mark the dough into ½-inch lengths. (The strips must be cut straight; for extra insurance, mark the opposite side of the square also.) With a long, heavy, sharp knife, cut the square into ½-inch strips. You will need twelve perfect strips.

Repeat with the remaining square of dough.

(There might be some leftover scraps of dough; if so, set them aside until later.)

Tear off a piece of plastic wrap or wax paper (I think plastic wrap is better for this) about 10 inches long and place it near the strips of dough.

To form the cookies: Place one strip of dark dough the long way on the paper or plastic. With a soft pastry brush, lightly brush one long edge of the strip with the beaten egg. Place a strip of light dough touching the egg-brushed edge. Brush the free long edge of the light dough with egg. Another dark strip, beaten egg, and then another light one. (You now have four strips of alternate colors touching each other, held together with a bit of beaten egg where they meet.)

Brush the top of the four strips lightly with the beaten egg. Place four more strips on top, placing dark over light and vice versa, and brushing a bit of egg between each strip as on the bottom layer. Be careful as you handle the strips and as you place them — they will not be easy to move because of the egg wash.

Brush the second layer with egg and then form a third layer, again dark over light, etc.

Now you have a three-layered bar, each layer made up of four narrow strips.

Wrap in the paper and refrigerate.

On a second piece of paper, form another three-layered bar. (Most of the egg will be left over — you will not need it for the cookies.)

Wrap the second bar in the paper and refrigerate. The bars must be refrigerated for at least half an hour, or until they are firm enough to slice, but they may be refrigerated for several days or they may be frozen — if they are frozen they must be thawed before they are sliced.

When you are ready to bake: Adjust two racks to divide the oven into thirds and preheat oven to 350 degrees. Line cookie sheets with aluminum foil.

Unwrap one bar of dough. Cut a thin slice off one narrow end to make it perfectly straight.

With the ruler and the tip of a small, sharp knife, mark the bar into ¼-inch lengths. With the knife, cut the cookies along the marks to ¼ inch thick. If the squares separate as the cookies are cut, put them back where they belong — they will go together in baking. Place the cookies ½ inch to 1 inch apart on the lined cookie sheets.

(Leftover scraps of dough may be shaped now or later. Press them together lightly to form a marbleized dough. Roll it out ¼ inch thick on the pastry cloth and cut into shapes with a cookie cutter or cut into squares with a knife. Or roll pieces between your hands into little sausage shapes with tapered ends; place on cookie sheet and form into crescents.)

Bake 18 to 20 minutes, until lightly colored, reversing the sheets top to bottom and front to back during baking to ensure even browning.

With a wide metal spatula transfer cookies to racks to cool.

Repeat with second bar, or reserve it to bake at some other time.

CHOCOLATE MACAROONS FROM MONTE CARLO

24 macaroons If these aren't the same as the ones I had on the Riviera, I can't tell the difference. Chocolate macaroons are one of my favorites. When I ate these and said they were the best ever, I could not get the recipe. This is the result of much experimenting. They are bittersweet and semi-soft/chewy. Almost like candy.

2½ ounces unsweetened chocolate

5 ounces (1 cup) almonds, blanched or unblanched

1 cup sugar

½ teaspoon vanilla extract

¼ teaspoon almond extract

⅓ cup egg whites (from 2 to 3 large eggs; measure carefully)

About 1 teaspoon additional sugar (for topping)

OPTIONAL: 6 candied cherries, cut into quarters

Adjust two racks to divide the oven into thirds and preheat oven to 325 degrees. These are traditionally baked on heavy brown paper. Cut two pieces (you can use grocery bags) to fit two 15½ x 12-inch cookie sheets. (The paper should be smooth; it can be ironed if necessary.)

Place the chocolate in the top of a small double boiler over hot water on moderate heat. Cover and let stand only until melted. Remove from the hot water and set aside, uncovered, to cool.

The almonds must be ground to a fine powder. This can be done in a food processor, blender, or nut grinder. Place the ground almonds in a mixing bowl. Add the sugar and mix well.

Add the vanilla and almond extracts to the egg whites and stir into the almond mixture. Then add the melted chocolate. Stir thoroughly. (The mixture should not be hard—or soft. It should be firm enough to hold a shape: semi-firm. It is a matter of proportion, and that is why it is important

that the egg whites—and the other ingredients, too—be measured very carefully.) Now, if the mixture is runny or too sticky to handle, chill it briefly (that will harden the chocolate and make it easier to handle).

Place a large piece of wax paper in front of you, preferably near the sink because you will have to keep your hands wet while shaping the cookies.

Form 24 mounds of dough on the wax paper, using a rounded spoonful for each.

The macaroons should now be shaped into balls by rolling them between your hands, which must be wet. Wet your hands; shake off water but do not dry, pick up a mound of the macaroon dough (use a metal spatula to pick it up if that is easier), and roll it into a ball. Place the macaroons 2 inches apart on the brown paper, but if you have used a grocery bag do not place the macaroons on the seam where the paper is double—macaroons on that double section will stick to the paper. Keep your hands really wet.

Sprinkle the tops very lightly with a bit of the additional granulated sugar. If you like, top each one with a quarter of a candied cherry, curved side up.

Bake for about 20 minutes, reversing the sheets top to bottom and front to back once to ensure even baking. When done, the macaroons should be dry (but slightly soft) on the outside, moist and soft in the centers. They will harden somewhat as they cool—don't overbake them.

Slide the papers off the cookie sheets. Let stand for about half a minute. Now the macaroons will be stuck to the paper. To remove them in the best classic manner, lift each piece of paper by holding two sides of it, and gently turn it upside down onto a work table or countertop. (Don't be afraid—it's OK. Pastry chefs do it all the time.) Brush the paper with water, using a pastry brush or a wet cloth. Let it stand briefly. As you see the paper dry out over the cookies, wet it a second time. Let stand for a few minutes until the paper can be lifted off easily without tearing the bottoms of the macaroons. If necessary, wet the paper a third time. Place the cookies right side up on racks to cool.

Store airtight with wax paper between the layers. Macaroons will stay fresh and soft for weeks in an airtight container in the refrigerator; they will be all right for several days at room temperature; or they can be frozen.

CHOCOLATE OATMEAL COOKIES

22 large cookies I have made enough varieties of chocolate oatmeal cookies (which have always intrigued me) to qualify as a self-proclaimed connoisseur. I think these are the best of all. So does my husband, and he claims to have eaten enough varieties of chocolate oatmeal cookies to put him in the *Guinness Book of Records*.

These are very oatmealy, coarse, crisp, and crunchy, with soft and chewy centers. They are easy to make and sturdy, but they must be stored airtight or they become limp.

⅔ cup *sifted* all-purpose flour

2 teaspoons baking powder

½ teaspoon salt

¼ cup plus 1 tablespoon unsweetened cocoa powder (preferably Dutch-process)

2⅔ ounces (5⅓ tablespoons) unsalted butter

1½ teaspoons vanilla extract

1¼ cups sugar

1 large egg

⅓ cup milk

2½ cups quick-cooking (not instant) rolled oats

Adjust two racks to divide the oven into thirds and preheat oven to 350 degrees. Line cookie sheets with aluminum foil and set aside.

Sift together the flour, baking powder, salt, and cocoa and set aside.

In the large bowl of an electric mixer, cream the butter. Add the vanilla and sugar and beat well. Add the egg and beat until smoothly mixed. On low speed, add half of the dry ingredients, then the milk, and then the remaining dry ingredients, scraping the bowl with a rubber spatula and beating only until smooth after each addition. Add the oats and mix until evenly incorporated.

Use a rounded large spoonful of the dough for each cookie; they should be moderately large. Place the mounds of dough about 2½ inches apart on the foil-lined sheets.

Bake two sheets at a time, reversing the sheets top to bottom and front to back once to ensure even baking. (If you bake only one sheet at a time, bake it on the upper rack. One sheet of cookies bakes in slightly less time than two.) The cookies will rise as they bake and then flatten. Bake for 22 to 24 minutes, until the tops of the cookies feel semi-firm to the touch. Do not underbake. These will crisp as they cool.

Let the cookies cool for a minute or so on the foil. Then, with a wide metal spatula, transfer them to racks to finish cooling.

Store airtight. I store them in the freezer (thaw before unwrapping) to keep them as crisp as possible.

CHOCOLATE SPRITZ COOKIES

60 to 70 cookies This recipe is for a cookie press, although you can shape the cookies many other ways (see directions below). They are rich, tender, fragile, and delicate.

NOTE

↓

These may be sprinkled before baking with coarse sugar or sanding sugar, especially appropriate for pretzel shapes. For other cookie shapes, you might use chopped nuts, or glazed cherries.

3 ounces semisweet chocolate

8 ounces (2 sticks) unsalted butter

¼ teaspoon salt

½ teaspoon vanilla extract

⅔ cup sugar

3 large egg yolks

2½ cups *sifted* all-purpose flour

Adjust two racks to divide the oven into thirds and preheat oven to 400 degrees.

Place the chocolate in the top of a small double boiler over warm water on low heat. Cover and let stand until melted. Then remove the top of the double boiler and set aside, uncovered, to cool slightly.

In the large bowl of an electric mixer, cream the butter. Add the salt, vanilla, and sugar and beat to mix well. Add the egg yolks and beat to mix, then the chocolate. On low speed, gradually add the flour. Beat only to mix after each addition.

Now place the dough in a cookie press; or place as much of it as will fit at one time in a cookie press and then repeat. Shape the cookies ½ to 1 inch apart on unbuttered, unlined cookie sheets.

Or, with your hands, roll the dough into small balls, flatten the balls, place them on a cookie sheet, and then press with a fork to form deep ridges going in one direction. Or, instead of a fork, press with a cookie stamp or a butter mold. Or shape the dough with butter paddles and flatten slightly. Or, with your hands, shape the dough into crescents and flatten slightly. Or roll the dough into long, thin tube shapes and then twist into pretzel shapes (see Note) or other curlicues. The cookies should not be more than about ⅓ inch thick; they may be thinner.

Bake for 8 to 10 minutes, reversing the sheets top to bottom and front to back once during baking to ensure even baking. (If you bake one sheet at a time, bake it on the upper rack.) With a wide metal spatula transfer the cookies to racks to cool.

Package these carefully, they are fragile. Store them airtight.

PETITS TRIANONS

16 squares or 12 to 14 bars This is a French recipe for small, plain fudge squares, similar to brownies without nuts. Mixed in a saucepan, they are quick and easy to make.

4 ounces (1 stick) unsalted butter, cut into 1-inch slices

2 ounces unsweetened chocolate

1 cup sugar

½ teaspoon vanilla extract

2 extra-large or jumbo eggs

1 cup *sifted* all-purpose flour

Pinch of salt

Adjust a rack one-third up from the bottom of the oven and preheat oven to 350 degrees. Prepare an 8-inch square cake pan as follows: Turn pan upside down. Cut a 12-inch square of aluminum foil. Center it over the inverted pan shiny side down. Fold down the sides and the corners and then remove the foil and turn the pan right side up. Place the foil in the pan. In order not to tear the foil, use a pot holder or a folded towel and, pressing gently with the pot holder or towel, smooth the foil into place. Lightly butter the bottom and halfway up the sides, using soft or melted butter and a pastry brush or crumpled wax paper. Set aside.

Place the butter and chocolate in a heavy 2- to 3-quart saucepan over low heat. Stir occasionally with a rubber spatula or wooden spoon until melted and smooth. Set aside to cool for about 3 minutes.

Stir in the sugar and the vanilla and then the eggs, one at a time, stirring until smooth. Add the flour and salt and stir until incorporated. Pour the mixture into the prepared pan and spread evenly.

Bake for exactly 28 minutes. Do not overbake; this should remain moist in the center. Cool in the pan for 5 minutes.

Cover with a rack and invert. Remove the pan and aluminum foil. The bottom of the cake will be slightly moist in the center. Cover with another rack and invert again to cool right side up. (The cake will be about ¾ inch thick.)

When the cake is cool, transfer it to a cutting board. With a long, thin, sharp knife, cut the cake into squares or rectangles.

These may be arranged on a tray and covered with plastic wrap until serving time. Or they may be wrapped individually in clear cellophane or wax paper. Either way, do not allow them to dry out. They may be frozen and may be served either at room temperature or about 5 minutes after being removed from the freezer—they're awfully good still frozen.

DUTCH CHOCOLATE BARS

16 or 18 bars These have a crisp, crunchy base with a thick, moist, baked-on chocolate topping. They are made without a mixer.

BOTTOM LAYER

- ⅓ cup *sifted* all-purpose flour
- ¼ teaspoon baking soda
- ⅛ teaspoon salt
- ½ cup firmly packed light brown sugar
- 1 cup old-fashioned or quick-cooking (not instant) rolled oats
- 2 ounces (generous ½ cup) pecans, finely chopped
- 2⅔ ounces (5⅓ tablespoons) unsalted butter, melted

TOPPING

- ⅔ cup *sifted* all-purpose flour
- ¼ teaspoon baking soda
- ¼ teaspoon salt
- 1 ounce unsweetened chocolate
- 2 ounces (½ stick) butter
- ¾ cup sugar
- 1 large egg
- 1 teaspoon vanilla extract
- 2 tablespoons milk

Adjust a rack to the center of the oven and preheat oven to 350 degrees.

For the Bottom Layer

Into a mixing bowl, sift together the flour, baking soda, and salt. Add the sugar and stir to mix thoroughly. Stir in the oats and nuts and then the butter. The mixture will be crumbly and it will not hold together.

Turn the dough into an unbuttered 8-inch square cake pan. With your fingertips, press the dough to form a smooth, compact layer.

Bake for 10 minutes.

For the Topping

Meanwhile, sift together the flour, baking soda, and salt and set aside.

Melt the chocolate and butter in the top of a large double boiler over hot water on moderate heat (or in a heavy saucepan over very low heat). Stir the chocolate and butter until smooth and remove from the heat. Mix in the sugar and then the egg, stirring until thoroughly mixed. Stir in the vanilla and milk. Add the sifted dry ingredients and stir until smooth.

Pour the chocolate topping over the hot bottom layer and spread smoothly.

Bake for about 35 minutes, or until a toothpick inserted in the center of the cake comes out barely clean and dry. Do not overbake; the chocolate should remain moist. Cool the cake completely in the pan.

With a small, sharp knife, cut the cooled cake into squares or bars.

These are best when very fresh. Wrap them individually in clear cellophane or wax paper or place them on a tray and cover airtight. Or pack them in an airtight freezer box. Just don't let them dry out.

Dutch
Chocolate
Bars

Viennese
Chocolate
Squares (page 180)

VIENNESE CHOCOLATE SQUARES

NOTE

↓

If you prefer a less sweet icing, use 1 ounce of unsweetened and 3 ounces of semisweet chocolate.

16 small squares These are small squares (petits fours) of almost flourless chocolate almond cake with a thin top layer of buttery dark chocolate icing. They are moist, not too sweet, and are both light and rich. They are easy, quite professional-looking, and delicious. You will like making them and will be proud to serve them. The recipe makes a small number, just right for a few people. If you double it, it must be baked in two pans.

4 ounces semisweet chocolate

1½ ounces (⅓ cup) almonds, blanched or unblanched

5⅓ ounces (10⅔ tablespoons) unsalted butter

2 teaspoons instant espresso powder or other powdered (not granular) instant coffee

1 teaspoon vanilla extract

1 tablespoon dark rum, Cognac, or whiskey

4 large eggs, separated

2 tablespoons *unsifted* all-purpose flour

¼ teaspoon salt

OPTIONAL: 2 or 3 tablespoons apricot preserves

CHOCOLATE BUTTER ICING

4 ounces semisweet chocolate (see Note)

2 ounces (½ stick) unsalted butter

½ teaspoon instant espresso powder (not granular) or other powered instant coffee

TO DECORATE (OPTIONAL)

½ ounce semisweet chocolate

16 walnut or pecan halves, or 16 whole toasted blanched hazelnuts, or 16 chocolate coffee beans (candy)

Adjust rack one-third up from the bottom of the oven and preheat oven to 350 degrees. Prepare a shallow 8-inch square metal baking pan as follows: Invert the pan, cover with a 12-inch square of aluminum foil, turn down the sides and the corners of the foil. Then remove the foil, turn the pan right side up, place the foil in the pan, and press it smoothly into place. Butter the foil using soft or melted butter and a pastry brush or crumpled wax paper. Set the prepared pan aside.

Place the chocolate in the top of a small double boiler over hot water on moderate heat. Cover until partially melted, then uncover and stir until completely melted and smooth. Remove the top of the double boiler and set aside, uncovered, to cool slightly.

The nuts must be ground to a fine powder. It may be done in a food processor, nut grinder, or blender. Set aside.

In the large bowl of an electric mixer, cream the butter. Add the espresso powder, vanilla, rum, and melted chocolate and beat until smooth. Add the egg yolks all at once and beat until smooth. Add the flour and then the almonds and beat until incorporated. Remove from the mixer.

In the small bowl of the electric mixer, add the salt to the egg whites and, with clean beaters, beat only until the whites barely hold a firm shape, not until they are stiff or dry. Gradually, in several additions, small at first, fold the whites into the chocolate mixture.

Turn into the prepared pan and smooth the top. Bake for 30 minutes. Cool in the pan for about 15 minutes.

Cover with a rack and invert. Remove the pan and foil, cover with another rack and invert again, leaving the cake to cool right side up. (The cake will be a scant 1 inch high.)

If you like, melt and strain the preserves. Spread the warm preserves on top of the cooled cake and let stand while you prepare the icing.

For the Icing

Place the chocolate and butter in the top of a small double boiler over hot water on moderate heat. Cover until partially melted. Then uncover and stir until completely melted and smooth. Stir in the espresso powder. If the mixture is not smooth, stir it briskly with a small wire whisk. Remove from the hot water and set aside to cool to room temperature.

Then let stand at room temperature or refrigerate, stirring occasionally, until only slightly thickened or thick enough so it will spread without running down the sides.

Place the cake upside down on a small board. When the icing is ready, stir it well and turn it out onto the cake. With a long, narrow metal spatula spread smoothly.

Let stand until the icing is set (it will not take long).

If you plan to serve the squares plain, when the icing is set use a long, thin, sharp knife to trim the edges and then cut the cake into 16 small squares.

Or, if you are going to decorate the squares, use the long knife, but only score the cutting lines, first the four sides and then the cutting lines for the squares.

For the optional decoration: Coarsely chop the ½ ounce chocolate and place in a small cup in a small pan of shallow hot water over low heat. Stir occasionally until melted.

Meanwhile, make a small paper cone. Place the melted chocolate in the tip of the cone and cut a tiny bit off the tip to make a small opening. Press out just a small dab of the

continues ⌄

chocolate on the top (right in the middle) of each square. (The chocolate is only to serve as a paste to hold the nut or coffee bean; it should not show — do not use too much.) Place nut half, whole hazelnut, or coffee bean on the chocolate.

Now trim the edges and cut the cake into squares.

Let stand at room temperature and serve at room temperature.

To store these overnight or to freeze them, pack in a single layer in a box or on a tray. Cover the squares airtight with plastic wrap. If you have frozen them, thaw before unwrapping.

BROWNIES

24 or 32 brownies These are the Brownies with which I started my reputation as a pastry chef when I was about ten years old. People who barely knew me, knew my Brownies. Since I always wrapped them individually I usually carried a few to give out. I occasionally run into people I never knew well and haven't seen in many years, and the first thing they say is, "I remember your Brownies." Sometimes they have forgotten my name — but they always remember my Brownies. I have continually revised the recipe over the years.

5 ounces unsweetened chocolate

6 ounces (1½ sticks) unsalted butter

1 tablespoon instant espresso or coffee powder

4 large eggs

½ teaspoon salt

2 cups sugar

1 teaspoon vanilla extract

¼ teaspoon almond extract

1 cup *sifted* all-purpose flour

10 ounces (2½ generous cups) walnut halves or large pieces

Adjust rack one-third up from the bottom of the oven and preheat oven to 450 degrees. Butter a 15½ x 10½ x 1-inch rimmed baking sheet, and then line it with aluminum foil as follows: Turn the pan upside down. Center a piece of foil 18 to 19 inches long (12 inches wide) over the pan, shiny side down. Fold down the sides and corners to shape the foil. Remove the foil, turn the pan right side up, place the shaped foil in the pan, and press it carefully into place. Brush the foil all over with melted butter.

Melt the chocolate and butter in a heavy saucepan over low heat or in the top of a large double boiler over hot water on moderate heat. Stir with a small wire whisk to blend. When melted and smooth, add the instant espresso or coffee and stir to dissolve. Remove from the heat and set aside to cool.

Meanwhile, in the small bowl of an electric mixer, beat the eggs and salt until slightly fluffy. Gradually add the sugar and continue to beat at medium-high speed for 15 minutes, until the mixture forms a ribbon when the beaters are raised. Transfer to large mixer bowl.

Add the vanilla and almond extracts to the cooled chocolate mixture. On lowest speed, add the chocolate mixture to the eggs, scraping the bowl with a rubber spatula and beating only enough to blend. Still using the lowest speed and rubber spatula, add the flour, again beating *only enough to blend*. Fold in the nuts, handling the mixture as little as possible.

Pour into prepared pan and spread smooth. Place in oven. *Immediately* reduce oven temperature to 400 degrees. Bake for 21 to 22 minutes. Test with a toothpick. It should come out just barely dry. Do not

continues ⌄

overbake. Brownies should be slightly moist inside.

Remove from oven. Immediately cover with a large rack or cookie sheet and invert. Remove pan and foil. Cover with a large rack and invert again. After 10 or 15 minutes, invert once again only for a moment to make sure that the Brownies are not sticking to the rack.

Cool completely and then chill for about 30 minutes or a bit longer in the freezer, or overnight in the refrigerator. Transfer to a large cutting board.

To mark portions evenly, measure with a ruler and mark with toothpicks to get the number and size you desire. Use a long, thin, very sharp knife, or one with serrated edge. Cut with a sawing motion into squares. I wrap these individually in clear cellophane, but you may package them in any way that is airtight — do not let them stand around to dry out.

WEST COAST BROWNIES

32 brownies I had heard about brownies called "Brownie Points" that were being sold in leading stores across the country. I was told they were very, very good. They were made in a bakery in Venice, California, by a young man named Richard Melcombe. I was delighted one day to open a California newspaper and see both the recipe and a picture of the baker, who calls himself Richmel.

This is my version of Brownie Points. Although they are rather thin (only ½ inch thick), they are extra chewy and moist. And the coffee and Kahlúa or Cognac give them an unusually delicious and exotic flavor, but one probably more appreciated by adults than by children.

1½ cups *sifted* all-purpose flour

1 teaspoon salt

1 teaspoon baking soda

2 ounces unsweetened chocolate

8 ounces (2 sticks) unsalted butter

¾ cup granulated sugar

¾ cup firmly packed dark or light brown sugar

2 large eggs

2 tablespoons Kahlúa or Cognac

1 tablespoon vanilla extract

¼ cup instant espresso powder or other

powdered (not granular) instant coffee

6 ounces (1 cup) semisweet chocolate morsels

3 ounces (⅔ cup) walnut halves or large pieces

3 ounces (⅔ cup) pecan halves or large pieces

Adjust rack to the center of the oven and preheat oven to 375 degrees. Butter a 15½ x 10½ x 1-inch baking sheet. Carefully line the pan with one long piece of wax paper, butter the paper, and set the prepared pan aside.

Sift together the flour, salt, and baking soda and set aside.

Place the chocolate in the top of a small double boiler over hot water on moderate heat. Stir occasionally until melted. Remove the top of the double boiler and set it aside, uncovered.

Cream the butter in the large bowl of an electric mixer. Add both sugars and beat well. Add the eggs, Kahlúa or Cognac,

vanilla, and instant espresso. Now add the melted chocolate and beat until blended. On low speed, mix in the sifted dry ingredients.

Remove the mixture from the mixer and stir in the chocolate morsels and nuts.

Turn into the prepared pan and smooth the top. Bake for about 25 minutes, until a toothpick inserted in the center comes out clean and dry. The cake will feel very soft. Do not overbake.

Cool in the pan, then cover with a large rack or a large cookie sheet. Invert, remove the pan and the paper, cover with a cookie sheet, and invert again, leaving the cake right side up.

Cut the cake into quarters. If the edges need to be trimmed (and they probably will), do it now after cutting the cake into quarters. Then cut each quarter into eighths.

Wrap each brownie individually in cellophane or wax paper. Or package them in an airtight box with wax paper between the layers.

WHOOPIES

13 very large cookie sandwiches These are chocolate drop cookies — large and cake-like — sandwiched together with a thick layer of creamy vanilla filling. They are monster cookies for cookie monsters.

I remember them as Whoopie Pies when I was growing up and going to school in New York. My husband remembers them as Moon Pies in Texas. They were also known as Cowboy Pies, Gobs, and Devil's Delights. But under any name, all children were crazy about them.

Until recently I never thought of making them at home. This recipe gives a large yield of large cookies that take a lot of room in the kitchen while you are baking. And a lot of time, since they are baked only five at a time on a cookie sheet.

If you are looking for something for a children's party, try these — but if the children are small you might want to cut each cookie sandwich into two or three pieces before serving. Teenagers and husbands devour them whole in no time.

3 cups *sifted* all-purpose flour

1½ teaspoons baking powder

1½ teaspoons baking soda

1 tablespoon cream of tartar

½ teaspoon salt

6 ounces (1½ sticks) unsalted butter

1½ teaspoons vanilla extract

1½ cups granulated sugar

2 large eggs

½ cup plus 1 tablespoon unsweetened cocoa powder (preferably Dutch-process)

1 cup plus 2 tablespoons milk

CREAMY WHITE FILLING

⅓ cup plus 3 tablespoons *sifted* all-purpose flour

1½ cups milk

12 ounces (3 sticks) unsalted butter

Generous pinch of salt

1½ teaspoons vanilla extract

3¾ cups strained confectioners' sugar

Adjust two racks to divide the oven into thirds and preheat oven to 375 degrees. Cut aluminum foil to fit cookie sheets (you will need six pieces of foil, or you can wipe one piece off and reuse it between batches).

Sift together the flour, baking powder, baking soda, cream of tartar, and salt and set aside.

In the large bowl of an electric mixer, cream the butter. Add the vanilla and granulated sugar and beat to mix well. Add the eggs one at a time, scraping the bowl

with a rubber spatula and beating until incorporated after each addition. On low speed, add the cocoa and then the sifted dry ingredients in three additions, alternating with the milk in two additions, scraping the bowl with the spatula and beating only until smooth after each addition. (Before all the dry ingredients are added the mixture might look curdled — it's all right.)

It is important for these cookies to be shaped evenly and as close to the same size as possible. Use a ¼-cup measuring cupful of the dough for each cookie. Use a narrow rubber spatula to fill the cup, level it off, and then to transfer the dough to the aluminum foil. Shape each mound of dough as round as possible — they will run and you want them to run into even circles. Place only five mounds of dough on one piece of foil — one in the center and one toward each corner. (During baking the cookies will spread to about 4½ inches in diameter.)

Slide a cookie sheet under each piece of foil. Bake, one sheet at a time, for 20 minutes, reversing the sheets top to bottom and front to back once to ensure even baking. The cookies are done when they spring back very quickly and surely when lightly pressed in the center with a fingertip.

Slide the foil off the sheet and let stand for a minute or two. Then, with a wide metal spatula, loosen the cookies carefully from the foil and transfer to large racks to cool. (The racks should be raised from the surface to make room for air to circulate underneath. Just place each rack on any right-side-up cake pan or mixing bowl.) If you don't have enough racks, as soon as some of the cookies have cooled they may be transferred to wax paper or foil.

You will have 27 very large cookies. If they are not all the same size, pick out the ones that match each other most closely and form them into pairs — there will be one cookie left over. Now lay them out in pairs, opened, with the flat sides up.

For the Filling

Place the flour in a 1-quart saucepan. Add the milk gradually, stirring with a rubber spatula. If the mixture is not smooth, strain it before cooking. Place it over moderate heat. Cook, stirring and scraping the bottom constantly with a rubber spatula, until the mixture becomes very thick and bubbles slightly. Simmer, stirring, for about 2 minutes. If necessary, beat with a small wire whisk to make the mixture smooth.

Stir in 1 tablespoon of the butter and set the mixture aside to cool to room temperature — stir it occasionally while it is cooling.

Place the remaining butter in the large bowl of an electric mixer and beat until it is slightly softened. Add the salt, vanilla, and confectioners' sugar (gradually) and beat well for about 2 minutes, scraping the bowl as necessary with a rubber spatula. Gradually, 1 large spoonful at a time, add the cooled flour and milk mixture. Then beat at high speed for a minute or two until the filling is smooth, light, and fluffy.

Now place a generous heaping large spoonful of the filling on the center of one of each pair of the cookies — use all of the filling. With the back of the spoon, spread the filling out to about ½ inch from the edges. The filling will be almost ½ inch thick. Top the filling with another cookie, flat side down. With the palm of your hand, press down gently on the top cookie.

Then hold a sandwich in your hands and with your fingertips press gently all around to spread the filling almost, but not completely, to the edges.

The filled sandwiches may be layered in a large shallow box or on a large tray with

continues ⌐

wax paper or plastic wrap between the layers and over the top. (Or they may be packaged individually in cellophane or wax paper, or in plastic sandwich bags, but it is best to do this after they have been refrigerated.) Store in the refrigerator or freezer.

These may be served either cold from the refrigerator or at room temperature. When they are cold, both the cookies and the filling will be firmer. At room temperature they will be quite soft, like the ones I used to buy.

PALM BEACH BROWNIES WITH CHOCOLATE-COVERED MINTS

NOTE

⊡

When you remove the cake from the pan you might see burned and caramelized edges. (You might not—it depends on the pan.) If you do, you can leave them or cut them off. I have friends who say that this is the best part. I cut them off, but then I can't resist eating them.

Makes 32 brownies This recipe is one of the two or three most popular recipes in all of my books. These are the thickest, gooiest, chewiest, darkest, sweetest, mostest-of-the-most chocolate bars with an almost wet middle and a crisp crunchy top. A layer of chocolate-covered mints in the middle stays whole (the mints don't melt), and they look and taste gorgeous.

The baked cake should be refrigerated for at least a few hours, or overnight, or frozen for an hour or two before it is cut into bars.

- 8 ounces unsweetened chocolate
- 8 ounces (2 sticks) unsalted butter
- 8 ounces (2 generous cups) walnuts
- 5 large eggs (1 cup)

- 2 teaspoons vanilla extract
- ½ teaspoon almond extract
- ¼ teaspoon salt
- 1 tablespoon plus 1 teaspoon instant espresso powder
- 3¾ cups sugar

- 1⅔ cups *sifted* unbleached flour
- 2½ (12-ounce) bags York chocolate-covered peppermint patties (miniature classics), unwrapped

Adjust an oven rack one-third up from the bottom and preheat oven to 425 degrees. Line a 13 x 9 x 2-inch pan as follows: Invert the pan and center a 17-inch length of nonstick aluminum foil, shiny side down, over the pan. With your hands, press down the sides and corners of the foil on the pan. Then remove the foil, turn the pan right side up, and place the foil in the pan. Very carefully press it into place in the pan. Now, to butter the foil, place a piece of butter (additional to that in the ingredients) in the pan, and put the pan in the oven. When the butter is melted, use a pastry brush or a piece of crumpled plastic wrap to spread the butter all over the foil. Set the prepared pan aside.

Place the chocolate and butter in the top of a large double boiler over hot water on moderate heat, or in a 4- to 6-cup heavy saucepan over low heat. Stir occasionally, until the chocolate and butter are melted.

continues ⌐

Stir to mix. Remove from the heat and set aside. (Or you may wish to zap this in a microwave one minute at a time at 50 percent power until melted.)

Break the walnuts into large pieces; set aside.

In the large bowl of an electric mixer, beat the eggs with the vanilla and almond extracts, salt, espresso, and sugar at high speed for 10 minutes. On low speed, add the chocolate mixture (which can still be warm) and beat only until mixed. Then add the flour and again beat on low speed only until mixed. Remove the bowl from the mixer.

Stir in the nuts.

Spoon half the mixture (about 3½ cups) into the prepared pan and smooth the top.

Place a layer of the mints, touching each other and the edges of the pan, all over the chocolate layer. (You will not use all the mints; there will be some left over.)

Spoon the remaining chocolate mixture all over the pan and smooth the top.

Bake for 35 minutes (but begin checking the brownies after 25 minutes to prevent burning, as individual ovens vary), reversing the pan front to back once to ensure even baking. At the end of 35 minutes the cake will have a firm crust on top, but if you insert a toothpick in the middle it will come out wet and covered with chocolate. Nevertheless, it is done. *Do not bake any longer.*

Remove the pan from the oven; let stand until cool. Cover the pan with a cookie sheet and invert the pan and the sheet. Remove the pan and foil lining.

Cover the cake with a length of wax paper and another cookie sheet and invert again, leaving the cake right side up.

Now the cake must be refrigerated for a few hours or overnight before it is cut into bars.

When you are ready to cut the cake, use a long, heavy knife with a sharp blade, either serrated or straight—try both. Cut the cake into quarters. Cut each quarter in half, cutting through the long sides. Finally, cut each piece into 4 bars, cutting through the long sides. (I think these are better in narrow bar shapes than in squares.)

Pack in an airtight box, or wrap individually in clear cellophane, wax paper, or foil.

These freeze perfectly and can be served very cold or at room temperature.

BITTERSWEET CHOCOLATE BISCOTTI

36 biscotti These are extra hard and crunchy — thicker than most — and especially dark and delicious, made with chocolate and cocoa.

After you mix and shape the dough, it will have to spend 45 minutes in the freezer before it is baked. It will then be baked twice for a total of 1 hour and 45 minutes.

9 ounces (generous 2 cups) blanched (skinned) whole almonds (see page 22)

6 ounces semisweet chocolate

1¾ cups *sifted* unbleached all-purpose flour

1 teaspoon baking soda

⅛ teaspoon salt

⅓ cup unsweetened cocoa powder (preferably Dutch-process)

1 tablespoon instant espresso or coffee powder

1 cup granulated sugar

3 large eggs plus 1 large egg white

½ cup firmly packed light brown sugar

1 teaspoon vanilla extract

Scant ½ teaspoon almond extract or ¼ teaspoon bitter almond extract

First toast the almonds in a wide, shallow pan in the center of a preheated 375-degree oven, stirring once or twice, for 12 to 13 minutes, until very lightly colored. Set aside to cool.

Chop or break the chocolate into small pieces and place in the bowl of a food processor fitted with the metal chopping blade. Let stand.

Into a large bowl, sift together the flour, baking soda, salt, cocoa, espresso powder, and granulated sugar.

Add about ½ cup of the sifted dry ingredients and about ½ cup of the almonds to the chocolate. Process for about 30 seconds, until the chocolate and nuts are fine and powdery.

Add the processed ingredients to the remaining sifted dry ingredients and stir to mix. Stir in the remaining almonds; set aside.

In a small bowl, beat the eggs and egg white, brown sugar, and vanilla and almond extracts until mixed.

Stir the egg mixture into the dry ingredients (you will think there's not enough liquid, but it will be OK). I use a large rubber spatula and push the ingredients together.

Place two 15- to 20-inch lengths of plastic wrap on the work surface. The dough will be thick and sticky. You will form a strip of it on each piece of the plastic wrap. Spoon half the dough in the middle — down the length — of one piece of plastic wrap to form a strip 12 inches long.

Lift the two long sides of the plastic wrap, bring them together on top of the dough, and, with your hands, press on the plastic wrap to smooth the dough and shape it into an even strip 12 inches long, 3 inches wide, and ¾ inch high, with squared ends.

Repeat to form the second strip.

Place the strips on a cookie sheet and put in the freezer for about 45 minutes, or until firm.

To bake, adjust two racks to divide the oven into thirds, and preheat oven to 300 degrees. Line two cookie sheets with baking parchment.

Open the two long sides of the plastic wrap on one strip of dough and turn the dough upside down on a lined sheet, placing it diagonally on the sheet; slowly peel off the plastic wrap. Repeat with the second strip and the second cookie sheet.

Bake for 1 hour, reversing the sheets top to bottom and front to back once during baking to ensure even baking. Reduce the temperature to 275 degrees and remove

the sheets from the oven. Immediately, while very hot, peel the parchment away from the back of a strip and place it right side up on a cutting board.

Use a pot holder or folded kitchen towel to hold the hot strip, and use a serrated French bread knife to cut. Cut across the strip, either straight across or on an angle (straight across is easier), cutting slices about ¾ inch wide. Place the slices, standing upright, on a cookie sheet.

Repeat with the second strip.

Bake at 275 degrees for about 45 minutes, until completely dry. Reverse the sheets top to bottom and front to back once during baking.

Cool and store in an airtight container.

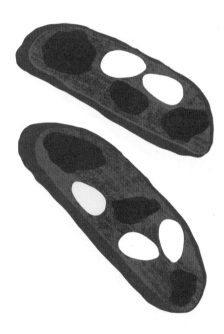

PASTRIES, PIES, PUDDINGS, AND MORE

CHOCOLATE SERENDIPITY

NOTE
⤷
Although this makes
20 portions, I have found
that it is not too much for
eight or ten people.

20 portions (see Note) This is a most unusual dessert —
chic, simple, elegant, and absolutely delicious. If they
serve chocolate and whipped cream in heaven, this
has to be on the menu.

It takes time and patience to put together but is great fun and can all be done a
day ahead. Plan it for a dinner party or a luncheon and once you have made it you
won't be able to wait to make it again.

It consists of a thin, thin layer of almost flourless chocolate cake, covered with a
thick, thick layer of whipped cream, then with a paper-thin coating of bittersweet
chocolate glaze. It is then cut into squares and refrigerated until it is served.

You will need a long, narrow metal spatula — mine has an 8-inch blade.

CAKE

- 5 ounces semisweet chocolate
- 7 tablespoons (1 stick minus 1 tablespoon) unsalted butter
- ½ cup granulated sugar
- 4 large eggs, separated
- 1 tablespoon plus 1½ teaspoons *sifted* all-purpose flour
- Pinch of salt

WHIPPED CREAM

- 1½ teaspoons unflavored gelatin
- 2 tablespoons cold water
- 3 cups heavy cream
- ½ cup strained confectioners' sugar
- 1 teaspoon vanilla extract
- OPTIONAL: 1 tablespoon rum or brandy

GLAZE

- 1 teaspoon instant coffee powder
- ½ cup boiling water
- ⅓ cup granulated sugar
- 1 tablespoon vegetable shortening (such as Crisco)
- 1 ounce unsweetened chocolate
- 4½ ounces semisweet chocolate

Adjust rack to the center of the oven and
preheat oven to 350 degrees. Butter a
15½ x 10½ x 1-inch baking sheet. Dust it
with flour and invert and tap to shake out
excess flour. Set the pan aside.

For the Cake

Place the chocolate in the top of a small
double boiler over hot water on moderate
heat. Cover until partially melted. Uncover
and stir until completely melted and smooth.

Remove the top of the double boiler and set
aside, uncovered, to cool slightly.

In the small bowl of an electric mixer,
cream the butter. Add the granulated sugar
and beat to mix well. Beat in the egg yolks
all at once, scraping the bowl with a rubber
spatula and beating well. On low speed,
add the melted chocolate and beat until
smooth. Add the flour and beat only to mix.
Remove from the mixer.

Add the salt to the egg whites in a small, clean bowl and beat until they hold a definite shape but are not dry.

Fold about one-quarter of the whites into the chocolate mixture. Then fold in half of the remaining whites, and finally the balance of the whites, being careful not to handle any more than necessary.

Turn into the prepared pan. Very gently and carefully spread the mixture to make a smooth and even layer — it will be very thin.

Bake for 18 minutes. If the cake puffs up in a few places during baking don't worry about it — it will settle down.

Let the cake cool completely in the pan. It will be only ⅓ inch thick (thin). If you want to do this ahead of time, the cake can be covered in the pan and frozen or refrigerated. It is best if the cake is really cold or even frozen when the whipped cream is put on.

For the Whipped Cream

Chill the large bowl of an electric mixer and the beaters in the freezer or refrigerator before whipping the cream.

Sprinkle the gelatin over the cold water in a small glass custard cup. Let stand for 5 minutes. Then place the cup in shallow hot water in a small pan over low heat. Let stand until the gelatin is dissolved. Remove from the hot water and set aside.

While the gelatin is melting, place about 2¾ cups of the cream (reserve about ¼ cup) in the chilled large bowl of the electric mixer and add the confectioners' sugar, vanilla, and optional rum or brandy. With the chilled beaters, beat until the cream barely starts to thicken.

Stir the reserved ¼ cup cream into the dissolved gelatin. With the mixer going, add the gelatin mixture all at once to the partially whipped cream and continue to beat until the cream holds a firm and definite shape. (In order to beat it enough and still avoid overbeating, which would turn it to butter, I suggest that you finish the beating at the end with a large balloon-type wire whisk.)

Place the stiffly whipped cream over the top of the cold cake and spread it evenly. With a long, narrow metal spatula spread it very smooth — it will just reach the top of the cake pan, and must be smooth.

Refrigerate the cake now for at least 1 hour, but it may be several hours if you wish.

For the Glaze

About half an hour before glazing the cake, in a small saucepan dissolve the coffee in the boiling water. Add the granulated sugar and shortening. Place over moderate heat and bring to a boil. Add both chocolates and stir until they are melted — don't worry about making it smooth.

Transfer to the small bowl of an electric mixer and beat briefly on low speed only until smooth. Then let the glaze stand until it cools to room temperature. Again beat briefly on low speed only until smooth.

Now, to cover the cream with a very thin layer of the glaze: Starting a few inches from one of the narrow ends of the pan, pour a thick ribbon of the glaze (about one-third of the total amount) over the whipped cream along the narrow end of the pan. With a long, narrow metal spatula,

continues ⌐

quickly spread it into a smooth, thin, even layer covering about one-third of the whipped cream. (You will find it best to rest the edge of the spatula blade on the rim of the pan as you spread the glaze. The glaze will actually be spread on the rim of the pan in some places.) Then immediately pour on the remaining glaze and spread that, covering all of the cream and smoothing the glaze evenly. This is not difficult, just unusual. The main thing is to work quickly and do not work over the chocolate any more than is absolutely necessary.

Refrigerate at least until the chocolate is firm enough to be cut. That will take only a few minutes, but it can wait longer if you wish — several hours or even overnight. Or place it in the freezer — this will cut more

neatly if it is frozen or partially frozen. However, frozen or not...superb!

With a small, sharp knife, cut around the outside of the cake to release. With toothpicks, mark a long side of the cake into five 3-inch lengths. With the small, sharp knife, cut through the cake forming five 3-inch-wide strips — wipe the knife blade after making each cut. Then, along a short side, cut down the middle, and then cut both halves in half again. (If this sounds complicated just cut it any way you wish, cutting the cake into about 20 portions. Cut carefully, and remember to wipe the blade after each cut.)

With a wide metal spatula, transfer the portions to a large serving platter. Refrigerate until serving time.

CHOCOLATE PASTICCIOS

NOTE
↓

A tip from a caterer friend who often makes these in large quantities: Bake the shells as directed, cool slightly, remove them from the tartlet pans and place them on a cookie sheet before filling them. In this way you can make many Pasticcios without so many tartlet pans.
^

30 pasticcios A dictionary definition of *pasticcio* is "In music, art, or writing, a medley made up of fragments of other works connected so as to form a complete work." These came about when I had a wonderful pastry and a delicious filling, both unrelated, and I put them together.

These are chic, elegant little pastries — they are finger food. Serve them at a tea party or as dessert for a luncheon. Or on a buffet. They are like miniature pies. The crust is a classic French pastry, the filling is a smooth, soft chocolate fudge. (How rich and creamy, dark sweet/bittersweet, etc., can chocolate be? From 1 to 10, this filling rates 12.)

This is not a quickie. On the contrary, it takes time and qualifies as a hobby or pastime.

You will need small, round (not fluted) tartlet pans. Mine are French. They measure 2⅜ (just over 2¼) inches across the top and just under ½ inch in depth. These are generally available in specialty kitchen stores or online.

It is best to make the pastry ahead of time. It should be refrigerated at least 1 hour before using, but it may wait in the refrigerator for a few days or it may be frozen.

PASTRY

- 1¼ cups *sifted* all-purpose flour
- ¼ cup sugar
- 4 ounces (1 stick) unsalted butter, cold, cut into small pieces
- 1 large egg yolk
- 2 tablespoons ice water

FILLING

- 3 ounces (¾ stick) unsalted butter, cut into pieces
- 12 ounces (2 cups) semisweet chocolate morsels
- ¼ cup light corn syrup
- 8 large egg yolks (the whites may be frozen for some other use)
- A few teaspoons of chopped, unsalted green pistachio nuts, walnuts, or pecans

The pastry may be put together in a food processor or in the traditional manner.

To make the pastry in the processor fitted with the steel blade: Place the flour and sugar in the bowl. Add the cold butter and process until the mixture resembles coarse meal. Add the yolk and water and process only until the mixture forms a ball.

For the Pastry

Place the flour and sugar in a medium-size mixing bowl. With a pastry blender, cut in the butter until the mixture resembles coarse meal. Stir the yolk and water together, add to the flour mixture, and stir with a fork until the mixture holds together.

Wrap the pastry airtight and refrigerate it for at least an hour, or even a few days if you wish, or freeze it.

The pastry crusts will be baked empty first and then again with the filling. When you are ready for the first baking, line up your little tartlet pans. This recipe is for 30 tartlets, but if you don't have enough pans the remaining pastry (and the filling) can wait (see Note).

Flour a pastry cloth and a rolling pin. Work with half of the dough at a time — reserve the balance in the refrigerator.

Place the pastry dough on the floured cloth. Flatten it slightly and turn it over to flour both sides. With the floured rolling pin, roll out the dough until it is very thin — it should be about $\frac{1}{16}$ of an inch. (During the rolling, roll the pastry up on the pin and then unroll it upside down in order to keep both sides floured.)

Cut into rounds with a plain 2¾-inch round cookie cutter, cutting them as close to each other as possible and making 15 rounds from each half portion of dough. As you cut each round, place it over a tartlet pan, ease it gently into place, and press lightly so that it touches the pan all over.

(If your fingernails are in the way, use a few scraps of the dough to form a little ball, dip the ball into flour, and press the ball all over the pastry to ensure that the dough is completely in place.)

Place the pastry-lined pans on a baking sheet or cookie sheet and transfer to the freezer until the dough is firm. (If you want to leave it overnight or longer at this stage, cover with plastic wrap or aluminum foil.)

While the tartlet shells are freezing, cut 30 small squares of aluminum foil, each one about 3 inches square.

Now, adjust a rack one-third up from the bottom of the oven and preheat oven to 400 degrees.

Line each tartlet shell with a square of the foil and press it firmly into place — keep the lined shells on the baking sheet or cookie sheet. In order to keep the pastry in place and keep it from puffing up, fill the foil with pie weights or dried beans. (You can use any kind of bean. Save them to use again for the same purpose.)

Bake the tartlets for about 12 minutes, reversing the pan front to back once during baking to ensure even browning.

After about 10 or 11 minutes, check on one of the shells — gently lift the square of foil with the beans in it. The shells should be baked until they are golden-colored. When done, remove from the oven and reduce the oven temperature to 300 degrees.

Gently remove the foil and beans by lifting two opposite sides of each piece of foil.

Either cool the shells completely or fill them while they are still slightly warm.

continues ↘

For the Filling

Place the butter and chocolate in the top of a large double boiler over hot water on moderate heat. Cover for a few minutes until almost melted. Then uncover and stir until smooth. Stir in the corn syrup.

In a bowl, stir the yolks briefly just to mix and then gradually stir in a few spoonfuls of the hot chocolate mixture. Gradually stir the egg mixture into the remaining chocolate. Reduce the heat to low and cook, stirring constantly, for 5 minutes.

Remove the top of the double boiler from the hot water. Transfer the mixture to a small bowl for easier handling. For best results use this filling while it is still warm.

Place a well-rounded spoon of the filling in each baked shell, placing it evenly in the center. (It is not necessary to spread the filling—it will run during baking. But place it carefully in the center. I find this is easiest to do by using two demitasse spoons, one for picking up and one for pushing off. But the amount should be the same as a well-rounded regular spoon—or 2 well-rounded demitasse spoonfuls.)

With your fingertips, sprinkle a few of the chopped nuts on the center of each Pasticcio.

Make sure that the oven temperature has reduced to 300 degrees—if not, the pastries can wait.

Bake for 12 minutes, reversing the pan front to back once to ensure even baking. The tops will feel dry to the touch but the centers will still be soft. Do not overbake!

Remove from the oven. Let stand until cool enough to handle, then use your fingertips to ease them gently out of the pans and place them on racks until completely cool.

These may stand at room temperature or they may be refrigerated or frozen. And they may be served either at room temperature or chilled or frozen. Try them each way and see which you like best. (The filling will be softer at room temperature, but even when these are frozen it will not be too hard. Of course, if it is too soft, chilling will firm it.)

If you are serving Pasticcios as dessert, plan on 3 to a portion.

CHOCOLATE TARTLETS

NOTE
[↓]
If you do not have enough molds to bake these all at once, the remaining pastry and filling may wait at room temperature.

60 to 75 tiny tartlets These are tiny cookie cups with a baked-in chewy chocolate filling. To make these dainty French cookies, it is necessary to use shallow, very small individual tartlet molds; they may be plain or fluted. Mine are French; they are assorted shapes and they vary in diameter from about 1 to 2 inches. There are also Scandinavian ones, generally a little larger, made for Sandbakelser cookies — they may be used for these tartlets. Or you may use plain round, shallow French tartlet pans about 2 to 2½ inches in diameter and ½ inch deep. These little pans should be washed with only hot soapy water; anything rougher would cause the cookies to stick. Don't make these if you are in a hurry; they take time.

FILLING

- 4 ounces (generous ¾ cup) blanched almonds (see page 22)
- 6 ounces (1 cup) semisweet chocolate morsels
- 2 large eggs
- 1 teaspoon instant coffee powder
- ¼ teaspoon almond extract
- ½ cup sugar

PASTRY

- 6 ounces (1½ sticks) unsalted butter
- Scant ¼ teaspoon salt
- 1 teaspoon vanilla extract
- ½ cup sugar
- 2 cups *sifted* all-purpose flour

For the Filling

In a food processor, blender, or nut grinder, grind together the almonds and the chocolate — these must be ground fine. (In a blender it will probably be best to do it in two batches, using half of the nuts and half of the chocolate in each batch.) Set aside.

In the small bowl of an electric mixer at high speed, beat the eggs for about 5 minutes, until very thick and pale in color. On low speed, mix in the coffee powder, almond extract, and sugar, and then gradually beat in the ground almond–chocolate mixture. Transfer to a small, shallow bowl for ease in handling and set aside at room temperature.

For the Pastry

In the large bowl of an electric mixer (with clean beaters), cream the butter. Mix in the salt, vanilla, and sugar and then gradually add the flour, scraping the bowl as necessary with a rubber spatula. The mixture will be crumbly. Turn it out onto a board or smooth work surface. Squeeze it between your hands until it holds together.

Form it into a ball. Start at the further side of the dough and, using the heel of your hand, push off small pieces (about 2 tablespoons), pushing against the work surface and away from you. Continue until all the dough has been pushed off. Re-form the dough into a ball. If it is not completely smooth, repeat the process again.

Adjust a rack one-third up from the bottom of the oven and preheat oven to 350 degrees.

With your fingertips, press a small amount of the dough into each tartlet mold (the molds do not have to be buttered). The pastry shell should be ¼ inch thick or a little less, and it should be level with the rim of the mold — use your fingertip to remove excess dough above the rim.

Place the molds on a cookie sheet or a baking sheet. With a demitasse spoon or a small measuring spoon, place some of the filling in each shell. The filling may be mounded a bit above the edges but only a very little bit or it will run over. It is not necessary to smooth the filling, as it will run slightly and smooth itself as it bakes.

Bake for 20 minutes, until the pastry is barely colored. Reverse the baking sheet front to back once to ensure even browning. Do not overbake these or the filling will be dry instead of chewy.

Remove from the oven and let stand until just cool enough to handle. Then invert each mold into the palm of your hand and, with a fingernail of the other hand, gently release and remove the mold.

VICTORIAS

18 tartlets These shells are made of classic French pastry dough called pâte brisée, which means "broken pastry." When you follow the directions for "pushing off" or "breaking off" the dough, you will understand its name. It is a joy — no problem to make and delicious. The dough may be baked in any size pan and used with any filling.

When I discovered these divine chocolate tartlets at Angelina's (previously Rumpelmayer's) on the Rue de Rivoli in Paris, I fell madly in love with them. I tried desperately to get the recipe but it was impossible. The recipe was a secret. After returning home, I wrote to Angelina's requesting that they mail some Victorias to me. They answered saying that Victorias should be eaten while still fresh, and, therefore, they were enclosing the recipe so that I could make them myself and have them whenever I wanted them. I think there's a lesson somewhere in this but I don't know what it is.

You will need individual tartlet pans 3½ inches in diameter and ½ inch in depth, and a 4-inch round cookie cutter. (I have also made tiny Victorias that are only 2¼ inches in diameter. They take time but are fabulous.)

PASTRY SHELLS

2½ cups *sifted* all-purpose flour

½ teaspoon salt

½ cup sugar

5 ounces (1¼ sticks) unsalted butter, cut into ½-inch pieces

1 large egg plus 2 large egg yolks

CHOCOLATE FILLING

8 ounces semisweet chocolate, broken into pieces

½ cup sugar

2 cups heavy cream, scalded

For the Pastry

Place the flour on a large board, marble, or other smooth work surface. Make a large well in the center and add all the remaining pastry ingredients. With your right-hand fingertips, work the center ingredients together. Gradually incorporate the flour, using a dough scraper or a wide spatula in your left hand to help move it in toward the center. When all the flour has been absorbed, knead briefly until the dough holds together and then finish by "breaking" the pastry as follows.

Form it into a ball. Start at the further side of the dough and, using the heel of your hand, push off small pieces (about 2 tablespoons), pushing against the work surface and away from you. Continue until all the dough has been pushed off. Re-form the dough and push it or "break"

continues ↘

it off again. Re-form the dough. Do not chill the dough.

Adjust the rack one-third up from the bottom of oven. Preheat oven to 400 degrees.

Work with half or less of the dough at a time. On a floured pastry cloth, with a floured rolling pin, roll evenly to ⅛-inch thickness. Reverse the dough occasionally to keep both sides lightly floured. With a 4-inch round cookie cutter, cut out rounds. Scraps of dough may be reserved and then rerolled together to cut out a total of 18 rounds. (You will have a bit more dough than you need — extra shells may be frozen before or after baking, or extra dough may be frozen unrolled.)

As the pastry rounds are cut, transfer them with a metal spatula and fit into 3½-inch tartlet pans. (See headnote; if you don't have enough tartlet pans to bake the 18 shells all at once, place the extra rounds on wax paper and cover them with wax paper or plastic wrap until you are ready for them.) Do not stretch the dough. Press it gently into place. Place the lined pans on a baking sheet or cookie sheet and freeze or refrigerate until firm.

Tear aluminum foil (against a ruler or table edge) into 4-inch squares. Line each frozen or refrigerated shell with foil, pressing it firmly against the bottom and sides. (Do not fold the foil down over the sides of the pastry.) Fill with small, dried beans or uncooked rice to keep the pastry from puffing up. Replace on baking sheet and bake for 10 minutes, until the pastry is set. Remove the shells from the oven and

remove the foil and beans or rice by carefully lifting opposite corners of the foil. Return to the oven to continue baking for a few minutes more, until the bottoms begin to color slightly and the edges are golden.

As the shells are baked, remove the pans from the oven individually with a wide metal spatula. With your fingertips, carefully remove the shells from the pans to cool on a rack. When cool, transfer to trays that will fit in the refrigerator.

For the Filling

In the top of a large double boiler over hot water on moderate heat, melt the chocolate. Stir in the sugar. Add the boiling hot cream all at once and stir and stir and stir with a wire whisk until smooth.

Cook uncovered over moderate heat for 30 minutes, scraping sides and bottom frequently with a rubber spatula. (Replace water in bottom of double boiler as necessary.) Remove from heat and place top of double boiler in ice water. Stir continuously and gently with a rubber spatula, scraping the sides and bottom in order not to let the chocolate start to set. Test the temperature frequently (I use the fingertip test). As soon as it is cold, pour it into a pitcher.

Pour the filling into the pastry shells, pouring carefully just to the top of each shell. They should be as full as possible, but be very careful not to let any run over in spots where the shells are lower. Carefully transfer to refrigerator. Refrigerate for a few hours. Serve chilled.

SERVING SUGGESTIONS

Victorias may be served very simply as they are at Angelina's, with just a light sprinkle of chopped green pistachio nuts right in the center, put on while the chocolate is still soft. Or they may be very elaborate, with whipped cream swirled on through a pastry bag and a star tube after the chocolate has become firm and then topped with candied roses or violet petals, or coarsely grated chocolate.

CHOCOLATE ÉCLAIRS

NOTE
↓

If the éclair shells have been frozen unfilled (they should be split before they are frozen), thaw them as follows: Place them, frozen, on a cookie sheet in a 350-degree oven for about 8 minutes to thaw and crisp. Cool on a rack.

12 to 14 dessert-size éclairs Homemade éclairs are not an everyday dessert—they are special. And with all the steps involved I consider them a creative art. Although they are not really difficult, I congratulate you when you make them. (This filling is unconventional—it is a combination chocolate pastry cream and chocolate Bavarian.)

The *pâte à choux* may be shaped and baked as soon as it is prepared, or it may be covered and may stand either at room temperature or in the refrigerator for an hour before using. The éclair shells are easy and fun to shape if you can handle a pastry bag, and they may be made way ahead of time and frozen (see Note). The filling and icing should be done the day they are served—or the filled and iced éclairs may be frozen.

You will need a 10- to 16-inch pastry bag and a #8 plain, round tube which has a ⅝-inch opening.

CREAM-PUFF PASTRY (PÂTE À CHOUX)

- 4 ounces (1 stick) unsalted butter
- 1 cup boiling water
- Pinch of salt
- 1 cup *sifted* all-purpose flour
- 4 large eggs

CHOCOLATE FILLING

- 2 ounces unsweetened chocolate
- 1 tablespoon (1 envelope) unflavored gelatin
- ¼ cup cold water
- 2 tablespoons *unsifted* flour
- 1 cup milk
- Pinch of salt
- ⅓ cup sugar
- 4 large egg yolks
- 1 teaspoon vanilla extract
- 1 tablespoon unsalted butter
- 1 tablespoon strong prepared coffee, or rum, Cognac, or crème de cacao
- 1 cup heavy cream

CHOCOLATE GLAZE

- 2½ ounces unsweetened chocolate
- ½ cup sugar
- 3 tablespoons plus 1½ teaspoons water (be very careful not to use too much—less is better than more)

For the Pâte à Choux

Adjust a rack to the center of the oven and preheat oven to 425 degrees. Line a 15½ x 12-inch or larger cookie sheet with aluminum foil. Place the cookie sheet on another, unlined one of the same size — the double sheets will prevent the bottoms of the éclairs from browning too much. (They will be a beautiful, smooth, shiny, pale golden color.) Set aside.

Place the butter, boiling water, and salt in a heavy 2½- or 3-quart saucepan over high heat. Stir with a heavy wooden spatula (cutting the butter as you stir) until the butter is melted and the mixture boils hard. (Do not boil unnecessarily or too much water will evaporate.)

Remove from the heat and immediately add the flour all at once, stirring vigorously with the wooden spatula until the mixture forms a ball and leaves the sides of the pan. If that does not happen within about half a minute, stir over low heat for a few seconds.

Turn the mixture into the small bowl of an electric mixer. Add the eggs one at a time, beating on low-medium speed after each addition until incorporated. After adding the last egg, beat for ½ minute more, scraping the bowl with a rubber spatula.

Fit a 10- to 16-inch pastry bag (large is better than small) with a #8 plain round tube. Fold down a deep cuff on the outside of the bag. To support the bag, place it in a tall, narrow jar or glass and transfer the warm (or cooled) pastry to the bag. Then unfold the cuff and twist the top of the bag closed.

Place the prepared cookie sheet on a table. (It is easier to work with a pastry bag at table height rather than at counter height.) Hold the pastry bag at an oblique angle to the sheet with the tube almost touching the sheet. Press on the top of the bag to press out a finger-shaped strip that is 5 inches long and ¾ to 1 inch wide (keep it narrow). At the end, retrace your direction with a quick jerk in order to cut off the pastry neatly. Continue to press out 12 to 14 strips about 1½ inches apart on the cookie sheet.

Bake for 20 minutes (at which time the éclairs should have finished rising — but the oven door should not be opened until they have finished rising or even a little longer).

Then reduce the oven temperature to 350 degrees and bake for an additional 30 to 35 minutes (total baking time is 50 to 55 minutes). The éclairs should be golden brown and crisp all over (including the sides, which are the last part to dry out and become crisp).

About 5 or 10 minutes before they are done, reach into the oven and, with a small, sharp knife, cut a few small slits in the top of each éclair to let the steam escape.

If they are underbaked the éclairs will collapse as they cool — it will not hurt to overbake them a bit.

As soon as they are done, with your fingers peel them carefully from the foil and place them on racks to cool. (If they cool on the foil they might stick.)

When they are cool, use a serrated knife and slice each one horizontally, cutting about one-third from the top, which will leave a deep bottom to hold the filling.

continues ↘

Do not mix up the tops and bottoms — keep them in their original pairs.

With your fingers, remove any excess soft dough from the inside of each half. Now either package them airtight and freeze, or fill them. Do not let them stand around or they may become limp. (They can wait for the length of time it takes to make the filling.)

For the Filling

Place the chocolate in the top of a small double boiler over warm water on low heat; cover and let stand until the chocolate is melted. (If the chocolate melts before you are ready to use it, uncover the pot and remove from the hot water.)

Sprinkle the gelatin over the cold water in a small custard cup and let stand.

Sift or strain the flour into a 1½- or 2-quart heavy saucepan. Add ¼ cup of the milk and stir well with a rubber spatula until smooth — if there are any lumps press against them with the spatula. When smooth, gradually stir in the remaining milk and then the salt and sugar.

Place over moderate heat and cook, stirring and scraping the pan with the rubber spatula, until the mixture thickens to the consistency of a thin white sauce and comes to a boil. Let boil, stirring, for 1 minute.

In a medium-size bowl, stir the yolks lightly just to mix. Gradually stir in about half of the hot sauce and then stir the yolks into the remaining sauce.

Cook over very low heat, stirring constantly, for 2 minutes. Do not let it get too hot or cook too long.

Remove from the heat. Stir in the melted chocolate and the softened gelatin. Beat with a wire whisk, electric mixer, or egg beater until smooth. If the mixture is not smooth, strain it. Then mix in the vanilla, butter, and coffee or liquor.

Partially fill a large bowl with ice and water. Set the bowl or saucepan of filling into the bowl of ice water and stir occasionally until cool and partially thickened.

Meanwhile, whip the cream until it holds a soft shape — it should be semi-firm, not stiff.

When the chocolate mixture starts to thicken to the consistency of a heavy mayonnaise, stir it briskly with a wire whisk and then fold the whipped cream into it.

Use right away or refrigerate briefly (if it is not firm enough to hold its shape and be pressed out of a pastry bag, it must be refrigerated to stiffen it a bit).

The filling will be put into the shells with a pastry bag; if the shells are on a slippery surface they will slide away from you while you fill them. I place them, open sides up, in matched pairs on a kitchen towel.

To fill the shells, fit a 15- or 18-inch pastry bag with a #8 plain round tube. Fold down a deep cuff on the outside of the bag. To support the bag, place it in a tall, narrow jar or glass and transfer the cold filling to the bag.

Unfold the top of the bag, twist it closed, and press out a heavy strip of the filling into the bottom half of each éclair. Then repeat, so you have two heavy strips of filling, mounded high, in the bottom halves.

Cover with the tops of the éclairs, pressing the tops down firmly so they stay in place — the filling should show on the sides.

Place on a tray and refrigerate while you prepare the glaze.

For the Glaze

Place the chocolate in the top of a small double boiler over hot water on moderate heat. Cover until partially melted. Uncover and stir until completely melted. Add the sugar and water and stir to mix.

Remove the top of the double boiler and place it over direct heat. Stir until the glaze comes to a boil.

Remove from the heat and stir briskly with a small wire whisk for a few seconds until the mixture is very smooth and only slightly thickened.

This should not be thick or stiff, but it should not be so thin that it runs down the sides of the éclairs. If it is too thick, add a few drops of hot water and stir well. If it is too thin, let it cool briefly and stir well. When it is right it will spread evenly and smoothly over the tops and will stay where you put it. Use the glaze immediately while it is still warm.

Hold an éclair in your left hand. With your right hand, use a spoon to pick up a rounded spoonful of the glaze, place it on the éclair and spread it with the back of the spoon. Use just enough to make a rather thin layer all over the top.

If the glaze thickens while you are working with it, place it over warm water, or stir in a few drops of warm water.

Return the glazed éclairs to the refrigerator.

Serve the same day, or chill until the glaze is dry and firm, then wrap individually in plastic wrap and freeze. Thaw in the refrigerator for a few hours before unwrapping. If the éclair stands too long after it has thawed the shell will lose its crispness.

CHOCOLATE FUDGE PIE

10 portions This is dense, dark, moist, chewy, and rich, rich, rich! It is best to make the pie early in the day for that night; it should be cooled and refrigerated before serving.

NOTE
↓

For a 10-inch crust, increase the amounts to 1¼ cups flour, generous ½ teaspoon salt, 3¾ tablespoons vegetable shortening, 3¾ tablespoons butter, and 3¾ tablespoons ice water.

10-inch partially baked pie shell (page 217, using ingredient amounts for a 10-inch crust)

FUDGE FILLING

4 ounces (1 stick) unsalted butter

3 ounces unsweetened chocolate

4 large eggs

Scant ¼ teaspoon salt

1½ cups granulated sugar

3 tablespoons light corn syrup

¼ cup milk

1 teaspoon vanilla extract

OPTIONAL: 1 tablespoon Cognac or rum

WHIPPED CREAM

2 cups heavy cream

1 teaspoon vanilla extract

OPTIONAL: 1 tablespoon Cognac or rum

¼ cup confectioners' sugar

For the Pie Shell

Follow the recipe for a baked pie shell on the opposite page, modifying it as indicated for a 10-inch shell. Note that for this pie shell, it is important to form a high rim with no low spots to hold all the filling. Before you bake it, make a change in timing since this will have additional baking when the filling is poured in: After you remove the aluminum foil and the dried beans and reduce the temperature to 400 degrees, bake for only 3 or 4 minutes (instead of 7 or 8) until the bottom of the crust is dry but not brown.

Let the partially baked crust cool slightly (or completely, if you wish) while you prepare the filling.

For the Filling

Adjust rack one-third up from the bottom of the oven and preheat oven to 350 degrees.

Place the butter and the chocolate in the top of a small double boiler over warm water on low heat. Cover until partially melted, then uncover and stir until completely melted and smooth. Remove the top of the double boiler and set it aside, uncovered, to cool slightly.

Meanwhile, in the large bowl of an electric mixer, beat the eggs well. Except for the chocolate and butter mixture, add all the remaining filling ingredients and beat well. Then beat in the chocolate and butter mixture.

Turn into the prepared, partially baked pie crust; the filling will come almost to the top of the crust. Handle very carefully and place in the preheated oven.

Bake for 50 minutes. Do not bake any longer even if the filling appears soft.

Turn the oven heat off, prop the oven door partially open, and let the pie stand in the oven until it is completely cool. (The filling will puff up during baking and then will settle down to a thin layer that will crack while cooling. That's OK.)

Refrigerate for several hours.

For the Whipped Cream

In a chilled bowl with chilled beaters, whip the cream with the vanilla, optional Cognac or rum, and confectioners' sugar until it will just hold a shape.

Shortly before serving spread the cream in a thick layer over the top of the pie.

Baked Pie Shell

Who ever said "As easy as pie?" Making a proper pie crust takes patience, practice, experience, and a thorough knowledge of the subject. Instructions teach you not to use too much or too little flour, too much or too little shortening and butter, too much or too little ice water. And especially not to handle the mixture any more than necessary. And to chill it properly. And to roll it very carefully. Etc., etc., etc. I hope this recipe will help you. Just follow the directions, and make a few crusts to practice before planning a finished pie. It will get easier.

This recipe makes a single 9-inch crust. For a 10-inch crust, see the Note. The ingredients may easily be doubled for two shells. I recommend using an ovenproof glass pie plate.

1 cup sifted all-purpose flour

Scant ½ teaspoon salt

3 tablespoons vegetable shortening (such as Crisco), cold and firm

3 tablespoons unsalted butter, cold and firm, cut into small pieces

About 3 tablespoons ice water

continues ⬎

If the room is warm, it is a good idea to chill the mixing bowl and even the flour beforehand.

Place the flour and salt in a large mixing bowl. Add the shortening and butter. With a pastry blender or butter knife, cut in the shortening and butter until the mixture resembles coarse crumbs — when partially cut in, raise the bowl with both hands, quickly move it away from you, up, and then toward you in a jerky motion to toss the bottom ingredients to the top. Search out any large pieces of butter and cut them individually with a knife. It is all right to leave a few pieces about the size of small peas.

Sprinkle 1 tablespoon of the ice water in small drops all over the surface of the dough. Mix and toss with a fork. Continue adding the water only until all the flour is barely moistened. (Too much water makes the pastry sticky-soggy-tough.) Do not ever dump a lot of the water in any one spot. When the water is partly added, repeat the raise-move-jerk motion to toss the dry flour to the top.

When adequate water has been added, the mixture will still be lumpy, but with practice you will know by the look of it that it will form a ball when pressed together. I have occasionally had to add a little more water, but very little — about 1 to 2 teaspoons.

The shortening and butter must not melt (they should remain in little flour-coated flakes) so do not handle now any more than necessary. Turn the mixture out onto a board or smooth work surface and, with your hands, just push the mixture together to form a ball. If the dough is too dry to hold together, do not knead it, but replace it in the bowl and use a knife to cut it into small pieces again and add a few more drops of water.

Lightly flour your hands, round the ball of dough, then flatten it slightly and smooth the edges. Wrap the dough in plastic wrap and refrigerate overnight or at least for a few hours. It may stay in the refrigerator for up to a week, or if you are in a rush it may be used after a few hours. Or it may be frozen now, airtight, for up to 2 months.

Rolling out the dough is much easier if you work on a pastry cloth. Flour the cloth by rubbing in as much flour as the cloth will absorb, then lightly scrape off loose excess flour. Lightly flour your rolling pin.

Place the flattened ball of dough on the cloth. If the dough is very firm, pound it sharply in all directions with the rolling pin to flatten it to a circle about 7 inches in diameter. If it is not too firm, just press down on it gently in all directions with the rolling pin to size. With your fingers, smooth the edges and pinch together any small cracks.

Start to roll, always from the center out. Do not roll back and forth and do not turn the dough over during rolling. Roll first in one direction and then another, trying to keep the shape round. If the edges crack slightly, pinch them together. If the dough cracks anywhere other than the edges, or if the circle is terribly uneven, do not reroll the dough; simply cut off uneven edges and use the scraps as patches. It may be necessary to reflour the pin occasionally, but the less flour you use, the better — too much flour toughens pastry.

Roll the dough into a round that is 13 inches in diameter for a 9-inch pie plate; 13½ or 14 inches for a 10-inch plate. The dough should be a scant ⅛ inch thick. It is important that the rolled-out pastry be exactly the same thickness all over so it will brown evenly.

If you have a cake-decorating turntable or a lazy Susan to place the pie plate on, you will find it much easier to trim and shape the crust. Roll the dough up loosely around the rolling pin to transfer it to the pie plate. With your fingers, ease the sides of the dough down into the plate — it is important not to stretch the dough or it will shrink during baking. The dough must touch the plate all around. With scissors, cut the edge of the crust evenly, leaving about a ½-inch overhang. With floured fingertips, fold the edge to the outside and down, forming a hem that extends about ½ inch over the rim. Press the hem lightly together between your thumb and forefinger knuckle, making it stand upright. (While you are handling the edges, if the kitchen is warm and the pastry becomes sticky, refrigerate it briefly.) With lightly floured fingertips, you may form a decorative edge on the pastry, or leave it plain.

With a fork, prick the bottom all over at ¼-inch intervals. Place the shell in the freezer for 15 minutes or more, until it is frozen firm. (This helps prevent shrinking.)

About 15 minutes before you bake, adjust a rack to the center of the oven and preheat oven to 450 degrees.

In order to keep the pastry shell in place during baking, cut a 12-inch square of aluminum foil. Place the foil, shiny side down, in the frozen shell. Do not fold the edges of the foil over the rim of the crust; let the corners of the foil stand up. Fill the foil at least three-quarters full with dried beans or with pie weights.

Bake the frozen shell for 12 to 13 minutes, until it is set and lightly colored on the edges. Remove it from the oven. Reduce the heat to 400 degrees. Gently remove the foil and beans or weights by lifting the four corners of the foil. Replace the shell in the oven and continue to bake about 7 or 8 minutes more, longer if necessary. Watch it almost constantly; if it starts to puff up anywhere, reach into the oven and pierce the puff with a cake tester or a fork to release the trapped air. Bake until the edges are richly colored — a too-pale crust is not as attractive as one with a good color. The bottom will remain paler than the edges. (During baking, if the crust is not browning evenly, reverse the position of the pan.)

Place on a rack and cool to room temperature.

CHOCOLATE PECAN PIE

8 to 10 portions The non-chocolate version of this pie is one of the most famous of all truly American recipes. The classic Southern pecan pie, often described as "utterly deadly," is rich, gooey, and sweet-sweet-sweet. The unsweetened chocolate and rum in this recipe cut the sweetness to just right. This is one of the best of all pies.

Traditionally, the filling is poured into an unbaked crust and then it is baked. I have never had one made that way that had a really crisp bottom crust. I like a crisp bottom crust, so the procedure for this is different: The crust is partially baked "blind" (without the filling), then it is baked again with the filling. It will have a crisp bottom crust.

And, traditionally, this amount of filling is used for a 10-inch crust or even for two 9-inch crusts. I like a thicker filling; this is baked in one 9-inch crust and it will be a thick filling.

When just right, the crust should be flaky, crisp, and buttery, and a rich golden color. The filling should be semi-firm in the middle with a consistency somewhere between a thick fudge sauce and smooth caramel; and the pecans, which rise during baking, should form a crunchy layer on the top.

9-inch partially baked pie shell (page 217)

FILLING

2 ounces unsweetened chocolate

2 ounces (½ stick) unsalted butter

4 large eggs

1 cup sugar

1¼ cups dark corn syrup

1 teaspoon vanilla extract

2 tablespoons dark rum

7 ounces (2 cups) pecan halves or large pieces

For the Pie Shell

Follow the recipe for a 9-inch pie shell on page 217. Because this pie has such a generous amount of filling, it is important to form a pie shell with an even, high rim with no low spots so the filling can't run over. Before you bake the pie shell, make a change in timing (since this will have additional baking after the filling is poured in): When you remove the aluminum foil and the dried beans and reduce the temperature to 400 degrees, bake for only 4 minutes (instead of 7 or 8), or until the bottom of the crust is completely dry but still pale and the edges are just beginning to color.

Let the partially baked crust cool slightly (or completely if you wish) and then prepare the filling.

continues ⌄

For the Filling

Adjust rack one-third up from the bottom of the oven and preheat oven to 350 degrees.

Place the chocolate and butter in the top of a small double boiler over hot water on moderate heat; cover until partially melted, then uncover and stir until completely melted. Remove from the hot water and set aside, uncovered, to cool slightly.

In a large bowl (you can use an electric mixer, a manual egg beater, or a wire whisk), beat the eggs lightly just to mix, then beat in the sugar and syrup just to mix. Add the vanilla, rum, and then the melted chocolate/butter, and mix. Now stir in the pecans.

Carefully pour the filling into the partially baked crust, watching the edges as you pour; if the rim is not high enough, or has any low spots, do not use all of the filling or it will run over.

Bake for 40 to 50 minutes. If you bake until a knife inserted in the filling comes out clean, the pie will be overdone. The top should still feel soft to the touch, and the middle should wiggle and shake if you move the pan slightly. Do not be alarmed — and

do not bake any longer. The filling will set and firm as it cools. Longer baking would spoil the sensational quality of the filling. (During baking, the top will rise and crack; it will settle down as it cools.)

Remove the pie from the oven, place it on a rack, and cool to room temperature.

Southerners are emphatic about the fact that pecan pie is best while it is still slightly warm (it takes about 3 hours to cool to room temperature). However, I think this particular pie is much better when it is cold — very cold. I refrigerate it and serve it cold.

WHIPPED CREAM VARIATION

Whipped cream is traditional with pecan pie. If you use it, for 5 portions, whip 1 cup heavy cream with only 1 tablespoon of granulated or confectioners' sugar, ½ teaspoon of vanilla extract and/or 1 tablespoon of rum or bourbon. Double the amounts to serve 10. Whip only until the cream holds a soft shape, not stiff. Pass it separately.

SALTED ALMOND CHOCOLATE PIE

6 to 8 portions When a new taste sensation hits the nation it doesn't take long to spread from coast to coast. All over the country, people discovered the taste appeal of chocolate that is both sweet and salty. It was new, it was tantalizing, and it is delicious.

This has a crisp crumb crust made of chocolate wafer cookies (I use Nabisco). The soft and gooey milk chocolate filling has marshmallows and coarsely chopped, chunky, roasted salted almonds. It is served frozen, at which point it is similar to ice cream (when the pieces of marshmallow in the filling are frozen they become wonderfully, deliciously chewy).

The crust can be made ahead of time and stored in the freezer, if you wish. The filling is quick and easy. The pie should be frozen for at least 3 hours before serving — although it can wait in the freezer for days.

CHOCOLATE WAFER CRUMB CRUST

- 6 ounces store-bought chocolate wafer cookies (to make 1½ cups crumbs); better yet, make your own Chocolate Wafers (page 151)
- 3 ounces (¾ stick) unsalted butter, melted

SALTED ALMOND CHOCOLATE FILLING

- 20 marshmallows
- 8 ounces milk chocolate
- ½ cup light cream
- ⅓ cup roasted salted almonds (in the nut section of most supermarkets; I buy Blue Diamond brand)
- 1 cup heavy cream

For the Crust

Adjust a rack one-third up from the bottom of the oven and preheat oven to 300 degrees. Line a 9-inch pie plate with aluminum foil.

Coarsely break up the chocolate wafers and spin them in a food processor — or pound them in a bag — to make crumbs. Mix the crumbs with the melted butter and turn into the lined pie plate; press into shape. Bake for 15 minutes. Turn off the heat, open the oven door, and let the crust stand in the oven to cool off slowly.

When it is cool, place the crust in the freezer for at least an hour. Remove the foil lining and refrigerate until ready to fill.

continues ↘

For the Filling

With wet scissors (dipped in cold water), cut 16 marshmallows into quarters (reserve the remaining 4 marshmallows). Place cut marshmallows in the top of a large double boiler. Break up the chocolate and add it, then add the light cream. Place over hot water on medium heat. Cover and cook, stirring occasionally, until the marshmallows and chocolate are melted.

Meanwhile, with wet scissors, cut the remaining 4 marshmallows into pieces about ½ inch in size. Set them aside.

Chop the nuts very coarsely; they should not be fine. Cutting each nut into 4 or 5 pieces is about right, but they should be uneven, with some larger pieces. I use a small rounded wooden chopping bowl with a round-bladed knife. Or you can chop them on a board with a heavy chef's knife. Set the nuts aside.

In a small bowl with chilled beaters, whip the heavy cream until it just holds a shape. Refrigerate the whipped cream until you are ready for it.

When the chocolate mixture is melted and smooth, remove it from the hot water and set it aside, stirring occasionally until completely cool. (To save time, place the top of the double boiler into a bowl of ice and water and stir constantly until cool.) The cooled chocolate mixture will be quite stiff. Fold in the nuts, the reserved marshmallows, and then the whipped cream in several additions. Do not fold any more than necessary: It is all right if some of the cream is not completely incorporated.

Turn the mixture into the crust. Smooth the top. Freeze for at least 3 hours.

Unless you plan to freeze the pie for days, do not cover it, because the wrapping might stick. If you are freezing for longer, place the pie in a box.

CHIFFON AND VELVET PIE

6 to 8 portions The "chiffon" is coffee sour-cream meringue, the "velvet" is smooth, dark chocolate filling, and there is a crunchy crumb crust. It is an elegant combination of textures and flavors.

The crust may be made way ahead of time (it has to be made somewhat ahead of time)—the filling and topping may be made early in the day for that night or the day before.

CRUST

1 cup graham-cracker crumbs

¼ cup sugar

½ cup walnuts, finely chopped (not ground)

2 ounces (½ stick) butter, melted

FILLING

8 ounces semisweet chocolate

2 tablespoons sugar

1 cup light cream

4 large egg yolks (reserve the whites for the topping)

1 teaspoon vanilla extract

TOPPING

2 tablespoons instant coffee powder

¼ cup boiling water

1 teaspoon unflavored gelatin

4 large egg whites

½ cup sugar

½ cup sour cream

For the Crust

Adjust rack to the center of the oven and preheat oven to 375 degrees.

Stir the crumbs, sugar, and nuts in a mixing bowl. Add the melted butter and stir with a rubber spatula, pressing the mixture against the sides of the bowl until thoroughly mixed. The mixture will be crumbly but it will hold together when it is pressed into the pie plate.

Using a 9-inch glass pie plate, press the crumb crust mixture halfway up the side of the plate. Bake for 8 minutes, until golden, then cool to room temperature.

For the Filling

Break up the chocolate and place it in the top of a large double boiler. Add the sugar and light cream. Place over hot water on moderate heat. Cook, stirring occasionally, until the chocolate is melted and the mixture is smooth. If it does not get smooth, stir it briskly with a small wire whisk.

Stir the yolks slightly in a mixing bowl just to mix. Gradually add about half of the chocolate to the yolks, stirring constantly, and then add the yolks to the remaining chocolate. Add the vanilla and stir well.

Remove from the hot water and set aside for 5 to 10 minutes, stirring occasionally.

Pour the filling (which may be warm) into the prepared crust. Cool to room temperature, then place in the refrigerator for about half an hour.

continues ↘

For the Topping

In a small cup, dissolve the instant coffee in the boiling water. Let stand until completely cool (refrigerate if necessary).

Sprinkle the gelatin over the cooled coffee. Let stand for about 5 minutes. Then place the cup in a small pan of shallow hot water over low heat until the gelatin is dissolved (stir with a metal teaspoon in order to see any undissolved crystals). Remove from the hot water and set aside to cool to room temperature.

In the small bowl of an electric mixer, beat the egg whites until they hold a very soft shape. Reduce the speed to medium and gradually add the sugar. Then increase the speed to high and beat until the whites are really stiff and hold a firm shape.

On low speed, very gradually add the cooled coffee-gelatin mixture, scraping the bowl with a spatula and beating until smooth.

In a mixing bowl, stir the sour cream with a rubber spatula until it is smooth and soft. Fold about 1 cup of the whites into the cream and then fold the cream into the remaining whites.

Spread the topping over the pie, mounding it high in the middle and thinner on the edges (the edges should not be heavy or they might run over the crust).

Refrigerate for at least 4 hours or overnight.

BLACK BOTTOM PIE

8 portions Marjorie Kinnan Rawlings, the Pulitzer Prize–winning author of *The Yearling,* also wrote a delightful cookbook, *Cross Creek Cookery,* which is a mouthwatering account of the food served in her house in central Florida. In it, she says of her Black Bottom Pie, "I think this is the most delicious pie I have ever eaten...a pie so delicate, so luscious, that I hope to be propped up on my dying bed and fed a generous portion. Then I think that I should refuse outright to die, for life would be too good to relinquish."

My sentiments are the same. This is glorious.

CRUST

- 1¼ cups graham-cracker crumbs
- 1 tablespoon granulated sugar
- 1 teaspoon ground ginger
- 1 teaspoon ground cinnamon
- 2 ounces (½ stick) unsalted butter, melted

FILLING

- 2 ounces unsweetened chocolate
- 1 tablespoon (1 envelope) unflavored gelatin
- ¼ cup cold water
- 1 cup granulated sugar
- 1 tablespoon cornstarch
- Salt
- 4 large eggs, separated
- 1¾ cups milk
- 2 tablespoons dark rum
- 1 teaspoon vanilla extract
- ⅛ teaspoon cream of tartar

WHIPPED CREAM

- 1 cup heavy cream
- ¼ cup confectioners' sugar
- 1 scant teaspoon vanilla extract

OPTIONAL: coarsely grated chocolate for garnish

For the Crust

Adjust rack to center of oven. Preheat to 375 degrees. Line a 9-inch pie plate with nonstick aluminum foil, shiny side down, pressing it firmly onto the plate.

In a bowl, mix the crumbs with the granulated sugar, ginger, and cinnamon and then add the melted butter. Stir with a rubber spatula, pressing the mixture against the sides of the bowl, until completely mixed. The mixture will look crumbly but will hold together when pressed into place.

Press the crumb mixture into the lined pie plate firmly and up the sides. Bake for 8 minutes. Cool to room temperature.

For the Filling

Melt the chocolate in the top of a small double boiler over hot water on moderate heat. Remove the bowl from the hot water and set aside.

continues ↘

Sprinkle the gelatin over the cold water and set aside.

In a small bowl, mix ½ cup of the granulated sugar (reserve remaining ½ cup sugar) with the cornstarch and a pinch of salt. Set aside.

In the top of a large double boiler, stir the yolks lightly with a small wire whisk or a fork just to mix.

Scald the milk uncovered in a small, heavy saucepan over moderate heat until you can see small bubbles on the surface. Stir in the sugar-cornstarch mixture. Pour very slowly, in a thin stream, into the yolks — stirring constantly. Place over, but not touching, hot water in the bottom of the double boiler on moderate heat. Cook, stirring gently and scraping the pot with a rubber spatula, for 12 to 15 minutes, until the custard thickens to the consistency of a medium cream sauce. Lift top of double boiler off the hot water.

Remove 1 cup of the custard and set aside to cool, stirring occasionally, for 5 to 10 minutes, until tepid.

Meanwhile, to the remainder of the custard in the top of the double boiler, immediately add the softened gelatin and stir until thoroughly dissolved. Stir in the rum and set aside.

Gradually add the reserved cup of custard to the chocolate, stirring constantly with a small wire whisk. Mix thoroughly until smooth. Add the vanilla and turn the mixture into the prepared crust. Spread level and refrigerate.

In the small bowl of electric mixer at moderately high speed, beat the egg whites with a pinch of salt and the cream of tartar until the mixture increases in volume and starts to thicken. While beating, gradually add the reserved ½ cup sugar and continue to beat until mixture holds a shape and is the consistency of thick marshmallow sauce.

Gradually fold the rum custard (which may still be warm) into the beaten whites. Pour gently from one bowl to another to ensure thorough blending.

Pour over the chocolate layer, mounding it high in the center. (If there is too much filling and it might run over, reserve some at room temperature. Chill the pie in the freezer for 10 to 15 minutes, or in the refrigerator a bit longer, to partially set the filling. Then pour on the reserved portion and it will not run over.)

Refrigerate pie for 2 to 3 hours.

For the Whipped Cream

In a chilled bowl with chilled beaters, whip the cream, confectioners' sugar, and vanilla until the cream holds a shape. Spread evenly over filling, or use a pastry bag with a star tube and form a heavy, ruffled border of cream.

If you like, if the cream was spread over the pie, sprinkle it with coarsely grated chocolate; if it was put on to form a border, fill the center with grated chocolate.

CHOCOLATE MOUSSE HEATTER

6 portions It has been said that chocolate is the sexiest of all flavors. If so, this is the sexiest of all desserts.

8 ounces semisweet, bittersweet, or extra-bittersweet chocolate

1 tablespoon instant coffee powder

⅓ cup boiling water

5 large eggs (see Notes), separated

Pinch of salt

MOCHA CREAM

1 cup heavy cream

¼ cup confectioners' sugar

1 tablespoon instant coffee powder

OPTIONAL: dark chocolate for grating

NOTES

In the interest of safety, use only the best-quality eggs and wash and thoroughly dry them before using.

I beat the egg whites with the salt in the large bowl of the mixer, beating at high speed only until the whites thicken or hold a very soft shape. Then I finish the beating with a large wire whisk so that there is less chance of overbeating.

This recipe may easily be doubled if you wish.

Coarsely chop or break up the chocolate and place it in a small, heavy saucepan. Dissolve the coffee in the boiling water and pour it over the chocolate. Place over low heat and stir occasionally with a small wire whisk until smooth. Remove from the heat and set aside to cool for about 5 minutes.

Meanwhile, in the small bowl of an electric mixer, beat the egg yolks at high speed for 3 to 4 minutes, until they are pale lemon-colored. Reduce the speed to low, gradually add the slightly warm chocolate, and beat, scraping the bowl with a rubber spatula. Beat only until smooth. Remove from the mixer.

Add the salt to the egg whites and beat with clean beaters only until they hold a definite shape but not until they are stiff or dry (see Notes).

Without being too thorough, gently fold about one-quarter of the beaten whites into the chocolate mixture, then fold in a second quarter, and finally fold the chocolate into the remaining whites, folding only until no whites show.

Gently transfer the mousse to a wide pitcher and pour it into six large wineglasses, each with about a 9-ounce capacity. Do not fill the glasses too full; leave generous headroom on each. (I always prepared this mousse in individual glasses and thought it had to be best that way. But it has been served to me many times at other people's homes from one large serving bowl, and it was fine.)

Cover tightly with aluminum foil and refrigerate for 3 to 6 hours. (The mousse may stand longer—12 to 24 hours if you

continues ⌄

wish. The texture will become more spongy and less creamy. Delicious both ways.)

For the Mocha Cream

In a chilled bowl with chilled beaters, beat the cream, sugar, and coffee powder only until the cream thickens to the consistency of a heavy custard sauce — not stiff.

Pour or spoon the cream onto the mousse to completely cover the top of each portion.

Refrigerate until serving time.

If you like, top with a light sprinkling of shaved or coarsely grated semisweet chocolate. Refrigerate until serving time.

CHOCOLATE POTS DE CRÈME

6 (½-cup) soufflé dishes or 8 pots de crème cups Another creamy, smooth, extra-rich baked custard—this is one of the most classic and popular of all French chocolate desserts (my favorite!). It is quick and easy to prepare. Make it just a few hours before serving or make it in the morning for that night. It may be served with a simple salad luncheon or a swanky dinner and, since it is made in individual dishes, it is easy to handle for a buffet. It may be made in pots de crème cups with covers, but I think those portions are too small—I use individual soufflé dishes (½-cup capacity). This recipe makes six ½-cup servings but it may be multiplied to make nine, twelve, or more.

2 cups light cream	6 large egg yolks	Pinch of salt
4 ounces semisweet chocolate	2 tablespoons sugar	1½ teaspoons vanilla extract

Adjust rack to the center of the oven and preheat oven to 325 degrees.

Place 1½ cups of the cream in a small, heavy saucepan over low heat. Place the remaining ½ cup cream and the chocolate in the top of a large double boiler over hot water on moderate heat. In a mixing bowl, stir the yolks lightly just to mix—do not beat until foamy.

When the cream is scalded (a slight skin formed on the top), stir in the sugar and salt and remove from the heat.

Stir the chocolate mixture with a small wire whisk until perfectly smooth. Off the heat, very gradually add the hot cream to the chocolate, stirring constantly to keep the mixture smooth. Then gradually stir the chocolate mixture into the yolks and stir in the vanilla.

Return the mixture to the top of the double boiler over hot water on low heat and cook, stirring constantly with a rubber spatula, for 3 minutes.

Pour the mixture through a fine strainer into a pitcher. Then pour it into the individual soufflé dishes or pots de crème cups—do not fill them all the way, leave a bit of headroom.

Place in a shallow baking pan. Pour in hot water to about half the depth of the cups. Place a cookie sheet over the top to cover the cups, or if you have used pots de crème cups put their covers on.

Bake for 22 minutes (individual soufflé dishes and pots de crème cups both take the same time). The usual test for baked custard is to insert a small, sharp knife halfway between the middle and the edge;

continues ↘

when it comes out clean the custard is done. However, with this recipe, if you bake it until the knife comes out clean the custard will be too heavy and firm by the time it is chilled. If your oven is right, 22 minutes is correct. The custard will look too soft but it will become firmer as it chills, and it is best if it is still slightly creamy in the center when it is served.

Remove the cover or covers, remove the cups from the water and place on a rack to cool. Then refrigerate for a few hours.

Serve as is or with a spoonful of sweetened and flavored whipped cream on top.

CHOCOLATE REGAL

NOTE

⤓

Remember that there is no vanilla, coffee, rum, Cognac, etc. in this recipe. The only flavor is the chocolate, so use a delicious one.

12 portions The ultimate chocolate extravaganza! WARNING: This should be served only to avowed chocolate lovers, preferably in small portions after a light luncheon or dinner. This looks like a cake and cuts like a cake, but there any similarity ends. Call it what you will, but it is simply wonderful and wonderfully simple. And easy and foolproof to make. It tastes somewhat like a rich pot de crème, only more so.

It may be made a day or two before serving. But before you start, you will need a 9-inch springform pan; it can be deep or shallow, but the sides and the bottom of the pan must fit securely or the mixture, which is thin, might run out. (If you doubt your pan, place it on a square of aluminum foil and bring the sides of the foil securely up around the outside of the pan. Unless the pan is in really bad shape, probably very little will run out anyhow.)

1 pound semisweet chocolate (see Note), broken into pieces

1 cup milk

Pinch of salt

12 ounces (3 sticks) unsalted butter (it must be soft, but don't melt it or cream it first), cut into pieces

7 large egg yolks (or 6 extra-large or jumbo egg yolks)

REGAL WHIPPED CREAM

2 tablespoons cold water

1 teaspoon unflavored gelatin

2 cups heavy cream

1 teaspoon vanilla extract

¼ cup honey

Adjust rack one-third up from the bottom of the oven and preheat oven to 350 degrees. Cut a round of baking parchment or wax paper to fit the bottom of a 9-inch springform pan. Butter the sides (not the bottom) of the pan and one side of the round of paper. Place the paper in the pan, buttered side up.

Place the chocolate, milk, and salt in the top of a large double boiler over hot water on moderate heat, or in a heavy 1½- to 2-quart saucepan over low heat. Stir frequently with a rubber spatula, scraping the bottom and sides, until the chocolate is completely melted—don't worry if the mixture isn't smooth.

Transfer to the large bowl of an electric mixer and beat on low speed only until smooth. Then let stand for 4 or 5 minutes to cool slightly.

On low speed, alternately add pieces of the butter and the egg yolks, scraping the bowl with a rubber spatula and beating only until

continues ↘

incorporated after each addition. Do not beat on high speed and do not beat any more than necessary — the mixture should not lighten in color.

When it is smooth, pour the mixture into the prepared pan.

Bake for 25 minutes, no longer. It will still be soft and shiny and will not look done. Remove it from the oven!

Let stand until it reaches room temperature. Then refrigerate for a few hours until completely firm. It may be kept refrigerated for a day or two if you wish.

With a small, sharp knife, cut around the sides to release — press the blade firmly against the pan in order not to cut into the dessert. Remove the sides of the pan. Cover the dessert with a flat cake plate and invert. Remove the bottom of the pan. (If it doesn't lift off, insert a narrow metal spatula or a table knife between the paper and the pan and gently and carefully work it around to release the pan.) Peel off the paper lining. The Chocolate Regal will be 1 inch high.

You can cover it generously with whipped cream now, or refrigerate it and add the whipped cream later.

For the Whipped Cream

Place the cold water in a small, heatproof cup. Sprinkle the gelatin over the top and let stand for 5 minutes. Then place the cup in a small pan of shallow hot water over low heat to melt the gelatin.

Meanwhile, in the small bowl of the electric mixer (the bowl and beaters should be chilled) whip about 1¾ cups (reserve about ¼ cup) of the cream and the vanilla. While beating, gradually add the honey and scrape the bowl with a rubber spatula — the honey might settle to the bottom. Whip only until the cream has increased in volume and thickened, but not until it is firm enough to hold a shape.

When the gelatin is dissolved, remove the cup from the hot water. Stir the reserved ¼ cup of cream into the gelatin and immediately, while beating, add it all at once to the partially whipped cream. Continue to beat until the cream holds a shape and is stiff enough to spread. But remember that it is always more delicious if it is a bit soft and creamy instead of stiff.

The cream may be put on simply and smoothly in a thick layer, or it may be swirled with a rubber spatula or the back of a large spoon. Or spread only a thin coating to cover the dessert, then use a pastry bag fitted with a star tube and, using the remaining cream, form either a lattice design on the top or decorate with rosettes or swirls.

SERVING SUGGESTIONS

A bit of shaved chocolate may be sprinkled over the top. Or a few chopped, unsalted green pistachio nuts. But there is something regal about keeping the decoration at a minimum.

continues ◥

Brandied black Bing cherries go well with dense chocolate desserts. They may be served with this, placing a spoonful of them alongside each portion. Use the store-bought ones or prepare your own as follows: A day or two before using, drain a can of plain pitted black Bing cherries. Add 2 tablespoons of Cognac and 2 tablespoons of kirsch. Let stand, covered, stirring occasionally — they may either be refrigerated or at room temperature.

MOCHA CHOCOLATE PARFAIT

6 portions This was one of my husband's favorites — he could not get enough. It is a creamy coffee-chocolate dessert frozen in individual wine or parfait glasses. It may be served the day it is made or it may be frozen for a few weeks.

Serve as is, or top each portion with Chocolate Curls (page 240), a few Chocolate Cigarettes (page 97), or simple finely grated chocolate. A bottle of Amaretto may be passed with this — a small amount poured over each portion is delicious.

You will need a candy thermometer.

2 ounces unsweetened chocolate	⅓ cup water
¾ cup sugar	4 large egg yolks
2 tablespoons instant espresso powder or other powdered instant coffee	2 cups heavy cream
	1 teaspoon vanilla extract
	1 teaspoon dark rum

NOTES FOR CHOCOLATE CURLS

If the chocolate is sticky when you start to form a curl, let it stand at room temperature for just a few minutes.

If the chocolate doesn't behave beautifully, the room is too warm or you have rolled it too thin or not thin enough. It may be remelted and rerolled. (Leftover scraps may be remelted, if you wish.)

After you have tried these you will see that they can be made any length, shorter or longer, and they can be made fatter or thinner.

Don't attempt more than 3 ounces of chocolate at a time, or the last pieces of chocolate will have stood too long and may crack while they are being formed.

Chop the chocolate into medium-small pieces and set them aside on a piece of wax paper.

Place the sugar, espresso powder, and water in an 8-cup saucepan (it must have at least an 8-cup capacity or the syrup will boil over). Stir over high heat until the sugar is dissolved and the mixture comes to a boil. Insert a candy thermometer and let boil without stirring until the thermometer registers 230 degrees — the thread stage. (The mixture will rise to the top of the pan and bubble hard — if necessary, reduce the heat slightly to keep the mixture from spattering.)

Meanwhile, place the yolks in the small bowl of an electric mixer and beat at high speed until they are pale lemon-colored.

When the sugar syrup is ready, add the chopped chocolate to it, remove from the heat, and stir until the chocolate is melted.

Then, very gradually, beating at a rather low speed, add the hot chocolate mixture to the yolks, scraping the bowl with a rubber

continues ↘

spatula and beating until smooth. Remove from the mixer.

Let stand, stirring occasionally, until the mixture cools to room temperature. Test against the inside of your wrist. (If it is the least bit warm it will deflate the whipped cream.)

Meanwhile, in a chilled bowl with chilled beaters, whip the cream only until it holds a soft shape — not stiff. Let it stand at room temperature until you are ready for it. (If it separates a bit while standing, stir lightly with a wire whisk until reincorporated, but not until it becomes any stiffer.)

When the chocolate has cooled to room temperature, stir in the vanilla and rum. Stir in one large spoonful of the whipped cream. Stir in another spoonful and then fold in half of the remaining cream. Transfer to a larger mixing bowl and fold in the remaining cream.

You will need six 8-ounce wineglasses or tall, narrow parfait glasses. Either spoon the mixture into the glasses or transfer it to a wide-mouthed pitcher and pour it into the glasses. Do not fill them all the way — leave a bit of headroom so the glasses can be covered without disturbing the top of the dessert.

Cover each glass tightly with aluminum foil. Freeze for 2 to 3 hours, until firm (although this is equally delicious, if not more so, before it is completely firm). Or freeze much longer, if you wish.

Freezer temperatures vary. If yours is down to zero the parfait may become too firm. Check the parfait ahead of time and if it is too firm transfer it to the refrigerator for about an hour or two before serving. It should have the consistency of a firm ice cream, but as this does not melt the way ice cream does, a little softer or a little harder is OK.

Chocolate Curls

You can make these curls with any semisweet chocolate. If you use real chocolate and not compound or melting chocolate, it is best to use the curls only for refrigerated desserts. If the curls stand at room temperature for more than a few hours they discolor, although they keep indefinitely in the refrigerator or the freezer.

You can make these curls only in a cool, dry room. If the room is warm and humid, the chocolate may be too sticky to handle. If your kitchen is not air-conditioned, wait for a cool, dry day and then make a lot of these.

For 16 to 20 (½-inch) curls — moderately sensational — coarsely chop 3 ounces semisweet chocolate and place it in the top of a small double boiler over warm water on low heat. Stir occasionally until the chocolate is partially melted. Then stir constantly until it is completely melted and smooth.

Tear off two pieces of wax paper, each about 12 inches long. Place one on a smooth work surface. Dry the underside of the section of the double boiler containing the chocolate so that no water drips. Pour the chocolate onto the middle of the wax paper and cover it with the other piece of wax paper. With your fingers, gently smooth over the top piece of wax paper, spreading the chocolate into a 6- or 7-inch squarish shape — don't worry about an even surface or exact edges, just make it rather square.

Then, with a rolling pin, preferably one that is not too heavy, gently roll over the top piece of paper several times in each direction to spread the chocolate into about a 10-inch square shape. Again, don't worry too much about the edges but now the chocolate must be as smooth and level as you can make it, and about 1⁄16 inch thick (thin).

Slide a cookie sheet under the bottom paper and transfer it to the freezer for a few minutes until the chocolate is set and the paper can be peeled away easily. Peel off the top piece just to release and then replace it. Invert both pieces of paper with the chocolate between them. Peel off the other piece of paper and do not replace it. Let stand for just a few minutes until the chocolate has reached room temperature and is flexible but not wet or sticky. (Don't walk away and leave it until later; if it stands too long the curls might crack as you roll them.)

With a small, sharp knife and a ruler, trim one side of the chocolate square to make an even edge; remove excess. With the knife and the ruler, cut strips 1½ inches wide, parallel with the trimmed side. Then cut those strips into 2½-inch lengths.

Using the knife as a spatula, transfer one of the strips to the edge of your work surface (the edge closest to you). Now use the handle of a large wooden spoon — the handle must be round and should be about 3⁄8 to ½ inch in diameter. A smaller diameter will make a tighter, less dramatic curl.

continues ↘

Don't touch the chocolate any more than necessary or the heat of your hands may melt it. Place the end of the handle along the 1½-inch edge of the chocolate nearest you. With your fingers, start the curl by loosely curling the end of the chocolate over the handle. Then roll the handle toward the other end of the chocolate, rolling the chocolate as you do. Do not roll too tightly or the curl will not slide off the handle easily.

Carefully slide the curl off the handle and place it on wax paper, seam side down. Shape all of the curls.

Slide a cookie sheet under the wax paper, transfer to the freezer or refrigerator until firm, and then place the curls in a small freezer box. Store the curls in the refrigerator or freezer.

CHOCOLATE BAVARIAN

6 portions This is a classic French *Crème Bavaroise au Chocolat*. If you attend a class at the Cordon Bleu Cooking School in Paris, you might make it just this way. It is a creamy gelatin mixture, traditionally made in a mold and turned out before serving. It is best to make this early in the day for that night, but if it is well covered in the mold it may stand overnight. This recipe may be doubled for a larger mold.

You will need a 5- to 6-cup thin metal mold. It is best to use a very lightweight tin mold—the heavier the mold, the slower and more difficult it is to unmold. It may be a plain shape or it may have a design.

1 cup milk	¼ cup cold water	Pinch of salt
2 ounces unsweetened chocolate	4 large egg yolks	1 teaspoon vanilla extract
2 teaspoons unflavored gelatin	½ cup sugar	2 tablespoons dark rum
	2 teaspoons instant coffee powder	1 cup heavy cream

Place the milk in a small saucepan, uncovered, and place over moderate heat to warm slowly (it burns over high heat).

Meanwhile, place the chocolate in the top of a small double boiler, covered, over hot water on moderate heat. Heat only until the chocolate is melted, then uncover, remove from the hot water and set aside to cool.

Sprinkle the gelatin over the cold water in a small custard cup and let stand.

Place the egg yolks in the top of a large double boiler off the heat. Add the sugar and beat with a handheld electric mixer or stir briskly with a small wire whisk for a minute or two, until the mixture lightens a bit in color and is smooth and creamy.

When a slightly wrinkled skin forms on top of the milk, add the milk gradually, very little at a time at first, to the egg-yolk mixture, beating or whisking as you add to keep the mixture smooth.

Pour hot (not boiling) water into the bottom of the double boiler and put the top, with the custard mixture, over it. Add the instant coffee and stir to dissolve. Cook, scraping the sides and bottom with a rubber spatula, for about 8 minutes, until the mixture thickens enough to coat a metal spoon (a candy thermometer will register about 175 degrees).

Remove the top of the double boiler, add the softened gelatin, and stir to dissolve. Then add the melted chocolate and stir to mix. Stir in the salt, vanilla, and rum. The chocolate will have a slightly speckled appearance. Beat briskly with an egg beater or an electric mixer until very smooth.

Set the chocolate mixture aside for a moment. Whip the heavy cream only until it holds a semi-firm shape—not until it is

continues ⌄

stiff. (If it is stiff it will make the Bavarian heavy.)

Now, put some ice and water in a large mixing bowl. Place the saucepan with the chocolate mixture into the ice water and scrape the bottom and sides constantly with a rubber spatula until the mixture is completely cool and starts to thicken slightly to the consistency of a heavy cream sauce. (It is best if the chocolate mixture and the whipped cream are the same consistency.) Remove the pot from the ice water. If necessary, beat again briskly with an egg beater or electric mixer until very smooth, and then quickly and carefully fold the chocolate all at once into the whipped cream. Fold only until thoroughly blended. If necessary, pour back and forth gently from one bowl to another to ensure thorough blending.

Quickly rinse a 5- to 6-cup thin metal mold with ice water, pour out the water but do not dry the mold. Pour the Bavarian into the wet mold — do not fill it all the way to the top or it will be difficult to dip into hot water to unmold. Refrigerate for about 3 hours (a larger mold may take a little longer). When the top is firm, cover it airtight with plastic wrap.

This may be unmolded a few hours before serving. Fill a large bowl or dishpan with hot (not boiling) water. With a small, sharp knife, cut about ½ inch deep around the upper edge of the mold to release. Dip the mold for 10 seconds (no longer) into the hot water. Remove it, dry quickly, cover with a chilled dessert platter, and invert. If the Bavarian does not slip out easily, dip it again as necessary but for only a few seconds at a time — a heavy mold will take longer to release than a thin one.

Refrigerate.

SERVING SUGGESTIONS

This beautiful unmolded dessert does not need any decoration — but it lends itself to whatever you want. Try a border of small whipped cream rosettes, each one topped with a chocolate coffee bean candy. Or surround it with any brandied fruit and serve soft whipped cream on the side.

4-STAR FRENCH CHOCOLATE ICE CREAM

About 3½ quarts This is luxuriously and extravagantly smooth, creamy, and rich. It is French ice cream times ten. It must be made in an ice cream maker. If you have never made real ice cream in an ice cream maker, you are in for an exciting good time and a delicious treat. If you don't have one, beg, borrow, buy, or steal one to make this great ice cream. You will need a 4-quart machine to make the full recipe, but it may be divided to make half (see Notes). (It is no more work to make the full amount; if you have a large enough ice cream maker, make it all — you will be glad you did.)

Like all homemade ice creams, this is at its best a few hours after it is made, or just as soon as it becomes firm. It will keep well for a few weeks, but it doesn't keep as long as commercial ice cream; there are no preservatives in this.

NOTES

You can use any semisweet chocolate in this recipe. If you use a bar chocolate, break it up; if you use 1-ounce squares, they may be chopped coarsely or left whole.

If you divide the recipe to make only half, the syrup will be too shallow to test with a thermometer — just time it; this smaller amount will need only 3 minutes of boiling. And for this smaller amount of ice cream, it will not be necessary to transfer the mixture to a larger bowl — it can all be mixed in the small bowl of the electric mixer.

- 7 cups heavy cream
- 12 ounces semisweet chocolate (see Notes), coarsely chopped or broken up
- 2 ounces unsweetened chocolate (see Notes), coarsely chopped or broken up
- 1 cup sugar
- ½ cup water
- Pinch of salt
- 6 large to jumbo egg yolks
- 2 teaspoons vanilla extract

Place 2 cups of the cream (reserve 5 cups) in a 6- to 8-cup heavy saucepan. Add both chocolates, place over low heat, and stir occasionally until the chocolate is melted.

Remove from the heat and beat briefly with a wire whisk, an electric mixer, or an egg beater until smooth. Set aside.

Place the sugar and water in a very small saucepan over moderate heat. Stir with a wooden spatula until the sugar is dissolved and the syrup becomes clear and comes to a boil. Wash down the sides with a brush dipped in cold water to remove any undissolved granules. Increase the heat to high and let boil without stirring for 5 minutes — a candy thermometer should reach 230 degrees.

continues ⌄

Meanwhile, in the small bowl of an electric mixer, add the salt to the yolks and beat for about a minute.

When the syrup is ready, add it gradually — in a thin stream — to the yolks, beating at high speed. Then continue to beat for several minutes until the mixture is pale and thick and forms a ribbon when the beaters are raised.

Transfer the mixture to the large bowl of the electric mixer. On low speed, add the warm chocolate cream and beat only until mixed, scraping the bowl frequently with a rubber spatula.

Add the vanilla; on low speed, add the reserved 5 cups of cold cream, scraping the sides and bottom of the bowl as you add the cream to keep the mixture smooth.

You may pour the mixture into an ice cream maker now and freeze it, or refrigerate it for several hours or overnight (it will become very thick) before freezing. Carefully follow the freezing directions for your machine. If your ice cream maker calls for rock salt, use a little less than usual. Otherwise the ice cream will harden too quickly; it is best if it hardens slowly.

Check the ice cream before serving; if it is too firm, place it in the refrigerator for 15 to 30 minutes or longer if necessary. To serve, scoop or spoon into chilled dessert cups or bowls.

VARIATIONS

This is perfect as it is; however, it lends itself to many variations. For a mocha flavor, add instant coffee to the hot cream. For a liquor flavor, add rum, bourbon, Cognac, Amaretto, Grand Marnier, Tia Maria, Kahlúa, crème de menthe, etc., to the cooled mixture before churning it.

Or add nuts to the churned ice cream when you remove the dasher; stir them in thoroughly. (Toasted whole unblanched almonds are delicious.) Ground toasted blanched hazelnuts may be added before or after it is churned.

To make **Rum-Raisin Chocolate Ice Cream,** place about 1 cup of raisins in a jar, add about ½ cup dark rum, cover with a tight lid, and let stand for a few days, turning the jar occasionally to keep all the raisins wet, or marinate in a closed plastic bag. Stir raisins and any un-absorbed rum into the ice cream after churning. Or do the same thing with chopped dates, using rum or brandy. For **Chocolate Chip– Chocolate Ice Cream,** finely chop (do not grind or grate) about 4 ounces of additional semisweet chocolate and stir it into the ice cream after it is churned. If you feel really exotic, use a liquor and nuts and chopped chocolate. Et cetera.

CHOCOLATE-CHIP-COGNAC-COFFEE ICE CREAM

NOTE

Rita said that Sam said the ice cream must be Häagen-Dazs. I can buy that brand easily so that is what I have been using. If you have trouble buying it, please use whatever good coffee ice cream you can get.

1 quart I got this recipe from Rita Leinwand, food editor of *Bon Appétit,* when she came to our home for lunch. She told me that she got it from Sam Aaron, wine connoisseur, writer, and owner of the Sherry-Lehmann Wine & Spirits store in New York City. Now you've got it. It is FAN-TAS-TIC!!! Thank you, Rita. Thank you, Sam.

2 ounces semisweet chocolate

1 quart coffee ice cream (see Note)

2 teaspoons dry powdered (not granular) instant espresso

4 ounces (½ cup) Cognac

On a board, with a large, heavy knife, chop the chocolate into fine pieces. The pieces do not all have to be the same size, some may be a little larger or smaller.

The rest of the instructions for this recipe are to simply mix all the ingredients.

It is necessary to soften the ice cream slightly, but no more than necessary — *do not allow it to melt!* (When ice cream is churned it absorbs a certain amount of air which makes it light and creamy. If you allow it to melt it will lose that air.)

Place the ice cream in the refrigerator for 15 or 20 minutes, just until it can be stirred. Or cut the firm ice cream into pieces and, very briefly, mix it in an electric mixer or process it in a food processor. Quickly stir in the chocolate, espresso, and Cognac and refreeze immediately.

FROZEN CHOCOLATE MOUSSE

NOTE
↓
In the interest of safety, use only the best-quality eggs and wash and thoroughly dry them before using.

12 to 16 portions My friend Joan Borinstein, of Los Angeles, is a prizewinning chocolate dessert-maker and a full-fledged chocolate dessert addict who once fulfilled a lifelong dream fantasy: She gave a New Year's Eve dessert-and-champagne party for which she prepared seventy-two desserts for one hundred guests. Her apartment that night was wall-to-wall desserts. This is Joan's smooth and creamy chocolate mousse (it tastes like ice cream) set in a chocolate-cookie crumb crust. It is a beautiful and delicious creation for an important occasion. It may be made up to two weeks before serving.

CRUST

- 8 ounces chocolate wafer cookies (The store-bought ones are sometimes called icebox wafers. Better yet, make your own Chocolate Wafers, page 151.)
- 3 ounces (¾ stick) unsalted butter

CHOCOLATE MOUSSE

- 1 tablespoon instant coffee powder
- ½ cup boiling water
- 1¼ cups granulated sugar
- 12 ounces semisweet chocolate: 12 (1-ounce) squares, coarsely chopped, or 3 (4-ounce) bars, coarsely chopped, or 2 cups morsels
- 4 large eggs (see Note), separated
- 3 cups heavy cream

  Pinch of salt
- ⅛ teaspoon cream of tartar

Adjust rack one-third up from the bottom of the oven and preheat oven to 375 degrees. Separate the bottom from the sides of a 9 x 3-inch springform pan; butter the sides only (if you butter the bottom the crust will stick to the bottom and it will be difficult to serve), and then replace the bottom in the pan and set aside.

For the Crust

Crumble the cookies coarsely and place them in a food processor or a blender and make fine crumbs (or place them in a plastic bag and pound and roll them with a rolling pin); you should have 2 cups of crumbs. Place them in a mixing bowl. Melt the butter and stir it into the crumbs until thoroughly distributed.

Pour about two-thirds of the mixture into the prepared pan. To form a thin layer of crumbs on the sides of the pan: Tilt the pan at about a 45-degree angle and, with your fingertips, press a layer of the crumbs against the sides, pressing from the bottom up toward the top of the pan and rotating the pan gradually as you press on the crumbs — they should reach the top of the pan all the way around. Then place the pan upright on its bottom; pour in the remaining crumbs and, with your fingertips, distribute them over the bottom of the pan to cover it. Press them firmly to make a compact layer.

Bake for 7 to 8 minutes, remove from the oven, and cool completely.

For the Mousse

Dissolve the coffee in the water in a heavy 2-quart saucepan. Add ½ cup of the sugar (reserve ¾ cup) and stir over moderate heat to dissolve. Adjust the heat to low, add the chocolate, and stir until it is melted and smooth. Remove from the heat and let stand for a few minutes to cool slightly. Add the egg yolks one at a time, stirring them in with a wire whisk. Set aside to cool completely.

In the large bowl of an electric mixer, whip the cream until it holds a shape but not until it is really stiff. Set it aside.

In the small bowl of an electric mixer with clean beaters, beat the egg whites until they are foamy. Add the salt and the cream of tartar and continue to beat until the whites hold a soft shape. Reduce the speed to moderate and gradually add the reserved ¾ cup sugar, one large spoonful at a time. Beat briefly between additions. Then increase the speed to high again and beat for a few minutes until the meringue is quite firm, but not stiff or dry.

Gradually, in two or three additions, fold most of the chocolate into the whites and then fold the whites into the remaining chocolate.

In a very large mixing bowl, fold together the whipped cream and the chocolate mixture.

Pour into the chocolate-cookie crumb crust, smooth the top or form a swirling pattern, and place in the freezer. After about an hour or so, cover the top airtight with plastic wrap. Freeze overnight or for up to 2 weeks.

The mousse may be removed from the pan just before serving or days before. With a firm, sharp, heavy knife, cut around the sides of the crust, pressing the blade firmly against the pan as you cut. Then release and remove the sides of the pan. Now, use a firm (not flexible) metal spatula (either a wide one or a long narrow one): Insert the spatula gently and carefully under the crust and ease it around to release the dessert completely from the bottom of the pan. The dessert will be firm and sturdy and easy to transfer. If you are serving it soon, place it on a large, flat dessert platter; if you are going to store it again in the freezer, place it on a large piece of plastic wrap and wrap airtight. In either case, return it to the freezer until serving time. It does not freeze too firm, and will cut beautifully and easily. Use a sharp, heavy knife.

OPTIONAL DECORATIONS

Just before serving, cover the top of the mousse with whipped cream and/or a generous layer of chocolate shavings and surround the whole dessert with a generous ring of large Chocolate-Covered Strawberries (page 281). When Joan made

continues ⌐

this for me and my husband, she made some beautiful chocolate leaves for decoration, some with dark chocolate, some with lighter milk chocolate, and some with white chocolate, and alternated them on top—it was gorgeous.

Or you can serve the mousse as is, and pass softly whipped cream as a sauce. Or serve it without whipped cream—it is wonderful just by itself.

VARIATION

Frozen White Chocolate Mousse: With the dark chocolate crumb crust, creamy white mousse filling, dark chocolate leaves, and red and green strawberries it makes a fabulous picture. And with or without the leaves and berries, it is a sensational dessert. Make the following changes in the Frozen Chocolate Mousse recipe:

1. Omit the instant coffee.

2. Do not add the ½ cup sugar to the water at the beginning. (Use only the ¾ cup that is added to the egg whites—therefore, use only a total ¾ cup instead of 1¼ cups.)

3. Use 12 ounces white chocolate instead of semisweet chocolate.

4. After melting the chocolate in the water, beat it with an electric mixer until smooth.

5. Add 2 tablespoons of white or natural crème de cacao to the cooled melted chocolate and egg-yolk mixture.

COLD CHOCOLATE SOUFFLÉ

8 portions This is an incredibly light and airy gelatin dessert made in a soufflé dish and extending generously above the top of the dish. It is especially dramatic in a clear glass dish, but is equally delicious and attractive in a classic white china soufflé dish. It may be made early in the day for that night, or the day before.

NOTES

In the interest of safety, use only the best-quality eggs and wash and thoroughly dry them before using.

The effect will not be so dramatic, but this may also be prepared in any serving bowl or in individual wineglasses or dessert bowls.

- ⅓ cup cold water
- 1 tablespoon (1 envelope) unflavored gelatin
- 1 teaspoon instant coffee powder
- ⅓ cup boiling water
- 1 cup milk
- 1 ounce semisweet chocolate
- 4 ounces unsweetened chocolate

- 5 extra-large or jumbo eggs or 6 medium or large eggs (see Notes), separated
- 1 cup granulated sugar
- 1 tablespoon vanilla extract
- Generous pinch of salt
- OPTIONAL: 1 ounce semisweet chocolate (for sprinkling on top)

WHIPPED CREAM

- 2 cups heavy cream
- ⅓ cup strained confectioners' sugar
- 1 teaspoon vanilla extract

First, prepare a straight-sided soufflé dish. For the soufflé to rise 1½ inches over the top, the dish should not have more than a 5-cup capacity. (My glass one measures 6 inches in diameter and 3 inches in depth. The closest white china soufflé dish measures 6½ [across the top] x 3 inches — and it works fine.) Prepare an aluminum foil collar: Tear off a piece of foil large enough to wrap around the dish and overlap a few inches. Fold it in half the long way. With a paper towel, brush vegetable oil over half of one of the long sides, brushing it along the half that has two open sides, not the folded edge. Wrap the foil tightly around the dish, oiled side to the top and inside. Fasten tightly with a string. Set aside.

Place the cold water in a small bowl or a cup with at least 1-cup capacity. Sprinkle the gelatin over the top and let stand for 5 minutes. Then dissolve the coffee in the boiling water, quickly add it to the gelatin, and stir to dissolve. Set aside.

Place the milk and both chocolates in the top of a small double boiler over hot water on moderate heat. Stir occasionally with a small wire whisk until the chocolate is melted and the mixture is smooth. Remove the top of the double boiler and set it aside.

continues ↘

In the small bowl of an electric mixer, beat the egg yolks with ½ cup of the granulated sugar (reserve remaining ½ cup). Beat for a few minutes at high speed until the mixture is creamy and pale-colored. Beat in the vanilla and then, on low speed, gradually add the warm chocolate mixture, scraping the bowl with a rubber spatula and beating until smooth. Gradually beat in the dissolved gelatin. Transfer to a medium-size mixing bowl (preferably metal) and set aside.

Prepare a large mixing bowl partly filled with ice and cold water and have it ready.

In the large bowl of the electric mixer (with clean beaters), beat the whites and the salt until the mixture increases in volume and starts to thicken. Gradually, while beating on moderate speed, add the reserved ½ cup granulated sugar. Then increase the speed to high and beat only until the mixture holds a soft peak — one that bends over slightly when the mixture is lifted with a rubber spatula. (If the whites are beaten until stiff or dry, it will be impossible to fold the chocolate into them without losing most of the air that has been beaten in.) Remove from the mixer and set aside.

Place the bowl of chocolate mixture in the ice and water and stir frequently until the mixture thickens to the consistency of a medium cream sauce. (This is an important step; if the chocolate mixture is too thin when it is folded into the whites, the chocolate will sink to the bottom — if it is too thick, it will become lumpy and the mixture will not be smooth. So pay close attention to it. Stir constantly after it starts to thicken slightly. It might take about 10

minutes, or a bit more. Actually, the chocolate mixture and the beaten whites should be of the same consistency — or as close as possible — for easy folding.)

Just as soon as the chocolate is ready, remove it from the ice water and fold a few large spoonfuls into the beaten whites. Repeat two or three times, folding in about three-fourths of the chocolate. Then fold the whites into the remaining chocolate. If necessary, pour gently back and forth from one bowl to another to ensure thorough blending.

Gently pour the soufflé into the prepared dish and place it in the refrigerator. To keep the air out, place a piece of plastic wrap over the top, letting it rest on the foil collar, not touching the soufflé. Let stand for 8 to 10 hours or overnight.

If you like, finely grate 1 ounce of semisweet chocolate and sprinkle it over the soufflé before removing the collar.

Do not remove the collar until shortly before serving. Peel it off very gently or, if it sticks, cut between the soufflé and the collar with a small, sharp knife. Wipe the sides of the soufflé dish and place it on a folded napkin on a flat plate.

For the Whipped Cream

Beat the cream, confectioners' sugar, and vanilla to make soft whipped cream and serve a large spoonful over each portion. (If the cream is whipped ahead of time it may separate slightly; if so, just stir it a bit to blend before serving.)

GLACÉ AU CHOCOLAT

1 scant quart This is a French chocolate ice cream—extraordinarily and outrageously smooth, rich chocolate. It is prepared without an ice cream maker and is not stirred during the freezing—it will need several hours to freeze, then it can be served right away or kept frozen for days.

The flavor depends completely on your choice of chocolate, as there is no other flavoring. The recipe may be doubled.

6 ounces semisweet or
bittersweet chocolate

1½ cups heavy cream
3 large egg yolks

⅓ cup water
¼ cup sugar

Chop the chocolate into rather small pieces and set aside.

In a chilled bowl with chilled beaters, whip the cream only until it holds a soft shape—not until it is stiff—and let stand at room temperature. (It should not be too cold when it is folded into the chocolate.)

In the small bowl of an electric mixer, beat the egg yolks until they are light lemon-colored.

Meanwhile, stir the water and sugar together in a 4- to 6-cup saucepan over high heat until the sugar is dissolved and the mixture comes to a boil. Boil without stirring for 3 minutes (no longer or too much water will evaporate).

Add the chopped chocolate to the sugar syrup, remove from the heat, and stir until the chocolate is melted. It will be very thick.

Now, gradually, on low speed, add the hot chocolate mixture to the egg yolks and beat until very smooth. It will be thick. Remove from the mixer and stir occasionally until cooled to room temperature.

If the whipped cream has separated a little, stir or beat it a bit with a wire whisk only to make it smooth but not long enough to thicken it any more.

With a rubber spatula, stir a large spoonful of the whipped cream into the cooled chocolate. One at a time, stir in two or three more spoonfuls until the chocolate is smooth and about the same consistency as the whipped cream. Then add the chocolate to the remaining cream and fold together. If necessary, pour gently from one bowl to another to ensure thorough blending.

Pour the mixture into an ice-cube tray or an 8- or 9-inch metal loaf pan (or any covered container), cover tightly with aluminum foil, and freeze for a few hours until firm.

Serve like any ice cream, but this is richer, so make the portions small.

AMERICAN CHOCOLATE PUDDING

4 to 6 portions If you think it doesn't pay to bother making your own pudding when you can buy a box and just add some milk, then you have not tasted the real thing. This has considerably more chocolate than a mix (as well as more cocoa), less sugar, and egg yolks that make it custardy and give it body. It is dense, dark, not too sweet, smooth, semi-firm, rich; it is marvelous.

Using cornstarch correctly is a delicate art. Overcooking or overbeating — even the least little bit — can cause the cornstarch to break down and make the mixture too thin. (Although I have written these words dozens of times, it recently happened to me.) Be very careful.

The recipe may be doubled, if you wish. And it was written for good old-fashioned generous portions. But actually they should be smaller if it is to be served after a dinner. Try serving the pudding in wineglasses, with the pudding filling the glasses only halfway and the whipped cream filling the remaining space to the top.

1 large or extra-large egg plus 2 additional egg yolks

2 ounces unsweetened chocolate

3 ounces semisweet chocolate

2¼ cups milk

½ cup plus 1 tablespoon granulated sugar

Scant ⅛ teaspoon salt

2 tablespoons *unsifted* cornstarch

3 tablespoons *unsifted* unsweetened cocoa powder (preferably Dutch-process)

2 tablespoons unsalted butter, cut into small pieces

1 teaspoon vanilla extract

OPTIONAL: 1 tablespoon dark rum

WHIPPED CREAM

1 cup heavy cream

2 tablespoons confectioners' sugar

½ teaspoon vanilla extract

Have 10- or 12-ounce stemmed wineglasses or dessert bowls ready. Cut rounds of wax paper to place on top of the pudding, actually touching it when it is poured into the glasses or bowls. Set aside.

In a bowl, beat the egg and yolks to mix and set aside.

On a board, with a long, heavy knife, chop both chocolates (coarsely or finely — either is OK).

Place 2 cups of the milk (reserve the remaining ¼ cup) in a heavy saucepan with a 2- to 3-quart capacity. Add ¼ cup of the

continues ↘

sugar (reserve the remaining ¼ cup plus 1 tablespoon) and the chopped chocolate. Place over moderate heat and whisk frequently with a wire whisk until the milk just comes to a boil (flecks of chocolate will disappear by the time the milk boils).

Meanwhile, sift the remaining ¼ cup plus 1 tablespoon sugar, the salt, cornstarch, and cocoa into a mixing bowl. Add the reserved ¼ cup of milk and whisk with a small wire whisk until smooth.

When the milk comes to a boil, pour (or ladle) part of it into the cornstarch mixture, whisking as you pour.

Then add the cornstarch mixture to the remaining hot-milk mixture. Stir to mix. Place over moderate heat.

Now, use a rubber spatula and scrape the bottom and sides constantly until the mixture comes to a low boil. Reduce the heat a bit to medium–low and simmer gently, stirring and scraping the pan, for 2 minutes.

Add about 1 cup of the hot chocolate-milk mixture to the eggs and whisk or stir to mix. Then add the egg mixture to the remaining hot chocolate-milk mixture, stirring constantly.

Cook over low heat, scraping the pan with a rubber spatula, for 2 minutes. Be sure that you do not allow the mixture to come anywhere near the boiling stage after the eggs are added. Remove from the heat. Add the butter, vanilla, and the optional rum. Stir very gently until the butter is melted. Without waiting, pour into the wineglasses or dessert bowls. Cover immediately with the rounds of wax paper, placing the paper directly on the puddings (to prevent a skin from forming).

Let stand to cool to room temperature. Then refrigerate for at least a few hours.

For the Whipped Cream

In a chilled bowl, with chilled beaters, whip the cream with the sugar and vanilla until it holds a soft shape, not until it is really stiff. (The cream may be whipped ahead of time and refrigerated; if it separates slightly, whisk it a bit before using.) Shortly before serving, remove the paper rounds and spoon the cream on top of the puddings.

CHOCOLATE BREAD

1 large loaf This recipe is a bread and not a dessert, but it should not be left out of a book of chocolate desserts. It is a huge loaf that makes giant-size slices, light and airy in texture, dark as pumpernickel in color. It has a few raisins and nuts. Serve it lightly buttered, or use it for cream cheese or peanut butter and bacon sandwiches, or serve it at the table with honey butter (mix ½ cup of honey into 4 ounces of unsalted butter).

¼ cup warm water (105 degrees to 115 degrees)

1 tablespoon plus ½ cup sugar

1 tablespoon (1 envelope) active dry yeast

1 cup milk

2 tablespoons unsalted butter, cut into pieces

About 4 cups *unsifted* all-purpose flour or bread flour

1 teaspoon salt

⅔ cup unsweetened cocoa powder (preferably Dutch-process)

2 teaspoons instant coffee or espresso powder (not granular)

2 large eggs

1 teaspoon vanilla extract

4 ounces (generous 1 cup) walnuts, cut into ¼- to ⅓-inch pieces

2½ ounces (½ cup) dark raisins

Generously butter a large bowl to have ready for the dough to rise in. Butter an 8-cup loaf pan (mine is 9¼ x 5¼ x 2⅓ inches). Set the bowl and the pan aside.

Stir the water and 1 tablespoon of the sugar (reserve the remaining ½ cup) in a 1-cup glass measuring cup. Add the yeast, stir briefly with a knife, and set aside for about 10 minutes, until foamy.

Meanwhile, place the milk and butter in a small saucepan over moderate heat until warm (105 degrees to 115 degrees). It is not necessary for the butter to melt.

Place a scant 4 cups of flour, the salt, cocoa, coffee powder, and the remaining ½ cup of sugar in a large mixing bowl. Stir to mix.

Beat the eggs just to mix, and add them to the flour mixture along with the vanilla, warm milk and butter, and the foamy yeast

mixture. Add the walnuts and the raisins. Stir as well as you can with a long, heavy wooden spatula. (Or mix these ingredients in a large-size food processor, or in a mixer with a dough hook.)

Turn out onto a lightly floured board and knead for 5 or 6 minutes, until smooth and elastic. (If you have used a food processor or an electric mixer, a minute or two of kneading will probably be enough.) Add additional flour (very little at a time), if necessary, to make the dough manageable.

Place the dough in the large, well-buttered bowl, turn the dough to butter it on all sides; cover with plastic wrap, and let rise at a temperature of 80 degrees to 85 degrees, until the dough has doubled in volume — it will take 1¾ to 2 hours.

continues ↘

Make a fist, punch it into the dough, knead the dough three or four times, and turn the dough out onto a lightly floured board. Cover with plastic wrap and let stand for about 5 minutes.

To shape the dough, form it roughly into an oval and, with a rolling pin, roll it out into a large oval 8 or 9 inches across the narrow width. Then roll it up the way you would a jelly roll, rolling from one narrow end to the other narrow end, and place the loaf, seam side down, in the buttered pan.

Loosely cover the pan with a piece of buttered plastic wrap, buttered side down. Let rise again until doubled in size — it will take 1¼ to 1½ hours.

Before the dough has finished rising, adjust a rack one-third up from the bottom of the oven and preheat the oven to 350 degrees.

Bake the loaf for 20 to 30 minutes, then cover the top loosely with foil to prevent overbrowning. Continue to bake for 30 to 40 minutes (total baking time is about 60 minutes).

Let the loaf cool in the pan for 5 to 10 minutes and then lift it gently with pot holders to remove it from the pan and place on a rack to cool.

CANDY, FUDGE, AND CHOCOLATE DRINKS

THE WORLD'S BEST HOT FUDGE SAUCE

1 cup This is very thick, coal black, as shiny as wet tar, and not too sweet. It will turn chewy and even thicker when it is served over cold ice cream — great! It may be served hot or warm, but at room temperature or chilled it will be too thick. It may be refrigerated for a week or two before serving.

½ cup heavy cream

3 tablespoons unsalted butter, cut into small pieces

⅓ cup granulated sugar

⅓ cup firmly packed dark brown sugar

Pinch of salt

½ cup strained unsweetened Dutch-process cocoa powder (it must be Dutch-process to have the right color and flavor)

NOTE

⬇

If you plan to store the sauce in the refrigerator, use a straight-sided glass jar or any covered container that flares out at the top. The sauce will become too firm when it is chilled to be spooned out of a jar. It is best to place the jar in hot water until the block of sauce melts on the outside and can be poured out of the jar. Then place the sauce in the top of a small double boiler over hot water, or in a small heavy saucepan over the lowest heat. With a wooden spatula, cut the sauce into pieces as you stir until completely melted.

Place the cream and butter in a heavy 1-quart saucepan over moderate heat. Stir until the butter is melted and the cream just comes to a low boil. Add both sugars and stir for a few minutes until they are dissolved. (The surest test is to taste; cook and taste until you do not feel any undissolved granules in your mouth.)

Reduce the heat. Add the salt and cocoa and stir briskly with a small wire whisk until smooth. (If the sauce is not smooth — if there are any small lumps of undissolved cocoa — press against them and stir well with a rubber spatula.) Remove from the heat.

Serve immediately or reheat slowly, stirring frequently, in the top of a double boiler over hot water, or in a heavy saucepan over the lowest heat.

This should be thick, but if it is reheated it may be too thick. If so, stir in a bit of hot water, adding very little at a time.

MILK-CHOCOLATE-WITH-ALMONDS-BAR SAUCE

1 cup Everyone loves this — be prepared with enough. One cup should be enough for four portions if it is served over ice cream, but I have seen times when 2 cups was not too much.

Yes, it is as easy as it sounds.

8 ounces milk chocolate bars with almonds (see Note)

¼ cup boiling water

Break up the chocolate and place it in the top of a small double boiler.

Milk chocolate must be melted very slowly or it may become lumpy, so place the top of the double boiler over *warm* water on *low* heat. Cover and let stand until melted. Milk chocolate holds its shape when melted — the only way you will know it is melted is by stirring it; stir with a rubber spatula.

When the chocolate is melted, add the boiling water all at once and continue to stir with a rubber spatula until the chocolate and water are smoothly blended.

Serve right away, or keep warm over warm water, or let cool and serve at room temperature, or reheat slowly over warm water.

If the sauce thickens too much while standing, stir in a few drops of water. (The thought that a chocolate sauce could be too thick reminds me of an old saying that Grandma Heatter used when someone complained about something that was too good: She would say, "The bride was too beautiful.")

This is especially popular served slightly warm over vanilla and/or coffee ice cream. Or anything.

NOTE

I use Hershey's Milk Chocolate with Almonds, but I don't see any reason you couldn't use any milk chocolate with nuts. Hershey also makes a super chocolate called Golden Almond bar. It is fabulous! Probably the best candy bar I have ever eaten. It has many more nuts than the regular bar, in fact it actually has equal amounts of chocolate and toasted almonds. It is divine for this sauce — or for whatever. Until recently it could not be bought outside of Hershey, Pennsylvania. Now it is available in finer stores throughout the country or online.

BASIC CHOCOLATE SAUCE (AND 8 VARIATIONS)

`2 cups` **This will not harden over cold ice cream — it will remain saucy. It may be kept for many weeks in the refrigerator.**

4 ounces unsweetened chocolate

1 cup sugar

⅛ teaspoon salt

1 tablespoon butter

1 cup light cream

½ teaspoon vanilla extract

Chop the chocolate coarsely and place it over the lowest possible heat in a heavy saucepan with a 4- to 6-cup capacity. (Remember that chocolate burns easily. If you don't have a really heavy pan, do this step in a double boiler, in which case the chocolate does not have to be chopped.) Stir frequently until the chocolate is melted. Stir in the sugar, salt, and butter and then gradually add the cream, stirring until smooth. (If you have used a double boiler, remove the bottom now and place the top over direct heat.)

Increase the heat slightly to low-medium and stir constantly for 4 or 5 minutes, until the sauce thickens slightly. Do not boil.

Remove from the heat and stir in the vanilla.

Serve this either warm or at room temperature — it may be kept warm in the top of a double boiler over hot water. If it is too stiff at room temperature, either warm it slightly or stir in a bit of cream, milk, coffee, or water. To reheat after refrigerating, stir it in the top of a double boiler over hot water.

Variations

LIQUOR CHOCOLATE SAUCE:

Add a spoon or two or more of any liquor or liqueur to the finished sauce. Rum, Cognac, and whiskey are the most common additions. Bourbon is good. Grand Marnier is good. Crème de menthe or crème de cacao or crème d'almond are all good. Amaretto is sensational with chocolate. Whichever you choose, add it slowly, tasting often.

MARMALADE CHOCOLATE SAUCE:

Melt ¼ to ½ cup orange marmalade. Add it to the sauce and, if you like, add a dash of Grand Marnier or Curaçao.

continues ⌄

MINT CHOCOLATE SAUCE:

Along with the vanilla, add a few drops of peppermint extract. Add very little at a time, taste it often and carefully, and make it as minty as you like.

CARAMEL CHOCOLATE SAUCE:

Use semisweet chocolate instead of unsweetened, and firmly packed dark or light brown sugar instead of granulated.

NUT CHOCOLATE SAUCE:

Add about ⅓ cup coarsely cut or broken walnuts or pecans, or whole unblanched almonds. Or toasted whole blanched or unblanched almonds. (To toast the almonds, place them in a small, shallow tin in the middle of a 350-degree oven. Shake the pan occasionally until the nuts are lightly toasted, about 10 minutes.)

MOCHA SAUCE:

Add 1 to 2 teaspoons instant coffee or espresso powder while stirring the hot sauce.

EXTRA-BITTERSWEET CHOCOLATE SAUCE:

This is strong, dense, thick, and *really* bittersweet. Use only ½ cup sugar instead of 1 cup. (That will reduce the yield to 1⅔ cups.) Since this is so dense, it should be served in small quantities.

BLACK FOREST SAUCE:

Chocolate, cherries, and kirsch are a magnificent combination. Use any kind of canned or frozen pitted cherries, well drained. Or use fresh ones if you have a cherry pitter. Add the cherries and kirsch, to your taste, to the basic sauce.

CHOCOLATE RAISIN CLUSTERS

1 pound These are so easy it is ridiculous. But they are delicious. You can make them in five minutes (so can a five-year-old), but they must harden for a few hours before serving.

8 ounces (two 4-ounce bars) Baker's German's Sweet Chocolate or semisweet chocolate (the clusters will have a less sweet flavor if you do not use German's chocolate)

⅔ cup sweetened condensed milk (see Note)

5 ounces (1 cup) raisins

NOTE

⤓

Condensed milk that stands on the shelf for a long time becomes very thick. If the milk you use is very thick, it is better to measure it in the metal measuring cups for measuring flour than in the glass cup for liquid.

Break up the chocolate and place it in the top of a double boiler over hot water on moderate heat. Stir occasionally until melted and smooth. Remove the top of the double boiler. Add the condensed milk and stir until smooth, then stir in the raisins.

Use a rounded spoonful of the mixture for each cluster, forming 24 clusters and placing them on a piece of aluminum foil.

Let stand at room temperature for about 3 hours or until they are firm. Then release each cluster and turn it over to let the bottom dry; they will dry quickly.

Store airtight. Do not let these dry out. They may be frozen. (If you freeze them, be sure to let them thaw before unwrapping or they will sweat.)

ROCKY ROADS

1⅓ pounds This is a quick, easy, and foolproof candy.

| 1 pound milk chocolate | 12 large-size (regular) marshmallows | 6 ounces (1½ cups) pecan halves or large pieces |

Prepare an 8-inch square cake pan as follows: Invert the pan and cover it with a 12-inch square of aluminum foil. Fold down the sides and corners of the foil. Remove the foil, turn the pan right side up, put the shaped foil in the pan, and gently press it into place.

Cut or break the chocolate into coarse pieces and place it in the top of a double boiler over warm water on low heat. (Milk chocolate must be melted very slowly, the slower the better — it should not ever get really hot.) Cover until partially melted.

Meanwhile, cut the marshmallows into quarters. (Some people use scissors; if they stick to the marshmallows, moisten them slightly in cold water.) Set the marshmallows aside.

Uncover the chocolate and stir until completely melted and smooth. Pour about half of the chocolate into the foil-lined pan and spread it to cover the bottom of the pan; it will be a thin layer. Sprinkle with about half of the nuts and then place the marshmallow pieces evenly over all. Stir the remaining chocolate well and drizzle it over the top. It will not cover the top completely but it should be drizzled on so that it holds the nuts and marshmallows in place. Now top with the remaining nuts.

Refrigerate until firm. Remove from the pan and peel off the foil. With a long, thin, sharp knife, cut the candy into 16 or 24 large squares. Wrap them individually in cellophane or wax paper. Or wrap the whole block securely in plastic wrap or aluminum foil and do not cut into squares until serving time. Or gift-wrap the whole block in one piece.

This should be stored in the refrigerator to keep the chocolate fresh-looking and to avoid any discoloring (it will keep for weeks). I think it is best to remove it from the refrigerator for a while before serving so the chocolate is not too brittle, but that is a matter of taste.

VARIATIONS

You can substitute 1⅔ cups miniature marshmallows for the cut-up marshmallows.

Walnuts or cashews are frequently substituted for pecans. And whole dried apricot halves (unchopped) or dried pitted prunes (unchopped) are often used in place of the nuts. I think any dried or candied fruits would be good either in place of or along with the nuts.

FUDGE

1¼ pounds One day recently in Palm Springs, California, I spotted a most attractive shop that sold only homemade fudge. The decor was all blue and white and in the window there was a huge shiny copper cauldron full of boiling fudge. I watched a man make the fudge right there in the window. It was a treat and I was so excited I could hardly wait for him to finish before I asked, "What causes fudge to be grainy?" He answered, "Cooking." So I said, "What do you mean?" And he said, "You either cooked it too long or not long enough or you cooked it too fast or too slowly. Or you didn't dissolve the sugar. Or it could be the weather."

"Thanks, Mister."

When I decided to write a fudge recipe, I called on my friend Virginia Heffington, then food editor of the *Independent Press-Telegram* in Long Beach, California. I was thrilled to hear that fudge was one of her favorites; she has made it since she was a child in Iowa, and she calls herself "the fudge lady." She was quite casual about saying that it is not difficult if you follow the rules. Here is Virginia's favorite recipe.

It begins with an emphatic warning: "CAUTION: Humidity causes fudge disasters. Pick a dry day!!!"

It is safer to make a small amount of fudge at a time. Unless you are an experienced fudge-maker, do not increase the recipe. But if you are, and if you do, increase it only by half. (In which case, cook it in a 3½- to 4-quart saucepan.)

Use a candy thermometer.

2 cups sugar

½ cup strained unsweetened cocoa powder (preferably Dutch-process)

⅛ teaspoon salt

⅔ cup heavy cream

2 tablespoons light corn syrup

2 tablespoons unsalted butter

1 teaspoon vanilla extract

2 ounces (generous ½ cup) walnuts, cut or broken into medium-size pieces

Generously butter the sides of a 2½- to 3-quart saucepan. Mix the sugar, cocoa, salt, cream, and corn syrup in the pan. Stir over moderate heat (stirring slowly and carefully to avoid splashing the mixture on the sides of the pan) until the sugar is dissolved and the mixture comes to a boil. Cover the saucepan for 2 or 3 minutes. (Covering the pan causes steam to form, which dissolves any sugar granules that may cling to the sides — one grain of sugar can start a chain reaction and turn the whole thing granular. And the buttered pan helps; incidentally, it also keeps the fudge from boiling over. If the pan has a spout and is therefore not airtight when you cover it, carefully hold a pot holder over the opening.)

Now uncover and place a candy thermometer in the pan. Boil without stirring until the thermometer reaches 236 degrees or the soft ball stage. (Professionals advise 234 to 236 degrees during cold weather; 236 to 238 degrees during warm weather.)

It is important now not to stir, mix, shake, or disturb the mixture. Very carefully and gently remove the saucepan from the heat. Do not remove the thermometer. Add the butter by simply placing it in the pan and letting it melt; do not stir it.

Let stand until the temperature drops to 110 degrees.

While the fudge is cooling, prepare a pan for it. I like to use a small loaf pan, which makes a 1¼-inch-thick layer of fudge. Mine is called an 8 x 4-inch pan, which measures 7 x 3½ inches on the bottom of the pan. If you use a larger pan, the fudge will be just as good but not as thick. Fold two pieces of aluminum foil to fit the loaf pan, one for the length and one for the width. Press them into place in the pan.

When the fudge has cooled to 110 degrees (at that temperature, the bottom of the saucepan will feel comfortably warm on the palm of your hand), remove the thermometer. Add the vanilla. Now, to beat the fudge, use a moderately heavy wooden spatula or wooden spoon. Virginia's system, which works very comfortably, is to sit and grip the pan between your knees, leaving both hands free to grapple with the spatula. First stir gently to incorporate the melted butter. Then start to stir steadily or to beat, and once you do, do not stop until the fudge is finished.

I think that knowing just how long to beat, and just when to pour, are the most important things in this recipe. And the most difficult to describe. To quote Virginia, "When the candy stiffens and loses its shine you are on borrowed time." But I think that if you beat until it is stiff or dull, it is too late. Beat until the fudge becomes very thick, or falls in thick gobs, or is thick enough almost to hold its shape when a little is dropped from the spatula. At this stage it should barely begin to lose its shine, but only barely. It should still be slightly glossy.

FIRST AID

If your fudge turned to sugar, or stiffened in the saucepan, or crumbled when you cut portions, you beat too long. Add 2 tablespoons cream and stir over very low heat (cutting up the fudge with the wooden spatula while you stir). Cook and stir only until warm and slightly softened but not until it is hot or thin. Remove from the heat, beat again until smooth and thick, and then turn it out of the saucepan again.

If you have fudge that didn't set, you didn't cook it long enough or you poured it too soon. If you think that you did not cook it long enough, add ¼ cup of milk or cream, then cook and stir constantly until it reaches 236 degrees again. Cool as above, and beat again.

But if you think that you cooked it enough and simply poured it too soon, transfer the mixture to a marble, tile, or Formica countertop. Then squeeze it and knead it as though it were bread dough until it is firm enough to hold a shape. Then roll it into a sausage shape, or form it into a square about 1 inch thick. Let stand for just a few moments and then slice the sausage shape or cut the square into portions.

continues ⌄

Quickly stir in the nuts and quickly, with the spatula, push the mixture into the lined pan. It will be too thick to pour. And Virginia says that you should not scrape the pan too well; scraping encourages grainy fudge. Quickly push the fudge into a smooth layer in the pan; it may be easiest to use your fingertips or your knuckles.

The fudge may be ready almost immediately (even while it is still slightly warm) to be cut into individual portions. As soon as it feels firm, but before it hardens, remove it from the pan by lifting the foil and, with a long, sharp knife, cut the fudge into portions. I like to make 12 large squares, but you can make 24 or more.

Do not let the fudge dry out. Immediately wrap the squares individually in cellophane or wax paper. Or package them in an airtight box.

Fudge is best the day it is made, but it will keep for a few days at room temperature if it is well wrapped. For longer storage, freeze it. It can be frozen for months.

VARIATIONS

Fudge may be varied in many ways. When the nuts are added you can also add ½ to 1 cup of raisins, cut-up dates, candied cherries, diced candied pineapple, diced candied ginger, or minced candied orange peel. Raisins or dates may be marinated in a bit of rum or bourbon. The nuts can be left out, or you can use any other kind of nuts (if you use almonds, they are best if lightly baked), or a variety, or sunflower or pumpkin seeds. A spoon or two of liquor or liqueur can be added along with the vanilla. (A friend makes it with Grand Marnier and candied orange peel.) Rocky Road Fudge has about a cup of miniature marshmallows mixed in with the nuts. Rum Raisin Fudge has 2 tablespoons of dark rum in place of the vanilla and about ½ cup of raisins in place of the nuts (marinate the raisins in the rum for a few hours or overnight). Apricot Fudge is made with whole dried apricot halves, and then there is prune and apricot.

EVERYBODY'S FAVORITE FUDGE

NOTE

↓

To toast pecans, place them in a shallow pan in the middle of a preheated 350-degree oven for 12 to 15 minutes.

A bit more than 2½ pounds — 24 large pieces My recipe for Fudge (page 272) is a classic, traditional fudge which, frankly, is temperamental and tricky to make. Since I first published that recipe, I continued to receive other fudge recipes from readers, recipes that are foolproof. They are all variations on a theme that includes evaporated milk, marshmallow, and chocolate morsels. This is the one that seemed to be everybody's favorite. It is never too soft to eat or too hard to handle or too sugary; always smooth and creamy.

OPTIONAL: 7 ounces (2 cups) pecans, toasted (see Note), or walnut halves or pieces

⅔ cup evaporated milk

1 (7-ounce) jar marshmallow cream

2 ounces (½ stick) unsalted butter

1½ cups sugar

¼ teaspoon salt

12 ounces (2 cups) semisweet chocolate morsels

1 teaspoon vanilla extract

Line an 8-inch square pan with aluminum foil as follows: Turn the pan upside down, center a 12-inch square of foil, shiny side down, over the pan, and press down the sides and corners of the foil to shape it to the pan. Then remove the foil, turn the pan right side up, place the shaped foil in the pan, and gently press the foil (with a potholder if you wish) into place in the pan. Set aside the lined pan.

If using nuts, pick over them carefully (sometimes they include a piece of shell), and remove and reserve about ½ cup of the best-looking halves or pieces to decorate the fudge. Set the nuts aside.

Pour the evaporated milk into a heavy 2½- to 3-quart saucepan. Add the marshmallow cream, butter, sugar, and salt. Place over low to medium-low heat and stir constantly with a wooden spoon until the mixture comes to a boil. This mixture

wants to burn; adjust the heat as necessary and scrape the bottom of the pan occasionally with a rubber spatula to be sure it is not burning.

As soon as the mixture comes to a full boil, start timing it: Let it boil and continue to stir for 5 minutes. (After the 5 minutes are up, the mixture will have caramelized slightly. It is not necessary to test the mixture with a thermometer — just time it — the temperature will be 226 degrees to 228 degrees when the boiling time is up.)

Remove the saucepan from the heat, add the chocolate morsels, and stir until melted and smooth — a strong wire whisk is a big help. Stir in the vanilla and then the 1½ cups of nuts if using. Quickly pour into the lined pan and smooth the top. Place the reserved ½ cup of nuts onto the top of the

continues ↘

fudge, spacing them evenly and pressing down on them enough so they will not fall off.

Let stand until cool. Then chill until firm. Remove the fudge and foil from the pan by lifting the corners of the foil. Or, cover the pan with wax paper and a cookie sheet, turn the pan and sheet over, remove the pan and foil, cover the fudge with a cookie sheet or a cutting board, and turn it over again, leaving the fudge right side up.

With a long, sharp knife, carefully cut the fudge into pieces. Wrap them individually in clear cellophane, wax paper, or aluminum foil. Or place the fudge in an airtight freezer box. If you want to store it for more than a few days, freeze it.

Fudge (page 272)

Everybody's Favorite
Fudge (page 275)

PHUDGE

1½ pounds This uncooked cream cheese fudge is quick, foolproof, smooth, dark, delicious, and so easy that children can make it.

4 ounces unsweetened chocolate

6 ounces cream cheese, at room temperature

½ teaspoon vanilla extract

⅛ teaspoon salt

1 pound (4 loosely packed cups) strained confectioners' sugar

3½ ounces (1 cup) walnuts or pecans, cut or broken into medium-size or large pieces

Place the chocolate in the top of a small double boiler over warm water on moderate heat. Cover until partially melted. Then uncover and stir occasionally until completely melted. Remove the top of the double boiler and set aside uncovered.

In the small bowl of an electric mixer, mix the cream cheese (or stir it by hand in a bowl) until soft and smooth. Add the vanilla and salt. Gradually beat in the sugar and then add the chocolate and beat until smooth. Mix in the nuts.

Now, either line an 8-inch square pan with foil or wax paper and press the fudge into the pan, or shape the fudge by hand on a piece of plastic wrap or wax paper into an even shape about 1 inch thick and 6 inches square, or roll the fudge into a sausage shape about 1½ inches in diameter.

Wrap and refrigerate until firm. It may chill longer. Cut into squares or slices and wrap individually or package airtight.

Refrigerate or store at room temperature. Serve cold or at room temperature. (I like it cold.)

FRENCH CHOCOLATE MINT TRUFFLES

NOTES

↓

The flavor of the chocolate is very important in these candies — use a delicious one.

↓

The truffles may be placed in little fluted paper candy cases.

20 truffles These are dense, bittersweet chocolate candies flavored with mint and shaped to resemble natural truffles. They are easy and fun to prepare and should be made at least a day before serving. Many truffle candies must be refrigerated until serving — these must not. They are served at room temperature. They may be served as dessert, with dessert, after dessert, or between meals. They are especially good after dinner with espresso and/or Cognac.

6 ounces semisweet chocolate (see Notes)

2 ounces (½ stick) unsalted butter, cut into small bits

2 large egg yolks

About ¼ teaspoon peppermint extract

Unsweetened cocoa powder (preferably Dutch-process)

About 2 ounces additional semisweet chocolate (for coating the finished candies)

Break or chop the chocolate into medium-size pieces. Place in the top of a small double boiler over hot water on low heat. Cover and let stand until partially melted. Uncover and stir until completely melted.

Remove the top of the double boiler temporarily. Add the butter, a few pieces at a time, and stir with a small wire whisk after each addition until smooth.

In a small bowl, stir a bit of the chocolate into the yolks and then stir the yolks into the chocolate. Replace over the hot water on low heat and stir gently with a rubber spatula for about 2 minutes.

Now, remove the top of the double boiler. Stir in the peppermint extract, adding just a few drops at a time. Taste it — make it as minty as you like (I make it strong), but add

it slowly and taste it carefully. Some mint extracts taste unpleasant if you use too much.

Place the top of the double boiler in a bowl of ice and water. Stir constantly with a small wooden spatula until the mixture is firm enough to hold a definite shape.

Place a piece of wax paper in front of you. Use a slightly rounded spoonful of the mixture for each truffle, placing them in 20 mounds on the wax paper.

If the portions are firm enough, the truffles may be rolled into shape immediately. But if they are too soft, let them stand uncovered at room temperature for about half an hour, or until firm enough to handle.

continues ↘

Spread out two more large pieces of wax paper. Onto one, strain a generous amount of unsweetened cocoa. Coat the palms of your hands well with the cocoa.

Pick up a mound of the chocolate mixture, roll it between your hands to form an uneven ball (real truffles are very uneven), then roll it around in the cocoa and place it on the other piece of wax paper. Continue to shape all of the truffles, coating your hands with cocoa before shaping each truffle.

Let the truffles stand overnight at room temperature, uncovered or loosely covered, so the outsides dry a bit.

The 2 ounces of additional chocolate must be ground to a fine powder; it may be done in a food processor, a blender, a nut grinder, or on a fine metal grater. Spread the ground chocolate on wax paper and roll the truffles around in it to coat them again.

These are best when they are very fresh, before they dry out too much and while they are still creamy soft in the centers. They may be kept at room temperature for a day or two but they should be refrigerated or frozen for longer storage. (Bring them back to room temperature before serving.)

VARIATIONS

Truffle variations are endless. Here are just a few. To make plain chocolate truffles simply omit the mint. Then, if you wish, vary some by adding ground or very finely chopped nuts (toasted hazelnuts are special) or chopped shredded coconut. Or rum-soaked raisins or dates, or cut-up soft, dried apricots. Or some diced candied (or drained preserved) ginger. Or chopped candied chestnuts. And/or a teaspoon or two of rum, Cognac, bourbon, Grand Marnier, Amaretto, whiskey, etc. For a coffee flavor, add coffee extract. Or roll the shaped truffles in very finely chopped nuts or coconut in place of the cocoa and ground chocolate. Et cetera.

———

CHOCOLATE-COVERED STRAWBERRIES

`1¼ pounds of dipped berries` **This is fun!**

Although they are the simplest thing imaginable — any child can make them — chocolate-covered strawberries have been featured by some of the country's most expensive, exclusive, posh candymakers, where they cost a fortune.

Since they are made with only strawberries and chocolate, their quality depends entirely on the quality of the berries and the chocolate.

Naturally these will be more dramatic if you use large berries, although small berries are very cute and are often more delicious. If possible, use berries with stems (which I have seen in other parts of the country but have never been able to buy in Florida). The berries must be ripe but not soft — do not use any berries that have soft spots. Do not wash the berries; just brush them gently with a dry pastry brush. (But if you would feel better about washing them, swish them around quickly in a large bowl of cold water and then drain on several thicknesses of paper towels for hours until they are completely dry.)

Some chocolate dippers refrigerate the berries for a few hours before dipping them: "If the berries are cold, the chocolate sets faster and there is less chance that it will streak or discolor." Others let them stand on a rack at room temperature for a few hours before dipping: "To dehydrate the surface." I've tried both and I don't see any difference.

You can use any kind of sweet, semisweet, bittersweet, or milk chocolate. It may be real chocolate or compound chocolate (see page 18).

These may be served as dessert, with dessert, or as a decoration for some other dessert. Or serve them as candy. They are perishable but will keep for a day.

Line the bottom of a tray large enough to hold the dipped berries with wax paper or aluminum foil.

One small "pint" box of berries will be enough to serve four people if you are serving these as a dessert. The

NOTE

↓

Candymakers also dip orange sections — you must be sure that the membrane is not broken and that they are seedless oranges; dip them to cover about two-thirds of the section. Or place toothpicks into 1-inch pieces of banana and dip to cover all or part. Or dip individual seedless green grapes on small stems. Or, or, or...

continues ↘

strawberries in such a box will measure almost 4 cups and will weigh 1 pound. For one such box you will need 4 ounces of chocolate.

Break up or coarsely chop the chocolate and place it in the top of a small double boiler over warm water on low heat. Cover until the chocolate is partially melted. Then uncover and stir until the chocolate is all melted and completely smooth.

If the melted chocolate is too thick (different chocolates are thinner than others when melted), add 1 scant tablespoon vegetable shortening (such as Crisco — not butter or margarine) for each 4 ounces of chocolate and stir until melted. It will not only thin the chocolate slightly but will also give it an attractive sheen.

Remove the top of the double boiler for easy handling, but if the chocolate starts to thicken replace it over warm water.

Hold a berry by the stem or by the green leaves (the hull) and dip it to about three-quarters of its length (not all the way — let some of the red berry show at the top). The chocolate coating should not be too

thick and heavy nor should it be as thin as on a Good Humor. Wipe excess chocolate off against the rim of the pot (but don't wipe so much that you leave that section uncovered). Place the dipped berry on its side on the lined tray. (If the chocolate gets too low to dip the last few berries, transfer it to a small custard cup or a small wineglass.)

If you have used compound chocolate, it will set quickly at room temperature and will not have to be refrigerated. If you have used real chocolate, place the tray of dipped berries in the refrigerator only until the chocolate is firm, no longer. Then gently lift each berry by the stem or leaves to release it from the paper.

Now, do not refrigerate these. They should be stored and served (within 24 hours) at room temperature. If they are refrigerated, the chocolate will sweat when returned to room temperature. And if they are cold when they are served, the chocolate will be brittle and the berries will be difficult to eat.

(If you have some leftover melted chocolate, save it and melt it again the next time you dip berries.)

CHOCOLATE FONDUE

6 to 8 servings *Fondue* is French for "melted"; a fondue is a melted food, and probably the most popular dish from Switzerland. Originally it was a melted cheese dish served with chunks of bread. The recipe has come a long way to this chocolate version — a fun dessert, created at the Chalet Suisse restaurant in New York City. It is especially good for a casual party.

To serve it properly, you need a fondue pot or some other way of keeping the chocolate warm. And it must be within comfortable reach of all the guests; on a very long table you need more than one fondue pot. (It is most cozy to serve this on a round table with a lazy Susan in the middle.)

You will serve the warm chocolate mixture and an assortment (few or many — it's up to you) of dunkable foods. The dunkables may be on one large platter, or many small ones, or each guest can be served a plate with an assortment. Fresh strawberries are wonderful. So are orange sections, apple wedges, banana chunks, ladyfingers, graham crackers, chunks of angel food or pound cake. And marshmallows, candied orange and grapefruit peel. Dried figs, dried apricots, pitted dried prunes and dates. And most especially (seriously, these are divine), saltines, pretzels, and plain salted but unflavored matzohs.

Long-handled fondue forks might or might not be necessary depending on the dippers you serve. Some of them (saltines, pretzels, graham crackers) are finger food. But some fresh fruits, some dried fruits, marshmallows, or squares of pound cake will require a fondue fork for each person.

I think it is best to make the chocolate mixture in the kitchen and transfer it to the fondue pot just before serving. Fondue recipes are very flexible. You can vary the chocolates and the liquors. Just remember to keep the mixture thick; it should coat the dunkable items heavily. Here are three different popular versions.

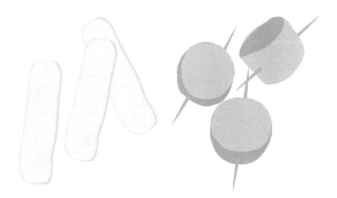

continues ⌄

12 ounces milk chocolate   **½ cup heavy cream**   **3 tablespoons light rum, kirsch, or Grand Marnier**

Break up the chocolate or chop it coarsely. Place it in a small saucepan with the cream over low heat. Stir frequently until melted and smooth. If necessary, stir briskly with a small wire whisk. (This may be done ahead of time and kept warm over warm water on low heat. Or it may be reheated.) Just before serving, stir in the liquor or liqueur and transfer to the fondue pot. The mixture should be thick, but if it is too thick add a bit more cream.

Variations

SEMISWEET FONDUE:

Substitute bittersweet chocolate for half of the milk chocolate.

HERSHEY FONDUE:

Use 1 pound Hershey's milk chocolate plus 4 ounces Hershey's Special Dark chocolate, ¾ cup light cream, and 3 tablespoons kirsch or ½ teaspoon almond extract.

HOMEMADE CHOCOLATE SYRUP (AND 18 DRINKS AND VARIATIONS)

NOTE

⌄

The amounts for a drink of this type are flexible. Use twice as much ice cream and half as much milk for an extra-thick and rich concoction. Or substitute very strong black coffee for all or part of the milk for a Coffee-Chocolate Frosted.

3½ cups syrup This syrup, thinner than chocolate sauce, is used for making hot or cold chocolate milk drinks. Store in the refrigerator and it will keep indefinitely. Use it to make either one portion at a time, or many.

1 cup strained unsweetened cocoa powder (preferably Dutch-process)

2 cups cold water (or cold black coffee)

2 cups sugar

¼ teaspoon salt

1½ teaspoons vanilla extract

In a heavy 2-quart saucepan off the heat, stir the cocoa and water or coffee until smooth (a wire whisk will blend them quickly). Place over moderate heat, change to a rubber spatula, and stir, scraping the bottom constantly, until the mixture comes to a low boil. Add the sugar and salt and stir until dissolved. Bring to a low boil again and let simmer slowly for 3 minutes. Remove from the heat and set aside to cool. Stir in the vanilla.

Store in airtight jars in the refrigerator.

Following this recipe are 18 different drinks (including variations), all of which call for the syrup. In this drink department you can be especially creative and make up your own. Any drink made with your own homemade syrup and homemade ice cream is divine, and the combinations are limitless.

Of course you know that children will adore these and will love you for making them.

But try serving thick shakes or frosteds to a bunch of adults who might not have had one in umpteen years, don't expect one, and don't even think they want one. After their first sips, just sit back, watch them enjoy, and listen to the compliments.

Cold Drinks

The colder the better for cold drinks. If you have room, chill the glasses in the freezer (or fill them ahead of time with cracked ice or ice cubes and let them stand awhile to chill). If the drink is made in a blender, it is good to chill the blender jar in the freezer, too. Or place the prepared drink in the blender jar in the freezer for about half an hour and then blend again just before serving. Or if you have prepared the drink ahead of time in a glass or a pitcher, and if you have room enough and time, place that in the freezer for about half an hour before serving; then stir from the bottom just before serving.

COLD CHOCOLATE MILK:

For a very chocolaty drink, stir ¼ cup of Homemade Chocolate Syrup into 1 cup of cold whole or skimmed milk for each serving. For a milder drink, use a bit less syrup or more milk. For a richer drink, use half-and-half in place of the milk, or use light or heavy cream in place of part of the milk.

CHOCOLATE FLOAT:

Add a scoop of chocolate ice cream to a large glass of Cold Chocolate Milk. Serve with a long-handled spoon and a straw.

CHOCOLATE FROSTED:

Place Cold Chocolate Milk in a blender with a scoop of chocolate ice cream for each glass of milk, blend until foamy, and serve quickly in a tall glass with a straw. Optional: Top with whipped cream.

GROWN-UPS' CHOCOLATE FROSTED:

Add about 2 tablespoons of dark or light rum, crème de cacao, or Kahlúa for each serving of Chocolate Frosted while blending.

continues ↘

CHOCOLATE SODA:

In a tall glass, stir ½ cup of cold milk with 3 to 4 tablespoons of Homemade Chocolate Syrup. Add ½ cup of carbonated water, stir lightly, add a scoop of chocolate ice cream, and, if the glass is not full, add more soda. Top with a generous spoonful of whipped cream. Serve with a straw and a long-handled spoon.

Variation: Use a scoop of half-chocolate and half-coffee ice cream (or use all coffee) in place of all chocolate.

CHOCOLATE BROWN COW:

In a tall glass, stir 3 tablespoons of Homemade Chocolate Syrup into ½ cup of cold milk. Add 1 cup of root beer, stir slightly, and add a scoop of chocolate or vanilla ice cream. If the glass is not full, add more root beer. Serve with a straw and a long-handled spoon.

Variation: For a **Black Cow,** substitute Coca-Cola for the root beer.

CHOCOLATE EGG MILK:

For each 1-cup (8-ounce) serving, place a raw egg in a blender or a mixer and blend or beat just to mix. Add 3 tablespoons of Homemade Chocolate Syrup and ¾ cup of cold milk. Blend or beat until foamy and serve quickly in a glass.

CHOCOLATE BANANA MILKSHAKE:

For each serving, purée about half of a large ripe banana in a blender. Add 3 to 4 tablespoons of Homemade Chocolate Syrup and ½ to ¾ cup of cold milk. Blend until foamy. Serve quickly in a tall glass. Optional: Sprinkle a bit of nutmeg over the top.

COLD RUM-CHOCOLATE MILK:

For each 1-cup (8-ounce) serving, dissolve 1 teaspoon of instant coffee powder in ¼ cup of boiling water, cool, and then chill. Mix ¼ cup of cold milk with 2 tablespoons Homemade Chocolate Syrup. Stir in ¼ cup heavy cream, the cold prepared coffee, and ¼ cup light or amber rum. (This drink is best when it is especially cold. If possible, place it in the freezer for 20 or 30 minutes and stir from the bottom before serving.) Optional: Top with a bit of whipped cream.

Variation: For a **Brandy Alexander Chocolate Milk,** substitute 2 tablespoons of brandy or Cognac and 2 tablespoons of crème de cacao for the ¼ cup rum.

GIRL SCOUT PUNCH:

Depending on the number of servings, mix Homemade Chocolate Syrup and cold milk (¼ cup of syrup to each cup of milk) in a punch bowl. Add a generous number of small scoops of chocolate and/or vanilla ice cream. Top with a generous layer of softly whipped cream (it should be soft enough to spread over the top of the punch), and a sprinkling of grated or shaved chocolate. Serve immediately.

Ladle into cups or glasses, including a scoop of ice cream with each portion. Serve with spoons.

Hot Drinks

The following (and all) hot chocolate drinks should be served in well-heated cups or mugs: Fill the cups or mugs with boiling water and let stand for several minutes before using.

HOT CHOCOLATE MILK:

Follow directions for Cold Chocolate Milk (page 287). Stir occasionally over moderate heat until it just comes to a boil. Beat or whisk until foamy. Serve in a cup. Optional: Top with whipped cream or a marshmallow. And for a surprise and an extra-chocolaty drink, put a small piece of semisweet or milk chocolate, or a few chocolate morsels, in the heated cup before pouring in the hot chocolate milk.

HOT MOCHA:

Mix equal amounts of strong black coffee and Hot Chocolate Milk. If you wish, add additional sugar or honey to taste. Just before serving, beat or whisk until foamy. Serve very hot, with optional whipped

cream or a marshmallow on top. Or top with a spoonful of candy chocolate coffee beans.

HOT CHOCOLATE CAPPUCCINO:

Prepare Hot Mocha, using extra-strong coffee. Pour into a heated cup, filling the cup only about three-quarters full. Add softly whipped cream to fill the cup to the top, sprinkle rather generously with unsweetened cocoa powder (through a fine strainer), and serve immediately. The heat will melt the whipped cream — that's OK.

CHOCOLATE HOT BUTTERED RUM:

For each serving, mix 3 tablespoons of Homemade Chocolate Syrup into ¾ cup milk, half-and-half, or light cream. Place over moderate heat and stir occasionally until it just comes to a boil. Stir in 1 generous teaspoon of instant coffee powder. Place 1 teaspoon of butter in a large heated mug or cup, and add ¼ cup light rum (I use

Bacardi silver label). Beat or whisk the hot drink until it is foamy and then pour it into the mug over the butter and rum. Serve immediately. Optional: Top with whipped cream.

Variation: I have also had **Chocolate Hot Buttered Brandy** made with Cognac in place of rum and it was equally wonderful.

NOTE

⊡

Chocolate Hot Buttered Rum is a cold-weather drink. I met it at a ski lodge in Colorado where the temperature was below zero. It was served at tea time in front of a roaring fireplace (hot toasted banana bread was served on the side). This will warm you all the way through in a hurry.

Chocolate Float
(page 287)

Chocolate Brown Cow
(page 288)

Hot Chocolate Cappuccino
(page 289)

Cold Chocolate Milk
(page 287)

index

about the author

Maida Heatter, dubbed the Queen of Cake by *Saveur,* was the author of several classic books on dessert and baking. Heatter was the recipient of three James Beard Foundation awards and was inducted into the organization's Hall of Fame.